THE BATTLE OF LOOS

THE BATTLE OF LOOS

Philip Warner

WORDSWORTH EDITIONS

First published in Great Britain in 1976
by William Kimber & Co. Limited

This edition published 2000
by Wordsworth Editions Limited
Cumberland House, Crib Street, Ware,
Hertfordshire SG12 9ET

ISBN 1 84022 229 8

Printed and bound in Great Britain
by Mackays of Chatham plc, Chatham, Kent.

CONTENTS

NOTE BY THE AUTHOR

THERE HAS NEVER YET BEEN a full account of the Battle of Loos, which was a critical battle of the war. This book describes the battle generally then shows the different sectors through the words of those who fought in them. It is an almost incredible story of courage and endurance and each account, even when it is describing an experience felt by thousands of others, is curious and strikingly different. The experiences of Captain Wyllie are unforgettable.

As well as all the other hitherto unpublished material the book has the advantage of being able to quote from Sir John French's diaries and to refer to his letters.

Acknowledgements

I N MAY 1975 the *Daily Telegraph* published a letter from me asking survivors, or relations of those who had fought in the Battle of Loos, if they would care to get in touch and let me see diaries or other reminiscences. Over one hundred and fifty wrote, and many more rang up. This tremendous response enabled me to reconstruct the battle as it appeared to the men who fought in it. The experiences of some seem almost incredible, and what may seem equally surprising is that the men could often preserve a sense of humour in such conditions. Perhaps the most remarkable feature of these accounts is that they all seem so individual and so different although all involved in the same battle.

My thanks are also due to Lady Patricia Kingsbury who kindly allowed me to read the diaries of her grandfather, Sir John French. I have quoted extracts from these in the text.

The Imperial War Museum gave me every assistance and showed me all their papers on the battle.

Finally, my thanks to Mr R.B. Goodall, who has the remarkable skill of being able to take an old, indifferent and faded photograph and produce from it a negative which can be clearly reproduced in a book.

LIST OF ILLUSTRATIONS

I

Battle of Loos

Loos is a small mining town between Lens and La Bassée. It lies directly north of the ill-famed Vimy Ridge and the important town of Arras. The French pronounce the word 'loss' but for the British it retains its army pronunciation of 'Looz'. On 25th September 1915, and for a few days after, it was the centre of one of the most intense and bloody battles of the First World War.

Although Loos was a critical battle it has been given little attention by historians and usually, when it has appeared in history, is remarked on for its mistakes rather than its extraordinary qualities. Its cost in casualties – about 60,000 – was appalling and most of these occurred in the first twenty-four hours. Although British troops captured eight thousand yards of German trenches and in places penetrated up to two miles, some hard-won ground had to be given up and the main objective – a large-scale breakthrough – was not achieved. This fact alone has probably caused Loos to be described as an 'expensive failure'. In terms of objective it was, but there are certain facts about Loos which need to be recorded and appreciated. Firstly, Loos was *nearly* a success, owing to the unbelievable courage of those who fought and died there. Secondly, if the initial gain had been used to enable 21st and 24th Divisions to break through the 2nd German line, the course of the whole war could have been different. Major-General Richard Hilton, who at the time was a Forward Observation Officer, said :

A great deal of nonsense has been written about Loos. The real tragedy of that battle was its nearness to complete success. Most of us who reached the crest of Hill 70 and survived were firmly convinced that we had broken through on that Sunday, 25th September 1915. There seemed to be nothing ahead of us but an unoccupied and in-complete trench system. The only two things that prevented our advancing into the suburbs of Lens were, firstly the exhaustion of the 'Jocks' themselves (for they had undergone a bellyful of marching and fighting that day) and secondly the flanking fire of numerous German machine-guns, which swept that bare hill from some factory buildings in Cité St Auguste [a suburb of Lens] to the south of us.

All that we needed was more artillery ammunition to blast those clearly located machine-guns, and some fresh infantry to take over from the weary and depleted 'Jocks'. But, alas, neither ammunition nor reinforcements were immediately available, and the great opportunity passed.

Nor was this the only part of the front where a breakthrough could have been made. Unfortunately more prominence has been given to reports of areas where penetration of the 2nd German line was clearly impossible. Of this, more later. But in view of the nearness of complete success it is worth considering what the results could have been.

In spite of the fact that the war had been in process for over a year there was very little preparation on either side for a long conflict, and the general feeling was that as the initial gambler's throw had failed – with German troops only twenty-three miles from Paris – that a peace settlement at this stage would be no bad idea. The slogging bitterness of the war was yet to come, on the Somme, at Verdun, and at Passchendaele to name but a few of the places which would see almost unbelievable bloodshed and hardship. A counterblast through the German lines in 1915 might not have produced a victorious Allied advance into Germany but it would have created a situation in which the guns could have stopped firing and peace be made. By this time both sides knew full well what the cost of victory was likely to be. But after 1915 no one could prevent the war grinding on to a murderous finish.

The possible difference to the world if the war had ended in 1915 stuns imagination. Millions of valuable lives would have been saved. America would never have come into the war at all. Russia might never have had its revolution. The break-up of the Austro-Hungarian empire and the Turkish empire would have been delayed, and the disruption caused by the 1919 Peace Settlements – which were trying to produce democratic order out of chaos – could have been avoided. These, though nobody could dream of it, were the stakes at Loos.

However what might have been the turning point of the war became the symbol of bad planning and inadequate staff work. Liddell-Hart described Loos as 'the unwanted battle', and this was a mild description compared to that given by others. 'Failure at Loos' was the headline given in one history of the war.

But whatever failed at Loos it was not men's courage. That, as will be seen in the accounts which follow later in this book, was almost incredible. Exceptional bravery was also shown on other fronts in France and other theatres of the war, but that does not make the performance by British troops at Loos less astonishing. Thrown into battle under the worst possible conditions they nearly made a success of it. 'They' were English, Scottish, Welsh and Irish. 'They' included some – there were not many left – of the old regular army and the first batch of the volunteers who had rushed to join the colours after the outbreak of war. They were committed to a task which seemed absolute madness to many officers of the British Higher Command. It is of course possible – perhaps probable – that if a complete breakthrough had been made it would not have been properly exploited. Sir John French was said to be opposed to a thrust by one or two divisions – he wanted to see the whole front moving forward at the same time. Perhaps the lack of trained staff officers would have caused any further gains to have been frittered away. Staff officers, though much criticized, are vital to the efficient conduct of operations and the lack of them had already been shown both in the advance to Loos and on the battlefield itself. It may be argued that on other fronts when a breakthrough was made it was never properly exploited – until 1918.

It is easy to apportion blame here and there for a lost battle and it is often justified. But war, like politics, is the art of the possible. In this account it is necessary to identify the mistakes made at Loos but that is not necessarily to say that they were avoidable. Mistakes are made in every battle. In very few battles in history have mistakes of planning and execution come so near to being redeemed by sheer courage as they were at Loos. This is what needs to be understood and remembered about Loos.

2

The Opening Stages

By August 1915, when the plans for Loos were being made, the war had been in process for a year. Even so there was no certainty on either side as to how it should continue, or, in fact, if it would continue at all. The Germans had made their opening thrust by implementing the Schlieffen Plan (drafted as long ago as 1905) and reached a point twenty-three miles from Paris. However, various factors, principally the battle of the Marne, had checked their attack and ruined their plans for a lightning war of the type they had previously launched against Austria and France; later such campaigns would become known as *blitzkriegs*.

The violation of Belgium's neutrality, necessary for the proper implementation of the Schlieffen Plan had, to Germany's surprise, brought Britain into the war. Both sides hastily began to construct trench lines, which ran from the Channel ports to Switzerland. The Germans would have liked to include Ypres in their area but the British were determined they should not. Ypres, being a Belgian town, represented the pledge Britain had made to Belgium in 1839 – to protect her neutrality. So far in the war Belgian neutrality had received short shrift but the British felt that their presence in Ypres was a moral obligation. It turned out to be an expensive one, for protecting Ypres meant holding a salient in the German line, and troops in the Ypres area were thus exposed to shellfire on three sides. Ypres was never lost to the Germans but the cost in lives of holding it was enormous. Tactically the British and French armies would have been better off without Ypres in the early stages of the war, but no commander likes giving up ground he feels he can hold.

'Wipers', as it was known to the British soldier, became the scene of continuous slaughter and of three major battles. 'First Ypres' took place in October–November 1914 and was an occasion when the Germans lost 20,000 killed and 80,000 wounded in a desperate effort to break through. (British losses were 8,000 killed and 40,000 wounded.) 'Second Ypres' was in April 1915 when the Germans used gas, achieved complete surprise, but failed to exploit the advantage it gave them. 'Third Ypres' was fought in the second half of 1917 and is more often known as the Battle of Passchendaele, for that small village, five miles north-east of Ypres, was one of the objectives.

While the early bitter and costly battles were going on, and as the belligerents began to realise the way the war was developing, considerable thought was given to methods of breaking the deadlock. The armies of both sides now saw it as a slogging match with a possible chance of a lucky breakthrough. However there were other minds at work and they felt that the steady slaughter of all their best young men was not the most sensible policy. On both sides therefore there were plans for bringing a quick ending to the war by invasion. The Germans had various ideas about the east coast of Britain and as early as 1914 had subjected Scarborough to a considerable naval bombardment. However bombardment is a long way from invasion and the Germans never attempted anything so ambitious as a landing on English soil.

The Allies were considering three possibilities for the invasion of Germany. One was to go via Holland (if the Dutch agreed), another possibility was via Borkum, and a third was planned via the Baltic and Pomerania to effect a rapid capture of Berlin. None was ever attempted.

In spite of the stalemate in France and the way the war appeared to be spreading to other areas there was no conviction in Britain that it would not all be over by Christmas. There is a perpetual belief (or hope) in any war that it will all be victoriously over by Christmas and the troops will be celebrating their success in Berlin, Tokyo, Rome, or wherever is the enemy capital. Only one dissident voice marred this general harmony of belief in Britain. It was Lord Kitchener's. He was quite firm in his conviction that this would be a long war and he began to raise armies to fight it. These, initially made up of volunteers and territorials, were the first hundred thousand. Soon they were joined by the second (K2) and third (K3).

But others took a more optimistic view. Among them was Marshal Joffre – commander-in-chief of the French armies on the western front. His prestige was high owing to his success in handling the Marne battle and by the summer of 1915 he was convinced that an assault by the French First and Tenth armies in the Lens-Arras region, accompanied by a British thrust in the La Bassée-Loos area, could bring rapid and devastating success. A parallel thrust would also be made by the French Second and Fourth armies in the Champagne region. There would also be subsidiary attacks on other fronts to keep the Germans occupied and prevent them from drawing off reserves for despatch to the main battlefields. Joffre firmly believed that once the German lines were penetrated there was nothing to stop the Allied advance. He was possibly right, although his allotment of a cavalry objective *fifty miles east* of Loos seems remarkably optimistic.

Surprisingly, one of the supporters of this grandiose plan was Lord Kitchener, whose Sudan campaign in 1898 had been the epitome of methodical caution. Kitchener was Secretary of State for War and gave a direct order to French that he should support Joffre's plan and thereby preserve the Entente Cordiale. Kitchener apparently felt that some positive action was required to offset the Gallipoli disaster and also to take the pressure off the Russians.

However, a bold strategic plan such as Joffre's is useless and dangerous if the local tactical situation is awry. There were two vital liabilities in the Joffre plan : one was the lack of artillery in the British sector and the second was the nature of the ground over which the British were expected to advance. The assault in all sectors was to be preceded by a 96 hour bombardment of the German lines. This was meant to cut all German wire, damage all their defences and destroy their morale. Unfortunately for the British forces they were desperately short of guns and shells. The French, in their sector, had 117 guns to the mile; the British less than half that number. According to Liddell-Hart, shell production in England was 22,000 a day compared to 100,000 in France and 250,000 by Germany and Austria. Making the situation worse was the fact that neither the British nor the French guns had the power to cut the German barbed wire and do the required damage to their defensive positions.

The lack of suitable artillery made the attack over open ground near-suicidal. Sir John French, the Commander-in-Chief of the British army, is always held to blame for allowing the attack to be launched in such unsuitable terrain, but in view of the fact that his orders came from Kitchener, he had no option but to agree. French had made his reputation at Klip Drift in the Boer War when by showing considerable expertise in the handling of his cavalry he had relieved Kimberley. However, had the Boers wired Klip Drift, as they might well have been expected to do, French's military career would doubtless have ended then and there. Because of the enormous casualties of the First World War it is often assumed that the generals were indifferent to the loss of human lives. This was not so – even with Haig who is often thought of as a cold-blooded automaton who sent thousands to their death without a qualm. A general whose task is to win a war knows that he cannot accomplish it without heavy casualties. Often his own friends and relatives are in units he knows must be sacrificed for the general good. Obviously he does not suffer like the troops involved, but this does not mean that he takes such decisions lightly.

Unfortunately for the British they took over the Loos section of the line from the French in August 1915. This was part of the general concentration for the offensive. Joffre was no doubt aware of the unsuitability of the ground for infantry attack – in spite of remarks about it – but to him it was only one of a number of unsuitable areas; any large-scale attack is bound to contain sectors which are certain death for infantrymen, even when they have plentiful artillery support. Nevertheless, neither French, Commander-in-Chief of the British Expeditionary Force, nor Haig, Commander of First Army which had been allotted the Loos sector, nor Rawlinson, Commander of 4 Corps whose front was over the most exposed portion, could regard the future with anything but gloom.

Joffre had told them, 'Your attack will find particularly favourable ground between Loos and La Bassée', but Rawlinson commented : 'My new front at Loos is as flat as the palm of my hand. Hardly any cover anywhere. Easy enough to hold defensively but very difficult to attack. It will cost us dearly and we shall not get very far.'

Rawlinson's corps contained two divisions of the new Kitchener army, the 15th (Scottish) and the 47th (London). They were the first of the newly raised Kitchener divisions to be committed to battle. Their story will be told more fully later.

The phrase as flat as my hand was in fact a figure of speech, as French and Haig both knew for they had both examined the ground personally. It could not have been worse if it had been completely flat and would have been marginally better for it consisted – and still does – of long gentle slopes, completely devoid of cover, broken at intervals by mine workings. The trenches ran north-south and at the southern end (right-hand of the attack) were a series of small villages such as Cité St Auguste and Cité St Emile, which were the northern suburbs of Lens.

Loos lies in a slight depression and due east of it was a low hill with bare slopes on all sides; this was Hill 70. Two miles north-west of Loos is the village of Grenay and the end of a low spur which became known as Lone Tree Ridge, for reasons which will be explained later. Behind the German lines here lay the village of Hulluch. Hulluch itself is just below the level of the surrounding land but from here to the La Bassée canal the German trenches were on higher ground than the British, thus giving them a considerable advantage in observation.

In this part of their line the Germans also had the Hohenzollern Redoubt, a strongly fortified hillock. It was linked to two other strong positions – the Dump and Fosse trenches – by two trenches which became known to the British as Big Willie and Little Willie. Big Willie linked the position with the Quarries. (See map.) The small villages in the area behind the battle front had to some extent been fortified by the Germans and this might have produced serious problems even after a large-scale breakthrough. The ground itself was chalk and thus difficult to dig into. Another disadvantage was that any digging was immediately obvious to the enemy by virtue of the whiteness of the chalk (see aerial photographs taken at the time).

The opposing trenches lay between two hundred and four hundred yards apart but overall the Germans had the advantage as regards observation. This was mainly because the area was used for coal mining. Principal mines were known as *fosses*, and auxiliary shafts as *puits*. Each had winding gear, towers rising to one hundred feet, which were invaluable for observation. Just beyond Loos there was a double pit-head which superficially resembled the London Tower Bridge. This gave excellent observation to the Germans and defied efforts by the British 18 pdrs to destroy it. When it came into British possession the German 5.9s made short work of it. 'Tower Bridge' was rebuilt after the war and still stands today though mining has ceased in this area. Even more of a problem were the *crassiers*, or dumps of mine waste. These could be used as observation posts or hollowed into caves and defensive positions. To the south-west of Loos was the notorious Double Crassier and to the south of the town was the Loos Crassier.

The British had two principal observation points. One was the Fosse 5 dump, near Grenay, which gave a good view of the German lines, and the other was the Fosse 9 dump, which was 135 feet high but two miles behind the British lines; however Fosse 9 was very useful to both British and French artillery spotters.

The battlefield is crossed by roads. The La Bassée-Lens road runs north-south through it and in approximately the centre of what was the 2nd German line is crossed by the Vermelles-Hulluch road. For the assault IV Corps would take the southern sector (from Grenay to Lens) and I Corps would take the northern section (Grenay-La Bassée). I Corps contained six divisions but IV Corps contained only four. Later the 21st and 24th Division from XI Corps would be put in to the central sector. XI Corps was the general reserve unit. Most of the units in these areas were short of battle experience and some were coming under fire for the first time. The ages of those on the Loos battlefield covered an astonishing range – the youngest known being $14\frac{3}{4}$ (he survived the war), the eldest being 61, a battalion commander who was killed in the battle.

Numerically the British had an advantage over the opposing Germans in the opening stages but the lesson which was driven home time and again in this war was that troops advancing over open ground against wired positions well equipped with artillery and machine guns were simply men being fed into a killing ground. This even applied on the Somme where the preliminary artillery bombardment was thought to have been adequate – but 40,000 men fell in the first three hours.

The organisation of the armies, which differs slightly from the modern pattern, requires some explanation here. Today men parade in three ranks; it used to be four. There are four companies to a battalion, but three battalions to a brigade. There are three brigades to a division, theoretically three divisions to a corps. Two or more corps make an army. However, even today this pattern may vary according to numbers available and need. There are also supporting units of special troops such as artillery, engineers, signals, ordnance, etc.

In 1915 numbers varied considerably. I Corps contained four divisions. Brigades contained from four to six regiments. The strength of a regiment was officially 750 men. There was a single division from III Corps and three from IV Corps. There were five divisions in XI Corps. There were three divisions from the Indian Corps, which contained Gurkhas, Punjabis, and Sikhs. There was a Cavalry Division (3rd) containing three cavalry brigades and a Royal Horse Artillery Brigade, and there were three wings of the Royal Flying Corps, which had 161 aeroplanes and 4 kite balloons.

The riflemen went over the top carrying 200 rounds of rifle ammunition, 3 sandbags, an iron ration and an extra cheese ration. Bombers (grenade throwers) carried 20 bombs, 120 rifle rounds and 3 sandbags. Every hundred men carried 25 picks and shovels and four wire cutters distributed among them. All wore a smoke helmet, a flannel bag with the front rolled up. With the front down men could scarcely see through the talc eyepieces; with it up in rain the chemicals washed into the eyes, causing irritation.

Haig was well aware of the madness of launching an attack on a wide front over open ground into prepared positions and initially wished to restrict the attack to two divisions on a narrow frontage. This might perhaps overwhelm the defence by sheer numbers and create gaps which could be widened by reinforcements. Most of the first two divisions would, of course, be killed. However this exercise in human slaughter was shelved for a better plan. The Germans had broken the convention of civilized behaviour by using gas at Ypres six months before. Now, it was decided, they should have a taste of their own medicine and the assault here would be launched under gas and smoke. If gas were to be used the right wind needed to be blowing, otherwise the gas would hang about in our own trenches. To have its full effect it needed to come as a surprise; in view of the labour of bringing some 5,500 gas cylinders into the trenches, a task involving 8,000 men, it is remarkable that the Germans did not realise that something unusual was going on, but they did not. Members of the Royal Engineers who were concerned in the handling of the gas cylinders felt, with some justification, that they had accomplished a major task. The personal reminiscences of some are given later. However, even 150 tons of gas was less than half the amount really required and the cylinders had to be used very economically.

In the event the wind proved unreliable. The gas was turned on at 0550 hrs. On the right sector it drifted slowly over the German lines, where it proved moderately effective; on the left it drifted back into our own lines. Many of the regiments in the 2nd Division (I Corps) were themselves gassed and those who were not were caught in the open by the German machine gunners who were waiting for them. The main assault had begun at 0630 hrs. All available units were thrown into the initial assault on the basis that a breakthrough was the essential objective and reserves would be forthcoming when it was effected. This assumption proved to be unwarranted for the reserve divisions were too far behind the lines to be immediately available, and when eventually they were committed the Germans had rushed up reinforcements, rewired their positions and were ready to receive them. The reserves were 21 and 24 Divisions and they were committed at 1100 hrs. on the 26th September – twenty-four hours too late.

However, the Germans too had miscalculated and though they fought with skill and determination seem to have been undeservedly lucky at Loos. They had known that a major attack was coming but had not completed their second line defences. According to Brigadier General Wilkinson, Commander of 44th Brigade in the 15th (Scottish) Division, the Germans had put up notices in their trenches asking the date and time of the British attack. As this had been postponed from August to September and then from the 8th to the 15th, and then from the 23rd to the 25th, their enquiries had some substance; at the same time it was clear the Germans were not taking the impending action too seriously. However, had the British not used gas and obtained the advantage of surprise, the German confidence in their ability to halt the assault when it had scarcely started could well have been proved correct. As it was, the arrival of chlorine in their trenches produced a state of panic, though not for long. As well as causing panic and confusion among men, gas rapidly rusted both rifles and artillery breech blocks, making them unusable.

This opening move was to be combined with attacks by the French army in the Champagne and Artois areas. The attacks in the former area had some success initially, the latter quickly came to a halt. In the Artois sector, which included Vimy Ridge, the attack did not begin till early afternoon of 25th September and then proved unsuccessful. In consequence the neutralizing of German gunfire from the Vimy heights did not occur and by the following morning the efforts of the French 10th Army to advance had been so ineffective that Joffre telephoned and cancelled the plan. However he gave instructions that no word of this cancellation must reach the British.

The progress of the battle is best described by working from south to north along the British line. The southern end was the IV Corps area and covers Loos itself; eventually IV Corps achieved the deepest penetration but this is no reflection on the efforts of I Corps which had a more heavily defended sector and also was unable to benefit properly from the opening gas attack. The southern sector was where the Higher Command expected the breakthrough to be made. The extreme right, or southern, portion was held by the 47th Division, which adjoined the French 21 Corps, which was not taking part in the advance. The 47th was a London Division and included 1/8th (Post Office Rifles), 1/15th (Civil Service Rifles), 1/17th (Poplar and Stepney Rifles), 1/18th (London Irish Rifles), 1/21st (Surrey Rifles) and so on. The 47th was a Territorial Volunteer division which had already seen action at Aubers Ridge and Festubert. It had therefore probably just the right amount of experience for this type of assault. Very experienced regiments move with clockwork precision but tend to lack the dash and initiative of novice units. Many of their members are skilled in ways of surviving the war – without in any way shirking their duties; such men contribute less than they might to winning it. The spirit of the 47th was shown by the 1/18th London Irish, who kicked a Rugby football ahead of them as they went over the top.

Further to the left were the East Surreys who would kick footballs ahead of them on the first day of the Somme (1st July 1916)*. The 47th gained all their objectives although they lost 1200 men in the first phase of the attack. Their task involved advancing over open slopes and also capturing the Loos Crassier, an enormous dump eight hundred yards long, and the Double Crassier (the waste from Fosse 11) which had been

*In 1944 when Major Roy Leyland, English Rugby international and former member of the East Surreys, was parachuting over the Rhine, he took a Rugby football with a view to kicking it on the parachute drop. It would have been the longest kick ever made but unfortunately the ball was forgotten in the general preparations for the drop.

made into two parallel embankments 1200 feet long by 100 feet high. Everything they did was observed by the Germans from 'Tower Bridge'.

However, the 47th made good use of smoke bombs from Stokes mortars. Stokes mortars had been invented the previous January by Mr Wilfred Stokes, and consisted (at this time) of a 4in. diameter steel tube. Out of it was propelled – first by an ordinary sporting cartridge – a smoke/gas bomb. Launching a projectile from the equivalent of a drain pipe might seem a somewhat haphazard business but in fact the missiles can be directed with amazing accuracy. Mortars were used with great success in the Second World War.

Units of the 47th had no slight difficulty in keeping direction, for the number of landmarks all looking much the same proved deceptive and misleading. This problem would be met elsewhere along the front. 47th Division was subsequently criticized for not pushing a defensive flank forward to the right of Hill 70. This would presumably have prevented 15th Division veering right and losing direction. However there was nothing in 47th's orders to indicate that pushing beyond their objective – the Loos Crassier – was expected of them.

Next to the 47th was the 15th (Scottish). An insight into the early experience and training of this admirable unit are given in Ian Hay's book *The First Hundred Thousand*. Students of military history – whether old soldiers or not – will not fail to note how little their experiences vary from nation to nation, from war to war, and century to century. Phenomena such as 'the fog of war' or MFU (Military Foul Up) know no frontiers of time nor space.

The 15th was a completely new and inexperienced division but it was given the task of advancing on a 1500 yard frontage to capture Loos itself, to cross Hill 70 and to occupy the Cité St Auguste. The reason why a division going under fire for the first time was given such difficult and important objectives was that Rawlinson considered them one of the finest he had encountered even without battle experience. The regiments which made up the division justified his confidence but paid a terrible price; some regiments, such as 7th KOSB*, were virtually wiped out. Loos was considered by the Germans to be an outpost defence to the important Hill 70 and all the way to the latter there were strongpoints and machine-gun emplacements which could take a heavy toll of any attacker. A feature of the German lines was their deep dugouts in which a machine-gun crew could sit out an artillery bombardment and emerge unhurt to mow down advancing troops when the barrage lifted. The Germans also made excellent use of the *Corons* which were miners'

*King's Own Scottish Borderers.

cottages built in terraces. Each possessed a cellar which made a very efficient dugout.

The regiments of the 15th Division had a bad start, for the gas scarcely cleared their own trenches. Many men put on their gas helmets but as these made breathing nearly impossible when moving they were soon discarded. It was a choice between being half-blinded and nearly asphyxiated, or being mildly gassed. Many men chose the latter alternative, though not wisely.

So great was the confusion at this moment that the line only began moving when the sound of the pipes was heard. These were played by Piper Laidlaw of 7th KOSB who marched up and down the parapet playing 'Scotland the Brave'. He was subsequently awarded the VC*. Another piper of the KOSB won the VC on 25th September. He was Pipe-Major Robert Mackenzie, then aged 60. He was wounded but kept on piping; then he was killed. He was with the 6th KOSB.

The lines were now moving forward with superb steadiness and discipline. Well placed machine-guns tore great gaps in the advancing ranks but the Scots kept moving on. Some of the Germans took refuge in the cellars of houses in the Loos area. Most of them were taken prisoner. Clearing an area of enemy snipers and machine gunners would have been easier if the grenades had been more serviceable. The new Mills grenade was only just arriving and most units had the inefficient and much disliked 'cricket ball' grenade. 'Pitchers' were another model of grenade but no more popular. Rifle grenades, such as the 'Pippins' were used, but the Pippins had an unfortunate tendency to explode if accidentally knocked or dropped.

However, even with all the disadvantages of a bad start and not very efficient mortar bombs and grenades, the 15th had managed to occupy Loos by 0800 hrs. By 0915 the KOSB had reached the Lens road. The advance continued but, as one observer recorded, many units had now strayed off their proper line of route and were mixed up with others. Many senior officers had been killed and the surviving junior officers were hesitant about assuming command without knowing whether battalion and company commanders were alive or dead. As it happened, they were dead.

Nevertheless, 'looking like a bank holiday crowd', some 1,500 began to move up the slopes of Hill 70. This was good, but what was not good was that in the confusion the whole advance of 15th Division was now drifting

---

*In September 1944, when Lieutenant M. H. Broadway of the Parachute Regiment was dropping on to the Arnhem battlefield, he heard the skirl of bagpipes. They came from 7th KOSB who had just landed by glider. Eleven years later the KOSB were the most highly decorated regiment in the Korean War.

to the south instead of heading east. The few hundred who did go over the hill and down the eastern slope found themselves trapped by enfilading fire in front of a broad high obstacle of uncut German wire. With an open slope behind them they were now hopelessly pinned down. Other units which could have helped extricate them and push on the attack had now veered too far south to do so.

This was one of the great disasters of the day, for the German second line was not complete and had there been enough troops to attack on a broader front the breakthrough could have been made and the Germans behind Hill 70 would themselves have been enfiladed. This was the time and place for one of the reserve divisions to be put in – if available. But that is another story.

Instead the Germans counter-atacked. Fortunately their counter-attack coincided with the opening attack by the French Tenth Army in their sector and the Germans, not knowing what this might portend, contented themselves with shelling Loos village and the Bethune-Loos road. The chance of a British victory in this sector had now been lost. And the cost in lives had been enormous.

Meanwhile 1st Division, also belonging to IV Corps, had been ordered to attack the Lone Tree Ridge area. The 'Lone Tree' was in fact a flowering cherry which had been heavily damaged by shellfire but somehow survived. Later in this book is a photograph of a section of this well-known tree which even managed to bloom again after the end of the war.

The nature of the ground over which the 1st Division attack must travel would create a gap between the 1st and 2nd Brigade. It was therefore decided to fill that gap with an auxiliary force under Lieutenant Colonel E. W. B. Green of the Royal Sussex, but this would be held in reserve till needed.

However initial progress in this area was slow. The gas moved very slowly and the advancing troops were soon themselves in it. Worse still, the German wire had escaped being cut by artillery and could not be cut by hand. The attack in the centre stopped completely. This was a serious setback but not a disaster. Unfortunately, instead of accepting the lesson that further attacks in this sector would be costly and unprofitable – if not hopeless – further assaults were intermittently made.

Much more success was obtained by the Gloucesters and Berkshires to the left. Casualties were appalling – only 60 men survived from the 10th Gloucesters. A mixed force was hastily arranged from the survivors of the Gloucesters, Berkshires and 1st Cameron Highlanders. Here an advance party found a gap in the German wire and entered Hulluch village. The Germans had deserted their trenches in this part of the line and were falling back. The news was thought to be too good to be true and no effort was made to switch Green's force or other reinforcements into the sector. In consequence the advance party, consisting of thirty Camerons, stayed in the village from 0900 hrs. till early afternoon. They were then driven out by the arrival of the German 157th Regiment.

Meanwhile, the other units of 2nd Brigade were hammering away at their objectives on this part of the front. The German defences were particularly strong here, the wire was mostly uncut, machine guns were positioned to take devastating toll of advancing troops and German morale in the area had been in no way affected by gas. In consequence the fighting which took place was fierce and bitter. Four VCs were awarded, but two of the recipients were killed while earning them. At the end of the day most of the units had lost from half to three-quarters of their numbers. The heaviest toll was from the 8th Royal Berkshire who lost 493. In all, of the six thousand who had begun the day only fifteen hundred were now to be counted. And without anyone realising it there was a gap of fifteen hundred yards between 3rd Brigade and 2nd Brigade. How this failed to be noted by HQ I Division is a mystery, but unnoted it was and thus I Corps and IV Corps made their plans for the 26th in ignorance of it.

The rest of the fighting on the first day had been in the I Corps area, that is from the Vermelles-Hulluch road to the La Bassée canal. This held the Quarries, a chalk pit which was twenty feet deep and a hundred yards wide. The Germans had tunnelled numerous dug-outs into the sides. It also held Fosse 8 with its *crassier*, known to the British as 'the Dump', and Auchy village. From the British line Auchy was on the left. Fosse 8 and the Dump were in the centre, protected by the heavily fortified Hohenzollern Redoubt, and to the right were the Quarries.

The area on the right was allotted to 7th Division under Major-General Capper. He was one of the three Divisional Commanders to be killed in the battle of Loos. Loos was a battle in which 'leadership was done from the front'. In consequence the casualties among senior officers was high. The assault of 7th Division gained no advantage at all from the guns, in fact the gas did them more harm than good. Nevertheless they pushed on, with Gordons and Devons in the lead. Soon after the attack began the 8th Devons had only two wounded officers and one hundred men still on their feet; the 9th Devons were in little better shape. But it is invidious to single out regiments. The South Staffords, the Warwickshires and the Royal Welch Fusiliers suffered no less. But by 1800 hrs. 7th Division HQ noted that the Quarries had been captured.

The centre, which included the Hohenzollern Redoubt and Fosse 8, was allotted to 9th Division under Major-General Thesiger. He too was killed in the subsequent fighting. The area has been described earlier in this book and the Hohenzollern Redoubt noted as the strongest point in the German line. There were a number of Scottish regiments in this division; they fought with the same selfless ferocity as their comrades in the 15th; they also paid the same price. 28th Brigade was commanded by Brigadier-General S. W. Scrase-Dickens. There is a reference to him later in the letters. 28th Brigade had the impossible task of capturing various strong points, e.g. Strong Point, Railway Redoubt and Mad Point. Casualties there were enormous and appalling. Six KOSB found themselves under heavy machine-gun fire in front of a wide barbed wire entanglement protected by a ten foot wide concealed ditch, also staked and wired. All the 20 KOSB officers were killed, all but one of the NCOs and over 600 men. The Highland Light Infantry fared no better. 28th Brigade had been destroyed as a fighting unit for very little gain at all.

However other parts of the front were more fortunate, even though all regiments had to pay a stiff price for success. General Gough, the I Corps Commander, firmly believed that if one of the reserve divisions, 21st or 24th could have been put in at this moment a complete breakthrough could have been effected in this sector of the line.

Second Division, which was holding the northern sector of the British line, in the La Bassée region, had the most dispiriting task of all for it had losses without compensating success. The day began disastrously with their own gas coming back into their faces. The attack was launched over ground made rugged by mining and counter-mining in the previous months. The Germans had a number of perfectly sited machine-guns and, behind these, belts of uncut wire. By the end of the day all ground captured had been given up again as it was too exposed to hold. The task of knocking the Germans out of their machine-gun posts proved impossible with the grenades available – the 'cricket balls'. Most of these refused to ignite. At best they were inferior to the German grenades.

In addition to the main attacks two feint attacks were organised for the Indian Corps north of La Bassée. The Indian Corps incorporated one entirely British division and two others made up of British and Indian regiments. The attacks were timed to begin up to two hours before the main Loos battle, with the object of tying down German units which might otherwise be switched to the southern area. The attacks could not be more than partially successful for there was insufficient artillery preparation and there were no reserves available to be used if a breakthrough should be made. The initial assault at 0600 hrs used gas but in a small quantity. The prevailing wind hardly moved the gas and smoke at all.

However, whatever the Gurkhas, Gahrwali, Punjabi and all the other regiments lacked it was not offensive spirit. Their success was their undoing, for they drove salients into the German line and thereby left exposed flanks which there were no reserves to hold. The communication trenches here were knee deep in mud. By 1600 the last units had withdrawn to their original position in the British line. It may seem astonishing that the great surprise weapon – gas – should have been used prematurely in a costly attack which could only prove abortive. Miraculously the Germans did not pass the word to their fellows further south that the British were now using gas. Possibly this was because the gas did not reach them and they were thus unaware of it.

Yet another attack further north was directed to Aubers Ridge. This time gas was not used. The only gain from this was that it enabled the British trench line to be straightened while the German attention was diverted.

At the end of the first day of Loos the general situation looked rather better than it was. In spite of the lack of artillery, resulting in uncut wire, and in spite of the partial failure of gas, much ground had been won. Considerable sections of the former German front line were now in British hands. However, casualties had been enormous – one sixth of all those engaged – and the new positions were in broken lines of trenches and thus highly vulnerable. Foch and Sir John French, looking at the gains on the map and seemingly unaware of the exhaustion and losses among the troops which had won them, felt that their bold plan had been justified. It seemed clear that the advantage should be pressed home the next day by using the general reserve.

The general reserve was 21st and 24th Divisions, the Guards Division and the Cavalry Corps. The first two had recently arrived in France; the Cavalry Corps was of course an anachronism in such conditions of war. The decision to use raw divisions at this stage in the battle when there were experienced divisions close at hand on the Somme is impossible to understand.

At this point it is appropriate to have a look at the definition of 'raw troops'. In one sense everybody on the battlefield area at Loos was 'raw'. The senior commanders, such as Haig and Sir John French, were raw because they had no previous experience in handling formations as large as the ones they were now responsible for. In wartime a man whose experience of command is based on a unit of 700 men can find himself responsible for many thousands. To command a force of up to half a million men, as a commander-in-chief could find himself doing at an early stage, he needs capable corps commanders, each responsible for some 40,000 men or more. In the divisions there was a need for men who could command up to 20,000 men, in the brigades between three and four thousand. In the regiments themselves there was a need for company commanders, platoon commanders, sergeants and corporals. And it is not enough merely to have experience at any of those levels; some people are good with very little experience and some men are useless at any level no matter how much experience they have. In the First World War there were many men holding higher appointments who were quite unfitted for them. In the first wave of expansion they had been promoted and appointed simply because there was no one else.

The army at Loos undoubtedly lacked experience but it had certain compensating virtues. It consisted for the most part of territorials and volunteers. Territorials were men who had joined volunteer units in peacetime on the understanding they would be used for home defence in emergencies only, and not sent abroad. Usually they consisted of sociable citizens who enjoyed a little drill, and marching and musketry – but not too much of it – and went to camp for a fortnight each year. They learnt to fire a rifle with reasonable accuracy but because they 'were only the TA' were given obsolescent or obsolete equipment. Their military pretensions were regarded with scorn by the Regulars but the Territorials, no whit abashed, felt that man for man they were better than the Regulars and one day would show them. The same attitude persisted until 1939 and even today the attitude lingers on in certain places. However, official policy today is to give every encouragement to Territorials, let them use the latest equipment and mingle with Regular units. Some territorial regiments are, of course, élite units and highly selective. Territorials have often paid a stiff price for being early in the field.

In October 1914 the London Scottish were engaged in the Battle of Messines. They had the Mark I Long Lee Enfields which, in theory, had been converted to take Mark VIII ammunition. Events proved otherwise for the new rounds all jammed in the magazine and the rifles could only be used for a single shot. The later Lee-Enfields held ten shots comfortably in the magazine. Less than twenty years before, troops fighting in the Sudan War had found their swords bent on impact owing to the poor quality of the steel used in their manufacture; there was no novelty about inefficient equipment.

During 1914, men flooded into recruiting centres for the new army. They were duly enrolled and found that in most places there were no arms, no uniforms and often no proper camps. They improvised as they survived. By 1915 there was no difference between the old Regular regiments, the Territorials and the Kitchener battalions. Whole regiments had been raised by patriotic citizens. They included the famous 'Pals' battalions, the Public Schools battalion and City battalion. Many of the recruits were valuable officer material but they joined as privates and thousands were killed while still in that rank. Later in the war there was a desperate shortage of junior officers, which is hardly surprising for the life expectancy of a subaltern (2nd Lieutenant or Lieutenant) was reckoned to be three months from the day he joined up.

In the early stages many officers had minimal training; in some cases no training at all. Their sole virtue was the courage and dedication which enabled them to lead a platoon over the top of the trench into deadly machine-gun fire. Anyone who crossed No-Man's-Land might find he was confronted with uncut wire; many of those killed at Loos died in attempts to cut wire which was too thick for the issued wire-cutters. But it would be wrong to minimize the influence of the young, unfledged, doomed officers. Before coming into the line they had untiringly supervised firing practice on ranges which were all too few for the purpose, they had supervised night operations on ground which bore no resemblance to the terrain they would meet later, and they had brushed on one side frustrations which could have damaged morale. On the whole they earned great respect, which is probably a vital component of leadership. There is, however, an enormous amount of knowledge needed to exercise command in wartime. It is not merely a matter of leading a bayonet charge. It is knowing about trench-feet and food and casualties and supplies and digging and what is needed to ensure that thirty men can give of their best.

Unfortunately the ranks at Loos were full of people who should not have been fighting in that capacity at all. There were business men and medical students, there were engineers and chemists, there were men whose experience and knowledge could have been used far more effectively elsewhere. One may argue that one life is as good as another, but in war one skill is certainly not as vital as another. One company in the 6th Cameron Highlanders was made up of the products of the Glasgow High School and University, and included men whose knowledge was desperately needed as engineers, gunners, signallers, and in other technical arms.

Furthermore, one of the great handicaps in training for the front was the shortage of practice equipment. It is possible to drill and learn discipline with wooden rifles but any skill in marksmanship can only be obtained by firing live rounds. In 1915 there were a million men under training in the United Kingdom. Ranges were built with astonishing speed but ranges are only of use when there is ammunition to fire on them – and there was too little of that. Of all firing practice the most important perhaps was for artillery, for if the co-ordination of artillery fire is wrong little else is right. Many recruits could shoot with shotguns or rifles before they enlisted, but no one could have had experience with field guns unless in an army unit. It was hardly surprising that there was not much ammunition available for practice for there was insufficient on the battlefield itself.

Yet with all these handicaps the British Army at Loos had made a tremendous dent in the German line and come within a fraction of complete success.

3

The Second Day–26th September

As mentioned earlier, the only reserves available to press home any advantage were the troops of the general reserve, that is, XI Corps. All the I Corps and IV Corps reserves had been committed in the battle itself. XI Corps consisted of the Guards Division, the 12th (Eastern) Division, 21st Division, 24th Division, and 46th (North Midland) – a territorial division. 12th and 46th were not yet in the area and would not be brought up till 29th September and 3rd October respectively.

The handling, and fate, of 21st and 24th divisions led to so much bitter recrimination that for many years the disasters of 26th September were ascribed to the obstinacy and personal antagonism of Haig and French. Haig believed that if he had had the reserve division under his command during the battle he could have used it to win the day; in fact, beforehand he was so sure of being able to use the general reserve that he committed all the Corps reserves in the battle itself, as we have already remarked.

French, however, had different ideas. He considered that XI Corps should stay as a general reserve – for there was no other, until a clear picture of the first day's events had been obtained. He was reluctant to commit such newly-arrived divisions – they had been in France for a mere fortnight. It is easy to be wise after the event and after Loos it seemed inexplicable that French should not have taken more experienced divisions from quiet sectors and used them in the attack; their normal places could have been taken over by the 21st and 24th.

In the event 21st and 24th had the worst of it all ways. Even the Guards Division – which was not put under Haig's command till 1600 hrs. on 26th September – did not get into the attack till 1600 on the following day, by which time 21st and 24th had been destroyed. The Guards, of course, had to be held in reserve for there was none other. Had the Germans managed to mount a full-scale counter-attack at this point the only unit left to stop it would have been the Guards Division. Their task might have been impossible, but it is a simple statement of fact to say that though other divisions might be equal to such a task, none could be better.

However the immediate concern is 21st and 24th Divisions. Both these (and the Guards Division) had been concentrated in the area west of St Omer. On 20th September the 21st and 24th received orders to march up, all movement to take place between 1800 and 0500. The Guards Division would follow a day later. The weather was hot and sticky, even at night. The first two nights each involved twenty miles straight marching but the third was more complicated as the divisional routes crossed before they arrived at their allotted billets at Lillers, some sixteen miles behind the Loos lines. One might perhaps wonder how anyone could plan a march up which involved two divisions crossing each other's paths in a night march. But there was even worse to come.

Had Sir John French been present during this march up it would have, in his mind, justified his statement written to the War Office the previous January, referring to the New Armies :

The experience I have gained during the war leads me to a very decided conclusion that it would not be advisable to organize troops so raised and trained, and having only such officers and staff as are available, in any higher units than brigades.

In short he believed that any unit of the new armies numbering more than three thousand would fall into chaos.

Nine months later he had decided that units of the new army might in some circumstances be more useful than experienced troops. The circumstances would be when the enemy was on the run; at such a time other soldiers would be reluctant to push too far forward, having developed a trench-hugging attitude. This was French the cavalry officer talking, and, as he was surrounded by cavalry officers, he would find no one to disagree. In the cavalry it is almost impossible for a large formation to be kept under proper control unless the commander and his officers are fully experienced; this can apply to infantry but is much less likely to do so. Equally, inexperienced cavalry troops often have a dash and vigour which their older comrades have lost. Nevertheless even the most orthodox cavalry officer would not leave his forces sixteen miles behind the line. It seems possible that French felt some compassion for what he regarded as fledgling troops and felt it was his duty to prevent Haig getting his hands on them and sacrificing them. In the event the delay meant they were in fact sacrificed.

Although General Haking, the XI Corps commander, subsequently blamed 21st and 24th Division for the hardships of their march, saying it was lack of march discipline, this unworthy criticism was simply untrue. Haking had commanded a division at Aubers Ridge the previous May and managed to lose most of it by the reckless handling of his brigade; however he had emerged with a reputation for forcefulness and was promoted to the command of XI Corps. French was probably well aware that if Haking had his way 21st and 24th would be thrown into the battle at the earliest possible moment. Loyalty to and consideration for his troops did not appear to have been characteristics of Haking.

At 1900 on the night of the 24th, 21st and 24th Divisions were ordered up into the line. Haking, at a conference earlier in the day, had told the divisional commanders to take away the cookers, which would not be returned till the night of the 26th/27th. Instead packs and greatcoats would be carried and each man would also carry one iron ration, one extra cheese ration, a piece of bread and cheese and some cold pea soup. They had already been scantily-fed and kept short of water on the march to Lillers, and, as everyone knows, marching by night and attempting to sleep by day is a tiring and frustrating process. In fact, they were already hungry, thirsty and weary before the last phase began. The horses were in a worse state than the men, for horses find night work especially tiring.

The roads to the line were narrow and not easy to find in the dark. As some forty thousand troops began to move up they were met by all the inevitable down traffic, ambulances, vehicles going back for supplies and ammunition, walking wounded etc. There were no designated 'up' and 'down' routes. It was, as the official history described it, like 'trying to push the Lord Mayor's procession through the streets of London without clearing the route and holding up traffic'. There were endless delays at cross-roads with all roads in use, and at level crossings which had long supply trains running over them. At one level crossing an accident held up 64th Brigade for an hour and a half.

Farcical though it may seem, 72nd Brigade was stopped by a military policeman on the outskirts of Béthune because the Brigade Commander had no pass to enter the area. Military police, although far from popular with other units of the army, do a vital job in traffic control. As they are normally stationed on crossroads, they have a high casualty rate if near the line. But at Loos they did little to earn popularity. Two regiments of 62nd Brigade were much delayed by an over officious military policeman at Nouex-les-Mines. He informed them that from there onwards they must conform to the routine of trench warfare and open out between sections. Lacking experience, they obeyed him. The instruction he had in mind referred to small units moving in areas likely to be under heavy

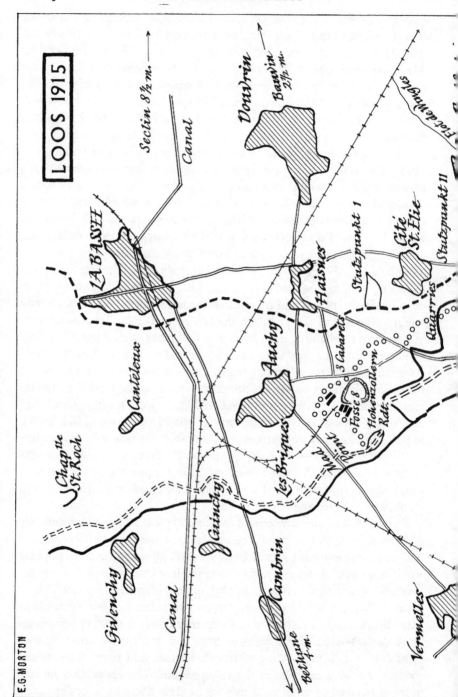

E.G.MORTON

LOOS 1915

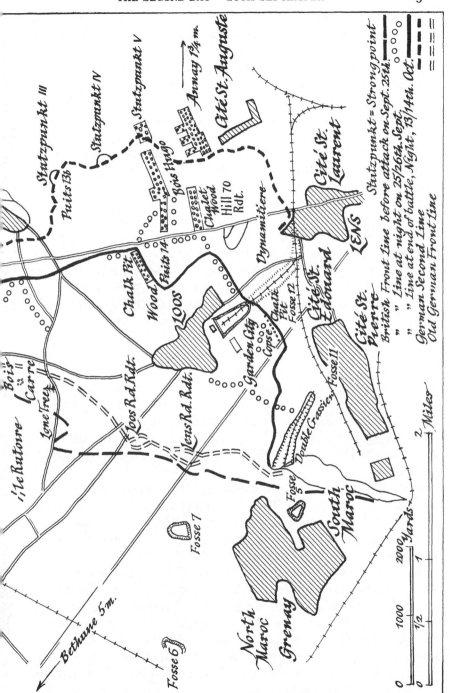

shellfire. Applied to units of a division – which closed up extended over fifteen miles of road – it would mean a delay of many hours as well as additional problems in keeping touch on congested roads.

It was raining all night and when the first units reached their allotted areas sleep was impossible as the Germans were now hammering the British line with the heaviest bombardment so far mounted in the war. At this time French and his staff were at Château Philomel, three miles south of Lillers. Here the Commander-in-Chief could telephone GHQ at St Omer but had no connection at all to his army units fighting the battle. To communicate with them he had to use messengers over the roads whose condition we have just described. Meanwhile the troops sat in the damp fields and thought about hot food.

In theory, while the battles of 25th September were being fought 21st and 24th Division were resting. In fact most of the men had had little sleep and not much food since 20th September. Undoubtedly much time which should have been spent resting and sleeping was spent exploring the district for food or other comforts. The fact that men were able to do this was due to the inexperience of the regimental officers. How much sleep they managed on 25th September, waiting for their turn in the battle, may be left to the imagination. That night 25th/26th was spent deploying in the positions in which they were expected to start the battle the next day. Nobody, including their staff officers knew the ground, and there were no large scale maps available. The problem of taking a regiment over unknown country, littered with trenches, debris and bodies, to a remote point in dark and drizzle might well be thought insoluble but somehow, by daybreak on 26th September, most of the units had found their allotted station in the newly-captured ground. Astonishingly, morale was still high.

In the higher command, and particularly with French and Haig, there was considerable optimism. The German line had been cracked and the pursuit could now begin. Haking had already informed the commanders of 21st and 24th Division that they were not to be used unless the Germans were actually retiring in disorder.

This assessment overlooked several vital factors. The troops of I and IV Corps who had been involved in the fighting of the 25th had suffered tremendous casualties which had effectively removed whole regiments from the battle. Furthermore all troops were exhausted : it was not only the fighting and lack of sleep which had exhausted them, it was also the effort of trying to secure their newly-captured positions by hacking trenches out of the stubborn chalk. The contribution the survivors of the battle of the 25th could make to the fighting of the 26th was thus strictly liimted. Much of this confusion and false deduction stemmed from lack of the means of communication. Radio communication was not possible and unless field telephone wires could be laid, and remain uncut, messages had to be delivered by runner. A runner could easily be killed or get lost; thus many messages between formations, in the line and from front to rear or vice versa, never reached their destination. Some of the critics of tactics in the First World War have overlooked the problem of communication.

The task of the signaller in this type of warfare was not enviable. Almost as fast as he laid lines they were cut by shellfire or other means. His job was then to go out and repair the damage. This usually meant going to the place where the shelling was most intense. While he was busying himself with the repair he also made an ideal exposed target for an enemy sniper.

Even more serious was the German reaction. At the start of the attack they had been surprised, but had contrived to retreat in reasonable order, taking their artillery with them. British Intelligence had calculated that at the best the Germans could rush no more than five divisions to this sector during the first day of the battle; in the event the Germans brought up nearly seven. These fresh troops busied themselves during the night with wiring the 2nd position and siting machine guns. What had the day before been an incomplete trench system with, in many parts, a single strand of wire in front, now had a strong entanglement, well-staked, 4ft high and twenty feet deep.

When 21st and 24th Divisions were launched into the attack at 1100 on 26th September they were advancing against uncut wire and un-damaged positions, for there had been no preceding artillery bombard-ment, furthermore they had no gas nor smoke to cover them but were expected to advance over open ground, littered with the dead and wounded of the previous day.

The situation of the newly arrived divisions requires some clarification at this point. Apart from weariness, thirst, hunger and frustration, there were more serious problems. The first was the lack of proper maps. In rain, mist and dark, units were expected to find positions, such as Hill 70, which were not even marked on the maps they had. Though the journey from Lillers to the line had been frustrating and wearisome the journey from the old British front line to the newly captured area made all that had gone before seem almost pleasurable. Even when they knew the location of their appointed destination it was still extremely difficult to reach. They had to cross the former trenches, both British and German, usually by using a single plank. When they came to gaps in the wire these were usually narrow. There were landmarks in the shape of pithead gear but they were so alike they merely added to the confusion; most units had to take a rough compass bearing on the light coming from the town of Loos itself, which had a number of burning buildings.

Had the units of the new division been told to act as reinforcements to the badly cut-up regiments already on the ground there would have been a fair chance of their reaching their required position without too much trouble. Instead 21st Division was ordered to deploy on a thousand yard frontage between Fosse 7 (on the Bethune-Lens road) and the Vermelles-Loos track (it was not a proper road). 24th Division was to occupy the thousand yards due north (i.e. on the left of the 21st) and this would take the left flank of the 24th on to the Vermelles-Hulluch road.

It will probably be no surprise to learn that meanwhile the 3rd Cavalry, which had been ten miles north of Lillers, had been ordered to take up an attacking position roughly north of Loos; their march brought them right across the path of the other two divisions. The cavalry were, of course, dismounted, and subsequently fought extremely well as infantry.

3rd Cavalry, incidentally, belonged to the Indian Corps which, as we have noted, went into action north of La Bassée in a feint attack which proved somewhat costly. The rain had poured down in the early part of the night and had been succeeded by drifting mist. Periodically the Germans shelled the area they had lost. On arrival at their destination digging proved impossible with the light entrenching tool carried by each man; the heavier digging equipment had been left at the rear. All this accumulating frustration would have been hard enough to bear for seasoned regiments with trained staff and experienced officers. In the circumstances the morale of the K division could have been expected to be at zero but it was far from it. Surprisingly the divisions were calm, and there were very few examples of units imagining they were being attacked by Germans and opening fire on their own comrades.

The Germans were well aware of the confusion among the British troops facing them and tried to exploit that confusion in various sectors. They made a bad mistake at midnight on 25th September, for three hundred Germans advanced along the Vermelles-Hulluch road hoping to recapture three guns abandoned earlier in the day. They came to a trench held by British troops and called out, 'Don't shoot, we are the Welch coming back.' Unknown to them, the trench was held by the 1st Battalion of the South Wales Borderers who indeed did not shoot – not until every German was well in sight. Few of the Germans got back to their own lines.

But all was not going so well elsewhere. Although the artillery were doing their best to support the infantry, some of their shells fell on lines still occupied by the British. Infantry often cynically imagine that most of the shells that fall on them come from their own guns. On the rare occasions when this happens it is often because the gunners have not received the latest information about their target areas.

When 62nd Brigade and 45th Brigade eventually reached Hill 70 they were badly intermingled and were already at the limits of physical endurance. Nevertheless they pushed the line over the top of the crest. 45th Brigade were cut down as they tried to advance further, for the area was now not only traversed by machine-gun fire but also accurately ranged on by German artillery fire.

Attempts to push the line further ahead proved unsuccessful, mainly because all the officers trying to lead were killed off. The Green Howards lost their commanding officer and the next three senior officers all within a few moments of each other. Even so, further attempts continued to be made until the Germans launched yet another heavy artillery bombardment on the hill slopes.

After that a number of stragglers began to wander back through Loos. They were not panicking but there was no one left to rally and re-group them; all were desperately thirsty, partly from lack of water, partly from the salty rations they had been issued with.

Further north the Germans had counter-attacked in the centre during the night just as some of the regiments of 21st Division were getting into their battle positions. The York and Lancaster Regiment took sustained casualties checking one attack; the West Yorkshire inflicted heavy losses on the enemy before themselves being enfiladed. Again it was the same story as on Hill 70. As one example, the Durham Light Infantry lost seventeen officers, which included the CO, the Adjutant, and all the Company Commanders. At 1200 hrs on 26th September, 1st Division made an attempt to capture Hulluch, using the Black Watch and the South Wales Borderers. To reach it they had to cross six hundred yards of open ground. Before they had covered the first hundred yards their numbers had been halved.

Regiment after regiment now tried to force its way ahead: King's Own Yorkshire Light Infantry, East Surreys, West Kents, Buffs, Essex, Sherwood Foresters. No one, not even the toughest veteran regiments would have done better, as their Divisional Commander recorded, but all were gradually scythed to a stop and had to return. The commanding officer of the Buffs, a militia officer, was 61; twelve other officers died with him. When men eventually fell back in disorder there was no difficulty in collecting and re-grouping them; cohesion had gone but not morale. As an example, when units of the 6th Cavalry Brigade were sent to reinforce the Hill 70 position they had no difficulty in collecting up stragglers (who had been on the move, fighting or digging, for 36 hours) and taking them back with them into the attack.

In the afternoon of 26th September it was decided at GHQ to put in the Guards Division to make a last effort to break through over Hill 70. Even this experienced division found the task of reaching the line almost impossible, and when they reached the battle area could not find either any headquarters or even the approximate location of the front line. Hill 70 was considered a vital area to capture for it dominated the newly captured line in the Loos valley.

Welcome though the arrival in the line of the Guards was, the fact that it did not take place till 27th September caused some comment. As the Guardsmen moved up that afternoon they were indignant to see stragglers. The 'stragglers' after two days bloody fighting were equally irate to see the Guards coming up 'late', as they put it. The exchanges were somewhat acid. However by 1700 the Scots and Irish Guards were themselves driven back; they were then joined by the Coldstream, after which all pushed forward and dug in. In two days this brigade lost 42 officers and 1266 other ranks. By the night of 27th/28th September the line along the British front was now stabilizing, although this also meant that the Germans were giving it all the shells that their artillery could manage.

On 28th September Sir John French made it very clear to General Joffre that his reserves were now used up and his right was exposed. If he were to continue the offensive the French must help by making diversionary attacks. The outcome was that the French took over the Loos sector thereby releasing 47th Division and two Guards brigades for a general reserve. However this did not stop the 2nd Guards Brigade (now at about half strength) being used on the 28th to try to push the British line further forward at Puits 14 bis, just north of Loos. The Coldstream were almost exterminated in the attack. The Guards eventually completed their tour in the line by digging trenches in almost solid chalk; it was considered to be one of the hardest pieces of trench digging in the war. On 30th September, Major General F. D. V. Wing of 12th Division was killed by a shell – the third General to be killed in this battle.

Meanwhile steady attempts were being made by the Germans to recapture the Hohenzollern Redoubt. On 3rd October they were successful. On 8th October the Germans made a further attempt to recapture lost ground by launching an offensive along the entire line. By nightfall they had abandoned the attempt after heavy losses. This was officially the end of the Battle of Loos.

Nevertheless on 13th October a final British effort was made to push the line a little further ahead before the winter rains set in; it eventually failed through lack of hand grenades. Haig thought that if the rains held off it might be possible to launch another general offensive on 7th November. However, the combination of heavy rains and accurate German shelling during the second half of October finally convinced him that the possibility did not exist. The battle of Loos was finally over. There were tangible gains, and lessons had been learnt.

The cost in terms of numbers was soon known. The ultimate cost in terms of the quality of men would become all too apparent later.

4

The Commander in Chief
Sir John French

EXTRACTS FROM HIS DIARY

The diaries of Sir John French, which were deposited in the Imperial War Museum by their owner Lady Patricia Kingsbury, were a private record and in no way a war diary in the conventional sense. Sir John French had kept a diary for many years but his diaries merely record events which interested him and with which he was personally concerned; they do not include general observations on the social and military scene. But both the diaries and the letters reveal him as a compassionate and kindly person, hating the carnage of war, and in no way resembling the caricature which has sometimes been made of him. On 26th September he visited the dressing station at Noeux-les-Mines and talked to many of the wounded and dying; it must have been an appalling sight and many generals would have shrunk from it.

The most interesting aspect of the diaries is that they record the information he received about the battle. On this he based his decisions. Some of it was wrong information. Like all commanders in history he made some right decisions and some wrong ones; he was forced into making an assault about which he had many misgivings and the result was a disaster. Sixty years later we can easily see the mistakes he made in handling the general reserve which resulted in XI Corps being asked to do the impossible. But at the same time it is worth bearing in mind that if Loos had resulted in a complete breakthrough Sir John French would have been considered one of the most enterprising and successful generals of history.

The following extracts include all the relevant references to Loos. The other portions of the diary deal with different sections of the front.

August 21st (1915) I had news from Kitchener late yesterday evening saying that they had it on the very best information that Germany was now very short of men. He asked me to urge Joffre to hasten his attacks.

August 24th I went to see Haig at his headquarters at 11.30 today. I intimated to him *the date.* I asked him to take every precaution to avoid waste of lives.

September 22nd The bombardment by I Army on enemy commenced yesterday. It was expected to be very effective in his trenches. The enemy's reply was weak. It was reported that three of his batteries were quickly silenced.

I went to see Haig at 2 . . . discussed the character of the wind and the state of the weather.

September 23rd I saw Foulkes [Colonel, R. E.] about the Gas coys. All is in order and all we want is a favourable wind. There is a marked change in the weather tonight which promises well.

September 25th I came to Advanced Headquarters at Lillers last night. There was a heavy cannonade all night. Much intensified towards 5 a.m.

The wind which was doubtful all night became fairly favourable at 5 and Haig ordered the gas to be started. Heavy volumes floated forward and *over* the enemy's lines.

The attacks arranged at Hooge started at daybreak and all the enemy trenches which were the objects of the attack were captured during the morning.

Some but not all of these gains were lost in a German counter attack that afternoon.

The attack by the 3rd and Indian Corps started at daybreak. They were both successful at first but later in the day the enemy brought up strong reserves and after hard fighting and variable fortunes they remained in their original positions at nightfall. They succeeded however in holding large numbers of the enemy.

French knew the overall position at 11 a.m. and went to Haig and decided to lend him 21st and 24th Divisions from XI Corps to support the attack. He told him he was holding the 3rd (Cavalry) Division in readiness to follow up and go through any gap made between Hulluch and Loos. He wrote I saw part of the 24th Division. They were a fine workmanlike-looking lot.

The diary goes on:

The 21st and 24th Divisions only reached the old trench line after dark and so were not available for attack today (25th). The Guards Division reached Noeux-les-Mines at 6 p.m. The Tenth French Army, on our right, delayed their attack till 12.20 thus losing many valuable hours.

September 26th The 21st and 24th Division beaten back and their situation became critical.

I went to see Haig at 11.30 and arranged with him to put the Guards Division and the 28th Division under his orders.

I spoke to a lot of wounded in the dressing station at Noeux-les-Mines. [*He spent two hours there*].

September 27th Foch came to see me this morning. I told him that if I was in the position of Commander-in-Chief of the whole Western Allied Front I should put every available man in front north of Hill 70 and rush a gap in the enemy. I should feel confident of success.

Clearly French did not know how much the German line had now been strengthened at that point.

Foch agreed in principle but said it would be very difficult to organize a big attack in so small an area with combined French–British forces. He suggested as an alternative that he should send the 152nd French Division to relieve 47th Division and thus enable me to put more troops into my eastern attack.

To this I agreed.

Eye-Witness Accounts

The following descriptions were written by men who were in the battle. A few of the general accounts have appeared in regimental association news letters, and one or two were included in regimental histories. The majority, as will be seen, are in letters written to the author of this book. Some divisions are very well represented; others, unfortunately, are not. With some exceptions those who fought in the battle were aged eighteen or over. This means that the youngest survivors are now seventy-nine. Although there are a few survivors in their nineties, most are in their eighties. Many who wrote to me apologised for their writing which they regretted had been spoiled by failing eyesight, arthritis and other ills, yet compared with most of the handwriting one sees today it was exemplary.

Many of the accounts and letters are grim and poignant reading. The battle of Loos, like others in the First World War, did not end within the period it was fought in; the effects lasted through following generations. The losses of these battles were not merely in men killed but in the extinction of marriages and hopes for marriage; there were hundreds of thousands of war widows, but perhaps an even greater tragedy lay with those whose potential husbands went off to the trenches and never returned.

The accounts begin with general descriptions, then work along the line from south to north, Lens–La Bassée.

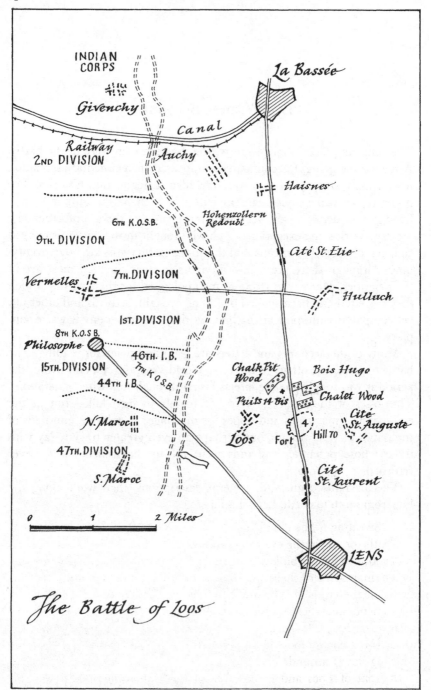

INDIAN
CORPS

La Bassée

Givenchy

Canal

Railway

2ND DIVISION

Auchy

Haisnes

Hohenzollern
Redoubt

6TH K.O.S.B.

9TH. DIVISION

7TH. DIVISION

Cité St. Elie

Vermelles

Hulluch

1ST. DIVISION

8TH K.O.S.B.

Philosophe

46TH. I.B.

15TH. DIVISION

7TH K.O.S.B.

44TH. I.B.

Chalk Pit
Wood

Bois Hugo

Chalet Wood

Puits 14 Bis

Cité
St. Auguste

N. Maroc

Loos

4

Fort

Hill 70

47TH. DIVISION

S. Maroc

Cité
St. Laurent

0   1   2 Miles

LENS

The Battle of Loos

Detail of the battlefield

5

General Accounts

Account from C. J. T. Johnson
The gunners were standing by their guns waiting for the order to fire. Slowly it seemed the minutes crept to Zero minus 5 – Then 4 'Hook your lanyards, 3, 2, 1 – FIRE! – Boom! Scrunch! – Red-Black Flash! – the quivering of the ground and the deafening crumps and spurts of earth and the smoke. The Battle of Loos had commenced, 5.50 a.m. the 25th September, 1915.

EVENTS OF THE FIRST DAY

The British artillery bombardment was not very impressive but there was no shortage of gas before the assault, over 150 tons were released from the cylinders.

The greenish-yellow gas hissed from the containers and rose into the air forming a cloud about 40 feet high and drifted very slowly forward towards the enemy. Now, above the din of the bombardment, was heard the dreaded pop and ping of German machine-gun bullets tearing across the top of the British trenches and more bullets striking the top bags of the parapet. Distress flares from the German lines soared into the sky – red and white. The assaulting troops, packed in their trenches waiting for the order to jump off, crouched down as the enemy shells came over at them. Sweating in the flannel gas masks covering their heads, barely able to breathe or see, as the eye-pieces misted over, they listened in dismay to the continued enemy bullets banging into the sandbag parados. Presently the German artillery shells were joined by mortar-fire. The strain on the nerves of the crouching British was mounting as direct hits smashed in the trenches and caused some casualties. 'When would the gas reach the enemy trenches and silence this fire?' The fact was the gas was not moving towards the enemy too well, it seemed to hang about in No-mans-land whirling slowly around.

In front of Loos and in the area of the Hohenzollern Redoubt the cloud of gas drifted fairly well over the German trenches but it moved much too slowly to be an absolute success; it was not thick enough by the time it reached the Germans. At the southern end of the attack front-age no gas had reached the enemy trenches after over 30 minutes dis-charge.

In the centre, in the Lone Tree region of attack, the chlorine vapour and smoke carried forward, on the slight breeze, towards the enemy at first but then the discharge began to drift back and into the British trenches which caused some casualties. Some of the men slightly raised the edge of their grey 'flannel bags' for fresh air, instead of which they caught a whiff of gas. Those of the infantry who got gassed were seen staggering about trying to vomit. They would tear off their masks and wildly grasp at the air. The release of gas was stopped at these places and smoke candles only used.

There was no great panic amongst the Germans and they quickly recovered. Sufficient gas did not reach them to do much harm.

Bayonets were fixed and at 6.30 a.m. the first wave of the assaulting troops of six divisions of the First Army scrambled out of their trenches in the fog of gas and smoke, barely able to distinguish a thing, loaded up with bombs, picks and shovels, extra ammunition etc. Some had their gas masks down as gas was still hanging about in places. Where possible their 'flannel bag', the improvised gas mask, was over their heads with the front rolled up. When the front was down and tucked into their tunics they could not see anything through the talc covered eyepieces and with the front rolled up the rain had caused the chemicals in the flannel to seep out and this made the eyes smart.

As they scaled the trenches several appeared to slip back into the trench again but on looking more closely it was seen these men's masks had a rent in them and the grey flannel was turning red. These men lay very still.

More and more troops were moving up the communication trenches and began to cough and splutter as they reached the front line where smoke and gas was hanging about. They climbed out and dashed along behind the parados looking for the bridges made over the trenches. This caused some congestion and confusion as the trenches were still under fire. At last, those who had not fallen, got across, extended and went for-ward after the first wave. Many did not get far and you could observe gaps in the line where they had dropped out, caught by the German machine-guns sweeping No-Mans-Land'. The advancing men now dis-appeared into the retarded motion of smoke and gas into which shells were now bursting throwing up clods of earth and some of the men with it. Bullets were flying about everywhere. The ground was strewn with the dead and the movements of wounded. Hands lifted among those still alive that were lying and crawling in the grasses, their tunics all torn. Some shouted for help and water. Those that were not so badly hurt asked when stretcher-bearers would be along. The reply was always the same, 'Help would be coming soon.' Other bodies were stumbled upon, lying quite still with staring eyes and pale faces.

To the right could be seen the red glow that was the village of Loos-en-Gohrelle on fire.

Another stop was made to check compass bearing and to find a gap through the German barbed wire, as just in front was the grey chalk of the captured German trenches. During the wait weary men sank down on the wet ground to rest. It was hard going over the shell-torn ground; packs and equipment were becoming a dead weight and most men were wet through. Now and again, as they waited, they could hear groans from the unseen wounded and cries of 'Water for Christ's sake.' '. . . Just a minute chum!' . . . 'Hi! Help! Oh-h-h, stretcher-bearers.' The men asked, 'Can't we do something for them?' 'Nothing,' was the reply; 'it will only bring false hopes and it is against orders to stop for the wounded, and we have no water.' 'For God's sake then let's get a move on! How do we get over these b—— trenches?' 'Find a plank or bridge. If not, scramble over!' Such were the snatches of conversation.

If only those reserves could have got up sooner and in daylight before the Germans came back with reinforcements. The front was then open. There was actually a lull in the fighting here. The only rifle fire was to the right beyond the 'Tower Bridge' on Hill 70 and on the left as far away as the Hohenzollern Redoubt. There was still a gap in this sector and it could have been filled before the Germans got there in any strength.

The figures giving the heavy losses suffered by the battalions in the line could hardly have reached the First Army Commander by nightfall.

The situation as Sir Douglas Haig and his staff saw it was that the enemy had been driven entirely from his first line defences and that the second and final system of defence behind the Lens–La Bassée Road (until it turned at right angles, west of and around Lens), was but weakly held and most trenches unprotected by barbed wire. If he could break through this last position in the centre, the German position around Lens would be turned.

Haig's original plan of action was to a great extent dependent on the French on the British right. Lord Kitchener had directed 'a continuous and vigorous attack' but an attack has vulnerable flanks that must be strongly protected. The enemy will always attempt to get round the flanks and so into the undefended back areas. This must be neutralized in advance by strong defensive flanks, so that the frontal attack may be made with assurance. On the right of the British attack the Tenth French Army failed to commence its assault until $5\frac{1}{2}$ hours after the First British Army's assault. It also failed when it did start at mid-day. The Vimy Ridge, over-looking the plain stretching away to the river Scheldt, remained in German hands. The French advance line was still 3 miles behind, so the advance by the British north of Vimy Ridge was endangered from the southern flank. This meant that the 47th and 15th British divisions would have to secure this flank by digging in and wiring their positions east of Loos and Hill 70 to stop any enemy threats into the southern side of the First Army's further attacks.

The First Army Commander decided to push on with the attack, to draw away German troops opposing the French and so help them to advance. General Haig's orders were accordingly circulated at 11.30 p.m. on the night of 25th from his Headquarters at Hinges to continue the attack. The 21st and 24th Divisions of the XI Corps were to attack at 11.00 a.m. the next morning, the 26th, break through the weak German second positions and line the Haute Deule Canal. The cavalry would then pass through the gap to the Flanders plain. Such was the general plan to be put into action. Field-Marshal Sir John French did not, apparently, repress General Haig, although he felt 'the futility of push-ing reserves through a narrow gap in the German defences', and informed his First Army Commander that the last reserves, the Guards Division, was on its way 'to be at his orders'.

While the order from First Army HQ to attack was being put into detailed orders at the Headquarters of the I, IV, and XI Corps, the Germans, apparently unknown to the British Staff, were busy bringing up still more reserves and sticking barbed wire in front of their positions, without any interference from the British. Other of the enemy were advancing to the straight Lens–La Bassée Road in the path of the XI Corps.

It took the East Surrey and Royal West Kents an hour to get through, and clear of, the old German line, with its narrow gaps in the wire and few single planks over the trenches. German dead were lying about and in one trench a batch of German prisoners was crouching guarded by a British sentry or two who asked for instructions but received nothing definite. Now clear of the trenches, the two battalions pressed on, head-ing straight for the enemy, whose precise position was not known, as no other British troops were directly ahead. The hungry men were, however, getting exhausted and water bottles were empty, so a rest was ordered. While resting many fell asleep despite the cold and wet.

About this time the alarming news came that Hulluch was entirely in German hands again. The 9th East Surrey Battalion, in endeavouring to maintain touch with the 21st Division had spread out too far to its right and was now ordered by Brigadier General Mitford, CB, DSO, commanding 72nd Brigade to close on its left and to dig itself in, in two lines facing east and about half a mile SW of Hulluch. The only casualties so far received by the E. Surreys were one officer and two men. It was now past midnight; the rain, however, had ceased and the tired, wet and hungry men attempted to dig trenches. Not with picks and shovels, they had none, but with the small entrenching tools that each man carries. These were utterly useless for digging a trench of any size and not effective on hard chalky soil. Anyway it did keep the men warm and resulted in some small scrapings in the chalk hacked out. This trench averaged perhaps 15 inches deep and wandered for about 200 yards beside the Lens–La Bassée Road which was about 500 yards ahead (see sketch). This was kept up till near dawn.

Owing to the delays and hold-ups it is not surprising that the XI Corps deployment was even now only about three quarters complete. These troops had now been on the move for over 18 hours, with hardly, if any, food or hot drink inside them. Another very serious incident befell the divisional artillery. The thick mist hanging over the area at dawn resulted in some of the division's guns getting into positions some half a mile in front of those assigned to them. When the mist cleared they found themselves in full view of the enemy batteries at Hulluch and Haines. So their guns were effectively neutralized from the very start.

Just before dawn orders were received by the East Surreys and Royal West Kents, attempting to dig themselves in, for a retirement to the captured German trenches and here the 72nd Brigade remained under occasional shell-fire which did no serious damage.

In spite of all ranks in this volunteer force now suffering from hunger and exhaustion – it will be remembered the East Surreys received their last solid meal on the evening of the 24th September, 36 hours before – their morale remained high. During the morning (26th) the cookers had at last caught up and dixies of greasy stew were brought up to the trenches. At 10 o'clock a.m. on 26th September, the Brigadier commanding received orders for the attack which was to commence an hour later. Although they had been told by Sir John French their job would be a long march in pursuit of a demoralized enemy on the run and even General Haking, the XI Corps commander, had said they would 'not be put in until the Germans had been smashed and were retiring', Haig's orders for the 26th September were quite definite – that *all* divisions were to continue the battle at 11 a.m. These orders, as you have read, were timed 11.30 p.m. on 25th September when the 21st and 24th Divisions were still struggling and stumbling about the captured German trenches and over the bodies of dead and wounded.

Since the previous afternoon and throughout the night the Germans had got their reserves up and into position and their second line of defence was as strongly held as had been his first line at the time of the first assault on the previous morning, with formidable barbed wire barriers erected and intact. The original attack on the previous day had been preceded by a four day artillery bombardment and a discharge of gas for half an hour along the whole front. Also the assault had been made by trained divisions who had rehearsed the attack some weeks beforehand. The unlucky newly formed 21st and 24th divisions, now filling the gap left on the 25th September, were expected to advance across a wide No-Man's-Land in broad daylight with no gas or smoke clouds for cover; with practically no artillery support and assault the enemy second position.

The area of the XI Corps attack contained a number of small quarries and mine shafts and a wooded copse named Bois Hugo. These had been evacuated by the enemy during the fighting of 25th September but were re-occupied as reinforcements came into action, and formed a German outpost line manned by machine-guns and snipers.

The tragedy of the situation seems to be that all this area and parts of the German second line defences could, as we have seen, have been captured for the asking in the afternoon, if the British reserves had been got up and properly handled.

It is now known that a German battalion in reserve coming up from Annay, to occupy ground between the Bois Hugo and Hulluch, were instructed to get forward as quickly as possible, as the British might have already entered it. So probable did this appear to be that the German battalion deployed about half a mile from it in extended order, just before dusk, only to find the sector empty of the British. This was the sector that the 24th Division were ordered to attack at 11 a.m. the 26th. During the night other opportunities were missed by the British. Immediately to the south of the above sector two more German battalions cautiously advanced into the Bois Hugo sector of their second line defences and then at dawn, under cover of the mist, went forward into the wood itself.

As soon as the early morning mist cleared, they attacked the British outposts at the western end of the wood and caused them to retire. The

British immediately north of the wood now came under enfilade fire and were forced back across the Lens Road. (This was on the 21st Divisional attack front). As the morning advanced the Germans were still busy reinforcing their line and filling up the gaps southwards and joining up with a further six battalions that had arrived to strengthen the Hill 70 position. Other minor local counter-attacks and small advances were carried out by the Germans to link up and improve their defensive positions. These movements of the enemy, more or less unmolested, would or should have been reported to British Corps and Army Headquarters, which surely would have told them that an unprepared attack by two untried divisions just out from home was not likely to succeed, not knowing what they were up against.

During the morning, in accordance with orders, the two new divisions prepared their order of battle. The final assembly points used were the captured German trenches of the previous day. Some of these trenches and dug-outs were pockets of gas, and in the old German front line were many German corpses, a horrible yellowish-blue colour. The stench was dreadful. Yet the spirit of these British volunteers was marvellously unshaken. The Official History states :

> They were delighted at the prospect of getting at the enemy after the exertions and frustrations of the last few days, although they had had hardly any food and no sleep for 48 hours.

At about 10 a.m. an apparently unmethodical pattern of artillery fire, nowhere near approaching or befitting the character of a bombardment, was put over at the German positions. Without their own artillery in position the new divisions were penalized by Haig's plan of 'flexible' distribution of guns for yesterday's first stage of the battle – relying on the gas to work wonders ! The guns were too widely spread and inadequate to support the offensive. Also the gunners could not have had any clear information of where the German emplacements were as they had been repositioned. It seemed that shells were fired at likely places. No shells cut the German wire and it is doubtful if they received any casualties. This fire only lasted approximately 20 minutes and merely alerted the Germans that we were coming. The front was then almost silent for half an hour.

Briefly the orders for attack received by the 72nd Brigade were :

1st Division to attack Hulluch.
72nd Brigade of 24th Division (with two battalions of 71st Brigade

and a Pioneer Battalion) to advance in a south-easterly direction past the southern outskirts of Hulluch and capture about 800 yards of German second-line trenches, which ran south from Puits No 13 bis.

21st Division to prolong the attack of the 72nd Brigade to the right.

Brigadier-General Mitford disposed the force under his command as follows :

First Line – 8th Royal West Kent Regiment on left; 9th East Surrey Regiment on the right, and to maintain touch with the 21st Division.
Second Line – 8th 'Queen's' on left; 8th 'Buffs' on right.
Third Line – 11th Essex on left; 9th Suffolk on right.
Reserve – 12th Sherwood Foresters.

At 11 a.m. precisely the East Surrey and Royal West Kents of 72nd Brigade scrambled out of the German trenches, without any artillery barrage, and formed up in lines of extended order at the correct spacing, in full equipment, including a weighty pack on their backs. On the order to advance to the attack, they went forward, all correct in line, like a field day before the General, at a walking pace, in full view of the enemy, which drew some German shell-fire and caused a few casualties.

The second wave, again correct in life, followed the first at about 400 yards interval. The East Surreys were on a two company-front. The distance to the German occupied trenches varied from about 1700 yards to 2000 yards.

At the beginning of the advance there was no intensity of fire, but as soon as the Lens-Hulluch Road was crossed the German artillery, machine-gun and rifle fire increased in volume, particularly from some houses on the southern outskirts of Hulluch and from a trench line close on the left of the advance and corresponding to it. The line of advance, therefore, became completely flanked at close range and the attackers began to fall, losses becoming heavy. There were also some German snipers up in the trees alongside the Lens–Hulluch Road, who caused many casualties, a large proportion being officers.

As the Brigades of the 21st and 24th Divisions advanced they came across the dead and dying of some of the men of the 1st Division and 15th Division that had pressed forward too far the previous day. Some of these wounded and delirious men raised themselves up and yelled at the advancing troops to stop and get back, or to bring stretcher-bearers, or to get down and join them in a shell-hole. But the discipline of the battalions held and they steadily went forward obeying orders.

In front of the lines walked the subalterns shouting encouragement – 'Come on boys we're nearly there' or 'We'll soon be among them, show them what we are made of' and so on. Courage and determination is required to go forward under a hail of fire with comrades getting shot up in front and alongside you but the men did not waver.

It is recorded that German look-outs watched column after column moving up in close formation at the crest of Lone Tree Ridge; in places even officers on horses could be seen marshalling battalions as they climbed out of German trenches and formed up in extended order in thousands. The effect was unnerving. Not since First Ypres had such dense masses of infantry deployed for an assault in full daylight over open ground. The very weight of numbers, would, it seemed, carry the British through the German outposts. A colonel of a German Reserve Regiment records, as he was walking in Hulluch a reliable NCO came running up and shouted out, 'Two Divisions . . . we shall be surrounded . . . we must retire . . .' A number of men followed, panic-stricken.

An officer who had been watching the British from a housetop look-out now reported and said the situation was not so very serious. 'We have terrific machine gun and rifle fire power from our position and it is impossible for any enemy to get across the open against it.' Swiftly, further German detachments were instructed and got into position. The Germans held their fire for almost a quarter of an hour, as the British new divisions deployed in lines of extended order and obedient to every order, set off at a walking pace down the slight slope towards the Lens–Hulluch Road.

It must have been a nerve-racking moment for the Germans, watching in silence, until, as the leading waves of the 72nd Brigade passed under the south-eastern front of Hulluch, at a range of about 900 yards, the command to fire was given.

The following is an extract from a German Regiment's diary –

Ten columns of extended line in perfect alignment could clearly be distinguished, each one estimated at more than one thousand men, and offering such a target as had never been seen before, or even thought possible. Never had the machine-gunners such straightforward work to do nor done it so effectively. They traversed to and fro along the enemy's ranks unceasingly. The men stood on the fire-steps, some even on the parapets, and fired in glee into the mass of men advancing across the open ground. As the entire field of fire was covered with the enemy's infantry the effect was devastating and they could be seen falling literally in hundreds.

In spite of some heavy losses the 72nd Brigade advanced with resolution in their straight lines. The East Surrey battalion, endeavouring to keep touch with the 21st Division, as ordered, was forced to incline to its right, leaving a gap between them and the Royal West Kents. This gap was immediately filled by the 'Buffs' and at about the same time the 'Queen's' pushed forward to reinforce the Royal West Kent as their left had suffered terribly from the flanking fire from Hulluch and that enemy-manned trench lying close beside the line of advance. The 'Queen's' also suffered a similar fate and the Brigadier ordered the Essex battalion up to deal with the infantry and machine-guns on the left, who put in some good service at this point.

Just before noon, regardless of the now heavy losses, the 72nd Brigade reached the German second defence lines, which proved a formidable obstacle. Contrary to earlier reports it was found to be wired and this pinned the Brigade down.

Early the previous evening the German position was, for a time, open and unwired, now it was protected by thick barbed wire, over 4 feet high and varied from 10 to 20 yards deep. The wire had been erected by newly arrived German reserves who had worked, without interference, throughout the night. It was excellently constructed, criss-crossed and staked with pit props driven deeply into the ground. Moreover it was entirely undamaged by our artillery.

Quoting again from the same German diary, it records with amazement as follows :

> In spite of the growing intensity of our fire the extended columns continued their advance in good order and without interruption. When they reached the Lens Road one of our companies advanced from the Hulluch trench in an attempt to divert the attack, but only a small party of the enemy stopped to meet it, the mass ignored it and came on regardless, past the southern front of Hulluch. Here they came under enfilade fire from our troops lining this position and also from the fire of a battery of the artillery concealed in the village. Their losses now mounted up rapidly and under this terrible punishment their lines began to get more and more confused. But they still came on doggedly right up to our wire entanglements.

This barrier was of tough steel barbed wire and the few hand-cutters issued made practically no impression on it. A few strands of wire were cut here and there but no gap could be made. In desperation men hurled themselves at it in furious folly; some even attempted to climb over it;

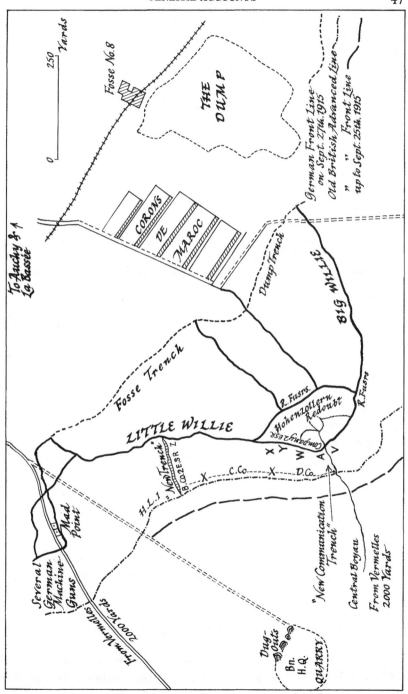

Defence of the Hohenzollern Redoubt by the 2nd Battalion, East Surreys, September 27th to October 1st, 1915.

others tugged at it; still more dashed about thinking to find a gap that the artillery should have made by shellfire until all were knocked or blown down by bullets, or bombs. No reply could be made to the German hand bombs, as at this time the British had but few bombs and these were of poor material.

In spite of the hopelessness of the attempts to penetrate the belt of thick wire, men persisted for quite a time trying to find a way through but it was impossible.

The strip of copse, known as Bois Hugo, lay on the right of the East Surreys. Here German machine-guns had been placed in the early morning and were now being used with great effect from the edge of the copse. The left battalion of the 21st Division, the Somerset Light Infantry and the East Surreys thus came under enfilade fire from this direction, while German field guns fired shrapnel and tear-gas shells over open sights from Hulluch. The East Surreys were now being cut to pieces and their lines rapidly thinned. Men hit with almost a dozen bullets at once would spin round as they fell. As they neared the wire men were falling thick and fast in the amazement of machine-gun death and the now thinned ranks faltered and laid down before the wire which defied all attempts to break through.

The German diary continues :

Confronted by this hopeless impenetrable obstacle and faced by continuous machine-gun and rifle fire the survivors began to turn and retire, though hardly one in ten that had come forward seemed to go back again.

Bodies of dead and dying lay thick outside the German wire, on the right or southwards, the 21st Division was cut to pieces in the same way.

Quoting from another German Regimental diary which refers to the 21st Division's sector :

Dense masses of the enemy, line after line, came into sight on the ridge, some of their officers even mounted on horseback, and advancing as if carrying out a field-day drill in peacetime. Our artillery and machine guns riddled their ranks as they came on. As they crossed the northern front of Bois Hugo, the machine guns positioned there caught them in the flank and whole battalions must have been utterly destroyed. The English made five consecutive attempts to press on past the wood and reach our second line defence position, but finally, weakened by their terrible losses, they were forced to give in.

The conditions at the other end of the wood and for the men struggling up the bare incline of Hill 70 were even worse. It is recorded that a commander of one German battalion said afterwards that, 'the massacre filled every one of us watching with a sense of disgust and nausea'; so much were they affected that they ceased fire when the English retired. They had before them the 'Corpse-field of Loos' as the Germans described it. As they watched dozens of forms in the English khaki rose up once more and began to crawl or limp back to their lines, 'no shot was fired at them from the German lines for the remainder of the day, so great was the feeling of pity and mercy for the enemy'.

The 24th Division was now entirely unsupported as the divisions on either flank had not succeeded in reaching their objectives. A withdrawal was therefore ordered and the 72nd brigade, after three-quarters of their numbers were either dead, dying or wounded, began to leave the battlefield, in full view of the Germans, across the open spaces, most of them walked slowly and upright, still in extended lines back to the trenches from which they advanced. It looked just as if the war was over and the Germans stood up and watched them go. There was not much German fire and it was held altogether after the Lens–La Bassée road was crossed except for a few shells. It was said to be on account of the wounded who were able to walk hobble or crawl, rising up and beginning to follow that caused the Germans to cease fire on most of the front. They had too many British wounded on their hands as it was with all those that had to be left lying on the ground in front of their wire, calling out, raising arms, crying for help.

As the remnants, with torn and chalk-mudded uniforms, reached the trenches they had left that morning, the slow and exhausted men were re-organized into a line of defence to meet any counter-attack.

Of the twelve or fourteen battalions of the New Army that actually went into the attack, at a total strengh of about 10,000, there were 385 officers and 7,861 other ranks casualties after $3\frac{1}{2}$ hours, about the time the battle lasted. The Germans reported no casualties.

The losses of the East Surrey battalion were 16 officers and 440 other ranks. Some of the wounded picked up died later whilst prisoners-of-war.

The batteries that took up wrong positions in the dark and mist suffered badly. Dead horses lay about, guns turned over, ripped and knocked at all angles by the Germans.

By evening, the remnants of the 21st and 24th Divisions had once again assembled around the Lone Tree Ridge and the Corps Commander, General Haking, went from one to the other enquiring how it went wrong and according to the Official History the general reply was, 'We

did not know what it was like. We will do all right next time.' This was the
kind of spirit these men had who answered to the call of Lord Kitchener's
'Your King and Country need you.' They were all volunteers. They were
the flower of the most powerful, the wealthiest nation of the world at
that time. They had a strong belief that triumph of right over wrong
would finally always prevail. The ordered childhood and principles of
Victorian times lay behind them, i.e. a notion of chivalry, a Christian
education, respectability, decency, correctness. These conceptions were
deeply absorbed in their minds. This was the first time in action of these
volunteers, but if their experience was 'the rules of the game' (the conduct
of war) well then, they would comply and adapt themselves.

When all the circumstances in which these two divisions entered the
Battle of Loos are considered – the long and trying marches to the scene
of action; men starved for 60 hours; dry-throated and the unpromising
nature of the mass attack, with no supporting artillery, obvious to the
youngest soldier – the staunchness of all ranks in the advance during the
attack and the steadiness in the final retirement, deserve credit.

German officers, who conversed with some of the captured wounded
East Surrey officers, spoke with the warmest admiration of the gallant
advance of this battalion (who later became known as 'The Gallants').

Early in the morning of the 27th September, at about 4 a.m. the 24th
Division was relieved by the Guards Division.

Incessant shelling and very severe fighting continued at this portion of
the front up to 8th October, when the battlefield of Loos once again
became static with no material gain to the British.

In London ugly rumours were rife, as the Red Cross trains arrived full
of the groaning wounded from the Battle of Loos. The very little gained
for such heavy losses was debated followed by murmurs of protest at the
slaughter of the 21st and 24th Divisions given an impossible task to per-
form. Reports were called for and eventually Sir John French and other
commanders and staff were re-called and General Haig was appointed
as Commander-in-Chief of the British Expeditionary Force on the
Western Front.

The lessons to be learned at Loos were :–

If it was at all possible to break through the Western Front, reserves
must be quickly and reasonably safely got forward to reinforce or exploit
penetration.

An advance must be kept going before the enemy has time to recover
and bring up general reserves.

Assaulting troops must be supported by a mass of artillery and means found for destroying barbed wire barriers.

Tools must be got forward quickly for consolidating ground gained – digging of trenches and converting and repairing captured trenches. Assaulting troops must not be weighed down with too much heavy equipment as it prevents quick movement.

Most of the equipment was left in front of the German wire at Loos to enable a quick getaway. Packs are cumbersome and heavy to fight in. (Although there were cases where they saved lives, bullets being found embedded in them instead of the man.)

Better means must be devised for getting back situation reports more quickly.

Staff work requires some improvement. Commanders and staff have yet to gain more experience in handling an ever increasing mass of men, especially at Brigade and Divisional levels, where most are new to their posts.

They left all that was dear to them, endured hardship, faced danger and finally passed out of the sight of man.

Let those who come after see to it that their names be not forgotten.

Letter and account by J. Chassar Moir

My brother was in that battle : he was reported missing and no further information was ever received although we learned that he had survived the first terrible day, and was lost early next morning when some advanced posts were given up.

My mother in despair wrote to everyone she could find who might be able to give information – but to no avail. Some letters were however of much interest and these came into my possession when my parents died. I made extracts from two of them and these were published in *The Scotsman* on the 50th anniversary of the Battle. I now send you this cutting.

My brother was a student at Glasgow Technical College, and 'joined up' when the appeal was made in September or October 1914. His platoon was composed entirely of University or Technical College students – privates all. Alas, few of them were to see Scotland again ('three years or the duration' was the promise then made – sadly ambiguous as events were to prove !).

Few people now understand the high motives and disregard for self interest that activated these young lads at that terrible time.

'Fifty years ago on 25th September at break of dawn a great concentration of Scottish troops leapt from the trenches in front of Loos, and one of the bloodiest and most heroic struggles of the First World War was begun. On this battle were staked the hopes of an early change of fortune : with it, alas, there perished all hope of easy victory. My brother was among those lost. In turning over correspondence received from his comrades – young lads all of them – I have found the following account of the charge across No-Man's-Land; it was written only four days after the event and dated September 29th, 1915.

The Charge came off on Saturday, 25th – it will be a red letter day to me all my life. All Friday night we were working getting our machine guns ready and in the handiest places, and we were so busy we did not get a wink of sleep.

We knew the attack was coming off, but nobody could tell us when, and it was only 5.30 we were told to fall in, and marched down to the trench we were to go out from. We were not long down when our artillery started pelting them with shells, and then they started also; it was hell let loose for half-an-hour.

We were all crouching in the bottom of the trench, ready for the order to go. About six o'clock every man was given a glass of rum to drink the King's health and success to our attack, but there was no doubt in any of our minds but that we would win the day. We had been told some days before this what we were to try to take – that was, their trenches – three lines of them – and a coal mine where they had some guns.

At 6.30 we got the order to go, and go we did. The Camerons were leading the attack at that particular part, with the Black Watch coming behind as supports, and the Seaforths were on our right, with the Gordons behind them. Well! no sooner did our Boys get over the parapet than the Germans began with big guns, machine guns, and rifle fire, and you never saw or heard anything like it in your life : you, nor anybody else who was not there, can ever imagine what it was like – you could not hear anything for the racket of the guns.

Then the Boys began to go down, it was not long before the ground was strewn with dead and wounded. It was awful! I don't know how any man was able to cross that 500 yards to reach the Germans. Anyway, when we did get there, we had not many more than 100 men, but we chased the Germans; took what we were told to take – went on again, and drove them out of all their trenches. When we finished, we had pushed them out of a village and into the open country without a trench to hide themselves in. We took five lines of trenches and a village – instead of three lines, and kept it with less than 100 men.

And you talk about officers – ours were splendid; every man led his own lot with Lochiel at the head of the battalion; he was a pure hero, every inch of him, and also every man who went down, dead or wounded. Poor chaps, it was awful! – one of the finest battalions that ever handled a rifle – practically wiped out. Lochiel was proud of his men, but he is more proud now, if he is able to be so with his sorrow.

We were relieved early on Sunday morning, after holding out against their repeated counter-attacks, and we were not out an hour when the lot that came in lost one of the trenches we had taken, and on Monday we had another charge and won it back. We came out of the trenches yesterday about 70 or 80 strong, out of the 1100 of the pick of Scotland.

Sir John French came along just as we were leaving our old billets to come to this one, and gave us a few words of praise, and, by jove! it was praise in earnest. He told us he was proud to meet us, and congratulated us on our fine work. He told us we had done what Camerons liked to do, and what they always did; he never knew the Camerons to fail in anything they had ever put their hands to, and we, it seemed, were no exception to the rule of Camerons. That was why he chose Camerons for his bodyguard.

Lochiel called for three cheers, and I think we made noise enough. Then some of the men called for three cheers, for Lochiel, and he fairly got it – the tears were in his eyes, and no wonder.

1st October 1915 We have had a sore time of it within the last few days – just imagine – two charges in three days. I don't know how there are any of us left; as it is, there are very few.

We captured some few hundred prisoners, in fact, they were glad to give themselves up. I was one of a party of four men and a sergeant who went out for wounded on Sunday night. We went right up to the old German trench, picking them up as we went along, and in one of the German dug-outs, we came across one of our own boys wounded in both knees, and, in the same dug-out were five Germans hiding. They had treated our fellow very well, binding up his wounds, and keeping him going in cigarettes, so we gave them food and water, and took them in. If they had not treated our fellow so well, I cannot say what would have happened to them, for we were all in a bad state of mind and could not stand tampering.

We got the Germans to carry the wounded man in. Shortly after we heard a moan on our left – we went away to investigate, and came across a Black Watch fellow in a very bad way indeed. We had only one stretcher and it was going to be a very painful job getting him in, so we told him we would be back as soon as possible.

On the Monday afternoon the Germans broke through the lines of the regiment who relieved us – an English regiment – and there was more trouble for us. We had to charge again, and in our weakened state, we thought we would never get them back, but we managed at last and kept them there till reinforcements arrived. We lost some more men then (Hohenzollern redoubt).

A German General was captured in that lot, and he told our officers when he was taken in, that, if they took away the kilties and the Guards regiments, they would wipe the earth with us. He was quite indignant at being captured and taken prisoner.

And Lochiel! he is a pure hero, and played a noble part in all the work that was done.

Diary of L. G. Mitchell of the Special Service Brigade, Royal Engineers (who was in charge of the gas cylinders).
September 23rd: At 4.45 p.m. today we started for the trenches. We made for Vermelles, as it is there that the communication trench begins. Vermelles is about five miles from Béthune. Somewhere about half-past five it started to rain in torrents, and kept on raining for the rest of our journey. As we got nearer to Vermelles, the noise of the guns got terrific. Our own heavy guns are placed just behind Vermelles town. This place is typical of the destruction wrought by the German guns. There is not a single house with a roof or four walls. Huge piles of bricks and debris are to be seen everywhere. Nearly every day someone is killed there.

As this is being written after the battle, I may as well describe here the nature of our work, as explained to us beforehand. It had to be kept absolutely quiet before the attack, in order to keep all knowledge of it from the Germans. We chemists are to turn on cylinders of gas, which are placed in our trenches, and direct the current of gas over the parapet by means of pipes. At Vermelles we were given the pipes, of which every two men had to carry six. I shall never forget that journey down the communication trench. In order to localise the effect of shell explosions, the communication trench is zig-zag from beginning to end. The result was that we had to carry the pipes right above our heads in order to get them along the trench, otherwise at every corner they would get stuck. The communication trench is $3\frac{1}{2}$ miles long and the journey took us between 7 and 8 hours. Rain was falling during the whole of the journey. In many places the trench was over a foot deep in water. When we arrived at our destination – the front line trench, I found my chum Stuart who had been left in charge of the cylinders of gas. These, by the way, had been put into place by some infantrymen a few days previous. I managed to crawl into Stuart's dugout, and, in spite of the fact that it was only supposed to hold two men, five others got in also. We were all in very cramped positions, but I was fortunate enough to get a few hours' sleep, all the same.

September 24th: Still raining! Everywhere in the trench there is water, varying in depth. In some places it is a foot or two deep. Our guns are going strong, and no mistake. They are directing their fire on the German front-line trenches, where they are trying to break the wire entanglements. Although the German trenches are 500 yards away from ours, the force of explosion is so great that our own shrapnel occasionally reaches us. The Germans send us a whizz-bang over occasionally, just to remind us that their artillery is still intact. This bombardment of ours is the biggest that has ever taken place.

The French are bombarding also, and have been doing so for twenty days, although we have only been doing so for four. We brought our food in sand bags with us, and although everything is sodden and cheese, bread, bacon and sultanas are mixed up together, we have had quite decent meals. We scratch a little crevice in the side of the trench, make a fire there and boil our tea and cook bacon – those who have any. This afternoon Stuart was hit by a piece of shrapnel, but was not hurt. All this evening a German has been sniping at us, and by the crack of his rifle, seems to be fairly close to us.

September 25th: We have 'stood to' all night, and now, at 6 a.m., we are just going to let off gas. The Germans are evidently expecting it for they are shelling us for all they are worth.

I was just unscrewing the cap off a cylinder when a shell exploded quite close to me. Fortunately I was not hit by shrapnel, but was struck on the left ear with some dirt, which made several little scratches, but nothing much. The smoke nearly suffocated me, but I rushed to another traverse and tied up the place with my field dressing. When I went back, poor old Stuart, with whom I was working, was half suffocated with our own gas. We all had gas helmets on, but they get so stuffy that the temptation is to remove them for 'a breath of air' which proves to be a breath of chlorine. Whilst we were gassing and when we had finished, smoke bombs were thrown over the parapet. These create a huge volume of smoke.

A few minutes were allowed to elapse after the final smoke-bomb throwing and then our infantry filed over the parapet. Those from the reserve trenches came first and were later on followed by the men from the front trench. They advanced with fixed bayonets in the same way as the French do in making their bayonet charges, i.e. one man leads and the others follow on behind, and not in line with him. It was a fine sight to see those fellows going along. They might have been strolling through town by the unconcerned manner of them. Those on our right and left were Scotsmen – the Camerons. The first two trenches were very easily captured. Most of the Germans in front of us had been gassed and the rest surrendered at first sight of the kilts. In a few minutes our men were strolling back, all in charge of one or two German prisoners. A few of the latter passed down our trench. They looked quite happy.

Last evening a German sniper was continually sniping at us. Immediately we had commenced to let gas off, he jumped into the traverse next to us and almost immediately died, although his respirator, if any good, should have prevented his taking any harm. Our trench continued to be shelled, even after the gas had been let off, so it was some time before we were able to make our way down the communication trench to Vermelles. Our trench has many wounded and dying men in it, and it was frightful to see them. They were patient, though. The whole of the communication trench was sprinkled with blood, and many poor fellows were trying to make their way to Vermelles to the dressing station there. At Vermelles I had to report at the dressing station, and after waiting for two or three hours, I was sent to a field hospital near Béthune.

September 26th: There is nothing serious the matter with me and I expect to be able to return to duty today or tomorrow. I am having hot compresses put upon my face, and they will soon draw the dirt out. The wounded are still streaming into here, and they give very good accounts of the progress of the battle.

September 27th: The MO examined me today, said that I can return to duty.

September 28th: I proceeded to distributing station – 'Home for lost dogs' – and was sent on thence to Gosse to the Chicory factory, our old billet. Most of the sections had returned, but one or two were still in the trenches for the purpose of making another attack. It appears that although the gas acted fairly well everywhere, we were not able to carry out the infantry charges successfully in all regions, on account of the strong reinforcements possessed by the Germans. Moreover the Germans kept their machine-guns in action by means of lighting big fires around them whilst the gas was going over. An infantryman has just told me that he *saw* the Germans chained to their machine guns!

September 30th: Today we have been sent to a village named Annaquin, quite close to Cambrin, where the Germans hold a very strong part of the line. Here we are to make another gas attack in the endeavour to shift the Germans from their strong position. We are billeted in an old *estaminet* and are able to keep a fire going, which is a luxury. I may mention that in order to keep the said fire going it has been necessary to pull down nearly every door and every bit of available wood in the house. The village has been shelled frequently but is now comparatively safe, although shells pass over us every day.

We have received the following encouragement from the Colonel

(Message from Colonel Foulkes to OC 186 and 188 Corps Royal Engineers) Please convey to the NCOs the following message from me : I have received reports from every one of the officers who took part in the gas attack of September 25th as well as from other officers who were in the trenches at the time of the very gallant and devoted way in which men of the Gas Corps Special Enlistment as well as old soldiers, performed their work.

I have mentioned this to the Commander-in-Chief and shall be proud to bring it to his notice in my Official Report of the operations.

I trust that the alterations that have recently been made in the equipment will result in your future work being carried out in circumstances of less difficulty than previously.

(Signed) C. W. Foulkes (Colonel)

October 13th: Since the date of my last entry the above date we have been sleeping at the same billet, but during the day-time we have been cleaning pipes and taking them to the trenches, putting cylinders in place and preparing generally for the second gas attack which came off today. This time we worked in fours and had 22-24 cylinders in each battery. Each cylinder has its own delivery and jet pipe, whereas in the last attack there were only two delivery pipes for us to get off all the gas and the smoke bombs too. I was put in charge of the bomb throwers. This time the gas attack was not followed up by an infantry charge but must have done a lot of damage. We were shelled all the time we were letting off the gas, and for some time before and after.

Of the gas, Corporal G. O. Mitchell, 28 Section, 188 Company, Royal Engineers, wrote:

There were only two pipes for each twelve cylinders so we had to change over when one was empty. God, what a game! The rotten apparatus they had given us was leaking all over the place and we were working in a cloud of gas. We sweated ourselves to death and only got 8 off. All gas had to be turned off at 6.28.

The Staffordshires went over where we were as if on parade with rifles at the slope and dressing by the right!

The Field Ambulance (Extracts from diary of A. E. Francis, 5 Fd Ambulance, 47 (London) Div.)

September 20th: My 25th birthday. What a place to spend it. Yet we have a good feed. I have two fine parcels and buy stores, often fruit, champagne, cigars etc. and we have a good spread in our bivouac.

September 21st and 22nd: Digging in front of our artillery. These being the first two days of slow bombardment, we come in for a very lively time.

September 24th: A and B Sections sent up the line. Our section held as mobile section to go and establish hospital in any captured place. A most terrific bombardment all day.

September 25th: We move to Les Brebis ready for working with the Advance which took place this morning. We pass crowds of prisoners being conducted back. We stay for the night in the French hospital – a fine place, beautifully equipped.

September 26th: We leave for S. Maroc. From here we work over the field of Advance clearing the wounded away. Horrible sights. Many Germans are dead in most chilling attitudes – some pointing a rifle straight at you, some in the act of throwing bombs. The gas affects our eyes and stomach and we have a few cases of our men gassed.

We have advanced beyond Loos now. So our work takes us beyond the Double Crassier. From there we work through the cemetery where there are piles of dead round the Crucifix. Our men here are showing the effects of their work, dead tired and I'm sure, couldn't move another step.

We go on through Loos beyond the Church and work between the lines. There is a deadly fire here which makes our work very difficult. An officer we rescue takes our names. All the wounded seem extremely satisfied and pay us many compliments. It is a pleasure to work for them.

We have to stop now it is light, and experience another danger, that of coming along the road which is open to the fire from the Slag Heap which is still in German hands. However we take to the trench and arrive back at our billet in Maroc quite safely. The 'Sniper's House' on the Vermelles Road is a terrible sight with about 30 dead bodies outside. One other is wounded there.

September 28th: We move to Loos and make our Advanced Dressing St. in the cellar of the château – now a mass of ruins. It is a filthy place and we clear it up a bit. Have to bury two men and a horse. The cellar is propped up in rather a dangerous way, and every time a shell falls near it shakes the place and covers us with dust. One falls just outside and casing and a ring come through the window, missing four of us very narrowly. Lucky for us that we have no direct hit on the place. The cellar is full of German lice and we very soon become 'cooty'. There are two cellar slopes which we convert into stretcher slides. Our staircase is under rifle fire from Hill 70, so we cannot use that.

We go out and bring in from the trenches and during the night evacuate to the cars on the Vermelles road. This is a very dangerous business during the daytime and the Germans make a few patterns round us. Evidently they haven't got the range of the road yet.

One night we have to get the inhabitants away. They are a mad crew and start flashing lamps about which brings bullets galore. They are terribly mean and even ask "deux-sous" for coffee during rescue work.

My duty to work the 'Primus' and get oxo and tea for the patients. Very nice job, but working day and night.

Saturday October 2nd: We are relieved by the French about 11 p.m. – a very dangerous business. On the road are crowds of troops and transport all congested, but we managed without the loss of a man.

We walk along the Lens–Béthune road to Scully-la-Bourse and pick up the cars. My God – How tired I am! Not a wink of sleep for 4 days! Still we go on and soon are landed at Hesdigneil.

Sunday, October 3rd: All of our party are showing signs of the strain of recent week. We have a Divisional Church Parade where Major-General Barter gives us HQ's appreciation of our work. 'All that was set the 47th Division was accomplished'. This is sufficient praise.

The aeroplane sheds are full of interest. The public again are very mean and ask for 'Money!' before we buy anything. We construct a fine bivouac but Bert Hoare comes in the party as well. We have a good feast on Price's birthday costing 28 francs. We have a grand time and honestly I must say the relaxation does us good. Later we move back again to Houchin.

Friday, October 15th: In action again Party No 1 – in trenches at La Rutoire; Party No 2 – Massingarbe trench baths; Party No 3 – Noeux-les-Mines Hospital.

I'm with No 3. I feel contented this time because I feel as if I want a change. So I'm put on Sanitary Police. The place is left in a filthy condition so we have 'beaucoup' scrubbing and cleaning. We have 'Mairie' for wounded hospital and a school for sick. I'm in charge of sanitary conditions of latter.

ADMS* congratulates us on having a hospital fit for London. That is indeed high praise especially coming from that person. *Billet* – an attic – changed to schoolroom and from thence to filthy barn of Mayor who objects to brazier being lit in spite of the cold and wet. We complain and

*Assistant Director of Medical Services.

have a fine attic in the *estaminet* at Madame Leroy's *Café l'Abbatoir,* rue de Labourse. Everything here is spotless, a fine billet indeed.

We have a steady stream of wounded among whom is Lance Corporal Keyworth vc who afterwards died. Hit in the head, penetrating.

The Cricket Ball Bombs (R. H. Torbet – letter from his wife)

R. H. Torbett was in 1/1st Battalion, London Regiment, Royal Fusiliers (T.F.) and was bombing corporal to the left of Loos 1915 at the early age of 19 on 25th May. Previously he was at Neuve Chapelle (approx March 10th) and Aubers Ridge (May 9th) near Fromelles.

He possesses no diaries or letters etc. referring to the battle – only his own memories. He remembers being on the extreme left of the Loos attack in thick mud to the knees and ordered to make a diversionary attack. Our weapons consisted of 'cricket ball' bombs, solid iron, with match substance on wrist bands for ignition, needless to say there was no possibility in the wet for the bombs to be ignited and it was only because of the order to retire when halfway to the enemy trench that they were saved annihilation. They were relieved in the evening by the Seaforth Highlanders and retired to rest on gravestones in a nearby cemetery. The bombs were about 3in. in diameter, heavy and unwieldy and were carried in pouches on a bomb waistcoat.

For my own part I am proud to say that in the following year he was awarded the MM for bravery in the field at Hebuturne – he was sergeant by then (*vide* London Gazette 9.11.1916).

I am afraid we cannot help you much in your research except to emphasize the heavy wet which made it impossible to drag one's feet out of the ground when advancing to the enemy's line in the incessant rain.

I have enclosed a rough drawing with the necessary particulars of the 'cricket ball' bomb and the approximate size and details as far as my husband can inform you. He says they were an improvement on the 'jam tin' bomb which was 2 gun cotton primers in an empty jam tin, packed round with stones and pieces of metal. A 5 second safety fuse was inserted in the primers which was lit with an ordinary match. (Used approximately in March 1915). The German reply was their tiny 'egg bomb' which could be thrown between 60–70 yards – but they were useless.

The only regular bomb used by us was the GS hand grenade which had a wooden handle similar to the German 'brush bomb' and was a percussion bomb eg. exploding on impact. The GS hand grenade was in such short supply and were so dangerous to the thrower that they disappeared as a weapon.

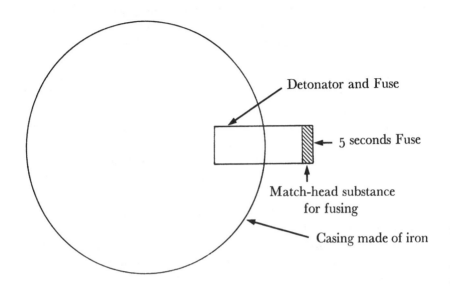

Details of Cricket Ball Bomb

Note: They were carried in a webbing waistcoat. My husband says he handled them once (a party of himself, corporal, and five privates) but they were never fired and he never saw them again, as the continuous rain at that time and the depth of mud made their working useless.

Striking A 'Match head' brassard was worn on the wrist and to ignite the bomb the end of the fuse was rubbed on the brassard to ignite. Needless to say the heavy rains soaked the brassard and bombs could not be ignited.

'The Hooge Draw Show': (Major J. R. Tuckett)
I was not actually at Loos but I have yet to read about the Battle of Loos and see any mention of the 'Draw Show' which was put on at Hooge, Ypres Salient.

This was advertised by a month's nightly bombardment of the German lines and their wire.

We dug assembly trenches in front of our line, where there had been a line of trenches of ours from earlier days. I had command of a working party of 600 from the Brigade the night we opened them up again. On the night of September 24th, or rather evening before we moved up into the trenches at Hooge we were told at a Battalion Parade the whole line was advancing the next day from sea to Switzerland. Well, the next morning when we went over we found our artillery had not hit their wire at all nor their front line, and we suffered really heavy losses, both in officers and men. I think if my memory still serves me, before we mustered approx 33 officers and 1100 ORs and after the 25th there were I believe about half a dozen officers and 150 ORs left. I was wounded here for the second time in the Ypres Salient, previously in February 1915 near Kemmel. After this battle my Division the 3rd was broken up and my Brigade the 7th was put into the 25th Division (a new one). One Battalion to each of two Brigades and one Brigade had two Battalions.

I have always understood that we advertised the 25th so well the Germans had a lot of reserves up there expecting us to break out of the Ypres Salient, but I have as yet to see any mention of it. The 3rd Div was of course one of the original BEF.

When I rejoined the Battalion in June 1916 we were on the Somme for 1st July and they remained there for four solid months and I was wounded and gassed there in October.

I do not know why there has not been any mention of our show at Hooge on 25th September, 1915. I think we went over the top two hours before they did down at Loos.

The Artists' Rifles (J. H. Johnson)

I wonder if you would be interested in a 'behind the scenes' event in the Battle of Loos.

On September 25th, the 1st Battalion 'The Artists Rifles', myself being one of them, was suddenly rushed up from St Omer to Arques and put on the job of changing the fuses on a consignment of several thousand 18-pounder shells. We worked, all of us without any experience, continuously in shifts, and finished in under four days. The correctly fused shells were loaded straight on to lorries and sent up to the battle.

The Nursing Service (N. Hill)

I went out to France as a VAD nurse early in 1915, and at the time of the battle was attached to No 10 General Hospital on the racecourse at Rouen. I have vivid recollections of the wounded from the battle arriving throughout the night straight from the trenches, still covered with mud. The ambulances poured into our hospital, and when we had no more beds, we put up tents over the stretchers and tended the wounded as they lay on the ground. Later, as I spoke German, I was allocated to the wounded prisoners' ward, with an armed guard at either end. I remember writing a letter dictated to me by a dying prisoner in German and he lay back dead as he finished it. It was after this battle that the Last Post, played at military funerals across the valley, became a familiar accompaniment to our daily work in the words.

I am now 83.

Letter from J. W. Palmer:
Infantry bombers were deprived of their rifle and given in exchange a small dagger with a handle which fitted round the back of the hand. It was a most primitive weapon, appeared to be made of iron, and certainly brought forth many sarcastic remarks in contempt for those who had thought of it.

Letter from Brigadier J. G. Selby, MC:
In September 1915 I was seconded to the Royal Flying Corps from the Gunners. I was then an observer, afterwards a pilot, later a Squadron Leader RAF commanding a Bristol Fighter Squadron.

On the morning of the battle I was being flown by Leveson Gower, since deceased, in a French Monoplane a parasol Morane.

It was the first time we used gas. We were flying about 8000 feet. The wind had changed and we could see the gas visible drifting over our trenches. My pilot throttled down the engine and turned round and said, 'Thank God we are in the Flying Corps, old Boy.'

The aerodrome was at a place called Ancre. In the valley below was a chateau which was turned into a temporary casualty clearing station. The ambulance stream had gone wrong and the hospital was overloaded. That evening the second in command of the hospital came up and saw our CO. They were short of accommodation and orderlies.

We picketed the aeroplanes in the open, struck the hangers and erected them in the hospital together with a workshop lorry for electric light.

We flew all day and the first night I had to hold up a guardsman who was gassed and not allowed to lie down.

On the second night I assisted a nursing sister looking after a soldier who had been shot through both thighs. The bullet had broken both thighs, turned round and made a large hole in his left leg. The whole thing was a mass of gangrene and the smell appalling. I said to the sister "hold hard a minute while I light my pipe".

I subsequently heard that the soldier did not die.

At the age of twenty all these events made a very distinct impression on my mind. The Battle of Loos was a complete failure altogether.

Letter from Miss Palmer

I lost my sweetheart at Loos who was killed only after being there two days. His name was Harry Richardson and he joined up with the Highland Light Infantry. He was made a sergeant. A friend of mine went to Loos and saw his name among the fallen on the Menin Gate and my sister saw his name in the Book of Remembrance at the Memorial in Edinburgh.

As you know, we lost the cream of our men folk in the 1914–1918 war. I am 89 years of age – my memory is still fresh of the two wars.

The Victoria Cross and the RAMC

Many Victoria Crosses were won during the battle of Loos, as in other battles. Some were posthumous awards. Undoubtedly there were occasions when men earned Victoria Crosses but never received them because the winner and all the witnesses were killed almost immediately.

It is not generally appreciated that the greatest number of VCs has been won by the Royal Army Medical Corps. Lieutenant G. A. Maling was awarded the VC at Loos 'for conspicuous bravery and devotion to duty in collecting and treating the wounded under heavy shell fire, continuing his work after being stunned by one shell explosion and wounded by another'. This occurred at Fauquissart. Maling worked for twenty six hours without break tending three hundred wounded men. He was also mentioned in despatches again the following year. Although he survived the war and had a practice in south-east London he died in 1929 at the age of forty. His son served in the infantry in World War II prior to becoming a doctor himself.

Although medical research gained something from the wars the losses among doctors and potential doctors were very high. Lieutenant-Colonel Heron-Watson fought at Loos with the 6th Cameron Highlanders which he writes 'started its first action with 28 officers and 1,000 men and was reduced to the junior subaltern (himself) and 40 men. Practically the whole of B Company were, like myself, 3rd and 4th year undergraduates and mostly medical.' Small wonder there was a shortage of doctors after World War I.

6

Gunners Supporting the Attack

A GUN SITE AT LOOS

By Brigadier E. Mockler-Ferryman, CB, CBE,MC, MA
At the time 19 and a Second Lieutenant in the Royal Artillery

We now felt that we should probably be left to ourselves for a few months – a very pleasant prospect after the numerous moves and changes which we had been undergoing for the last few weeks.

I was at first left in charge of the wagon-line, where life is never varied nor interesting. The work consists of exercising, watering, stables, and harness-cleaning. At Henu exercising and watering were carried out together, as twice a day we had to go to Pas to water the horses. I was very glad when, after ten days at the wagon-line, I was relieved by Holiday, and went off to the gun-line. But I was only destined to remain there two days, which gave me just sufficient time to make myself thoroughly acquainted with the battery position, but not to discover anything of our OPs* and the trenches in front of us.

The battery was in action on the north-west side of Foncquevillers. The orchard in which we were was not a large one but contained a great number of thick trees, affording us excellent cover from aeroplane observation.

The second line of defence ran through the orchard, so there were plenty of trenches in which to move about without trampling down the grass round the position. At the back edge of the orchard there ran a road, by which rations and ammunition were brought up. The guns were not dug-in in accordance with the rules laid down in FAT†, i.e. in dressing and 20 yards apart. No 1 was dug-in in the open field to the right of the orchard, and made to look like a *place d'armes* in one of the trenches; while the other three guns were in a long trench under cover of the trees.

*Observation Posts.
†Field Artillery Training.

The emplacements were strongly built, with logs supporting a roofing of 4 or 5 feet of sandbags, and earth and broken bricks on the top. I think they would have kept out a 4.2-inch shell. The trenches had to be widened considerably in places, to allow the guns to be got in, and to enable us to get them out quickly should the necessity arise. The dug-out for the officers when I arrived could hardly be called a 'dug-out', 'lean-to' would have been a more appropriate name. There had been no time to dig a proper one, and all we had was a small portion of trench widened, blocked at both ends with sandbags, and a layer of corrugated iron and earth on top. It was most uncomfortable, as the wind and rain drove in without the least difficulty.

In the bank of the road running behind the orchard were two dug-outs, built by a French '75' battery, which had been in action close by. One of these we used as a telephone exchange, while the signallers lived in the other. The gun detachments had to sleep in the emplacements. A cook-house had been constructed out of corrugated iron, well away from the Battery, in the orchard over the road to the right, so that there should be no smoke in the gun position.

The trees in the orchard were covered with small and sour cider apples, of a most brilliant red colour. These made excellent stewed fruit, though quite unfit to eat raw – a fact which caused much sorrow and not a few pains among the men of the battery.

Although we were only 1000 yards from the German trenches, we never fired at a range of less than 3000. This was due to the fact that we were employed to bring an enfilade fire to bear on the trenches to the north-east near Moreby, while another battery, away to our left, enfiladed these directly in front of us.

As to the position of the 18-pounder batteries, of which there were 12 : they were in action in the open, and were more or less in a straight line, extending over a front of about $2\frac{1}{2}$ miles. One of the batteries was about 400 yards in rear of us, and we used to get the full benefit of their prematures, which they had pretty frequently.

About 300 yards in front of us were the ruins of Foncquevillers Church, a large building dating back to the latter part of the 16th Century. There was very little left of it, except one wall on which hung a life-sized image of the Saviour. This image had remained untouched by shot or shell through twelve months of the war, during which time the village had been lost and retaken by the French. About a month later, a machine-gun had evidently been playing on the building, for, as I passed, I noticed that it had been pierced in more than a hundred places.

The battery was doing very little firing – not more than about 10 rounds a day, but the men were kept busy bricking the bottoms of the trenches before the wet weather set in. The collecting of the bricks required much skill and caution, as the RE in Foncquevillers (who belonged to the 48th Division on our right) had an idea that all buildings, however badly knocked about, belonged exclusively to the sappers, and were urgently required for defensive purposes. However, our men soon became highly proficient in the art of 'pinching' and it did not take long to get several hundred yards of trenches laid with a double layer of bricks. These bricks were a great blessing not only for keeping us moderately clean and dry, but they also enabled us to get the guns out in a little over a quarter of an hour.

Two days after I arrived at the guns rumours began to filter through that the British were going to attack in some part of the line, and that we should probably do a good deal of crumping on our own particular front for a few days preceding the attack. Now, I knew nothing of our trenches, nor of the views of the country from our OP's, whereas Holiday and Sullivan had spent 10 days in choosing OP's and registering various points in the German trenches. Consequently, I was sent back to the wagon-line, and Holiday was brought up to the guns.

The next week at the wagon-line was a most unpleasant one. The battery fired about 100 rounds a day – a large allowance in those days of shell-shortage – and I had orders to keep the wagon-line in readiness to move at any moment, with harness behind the horses. As it rained continuously, the harness soon became coated with rust, and the leatherwork sodden and hard. We were not allowed to go to Pas for water, but had to water from a well on the road outside the billet – a proceeding which wasted some 8 hours each day.

On the morning of *September 25th*, I got orders to move forward to the advanced wagon-line position. We packed and harnessed up, and proceeded at once to a field on the front edge of Sonastre about 1500 yards behind the battery. Here we waited, harnessed-up, the entire day in drenching rain. In the evening we returned to our billet. When at last things settled down peacefully again, the harness was white and rusted beyond recall; the men were soaked, and everybody generally out of temper and thoroughly miserable.

On *September 28th* to my great relief, I again went up to the gun line – this time for a longer stay than previously. For about the first three weeks that we were in action and while we were still feeling energetic and interested in the novelty of the situation, there was an order that each battery was to man one of the OP's (Observation Post) at dawn and dusk, to observe for flashes (as the half light of morning and evening renders the flashes most conspicuous). Sullivan and I, therefore, took it in turns to get up early, which meant getting up at 4.30 a.m., so as to be at the OP before it was light. These early morning jaunts were made to No 1 OP, situated on the front edge in front of Foncquevillers (E.21 d.33) some 700 yards behind the front line trenches. It was a highly dangerous place, as the enemy were continually sweeping the trees with machine guns. To get to it one had to cross the High Street and enter a long communication trench called Rotten Row – a very fitting name, as it was always about a foot deep in slush. In the evenings one was frequently sniped when entering the trench.

One evening, on entering this trench, I noticed a pile of bricks about 18 inches high, on a base of 2 bricks square. This pile was usually knocked down during the daytime, but every evening they were piled up again – by whom we never discovered. The idea was that there was a German sniper at night-time somewhere in the trees close by, and that his rifle was laid on to the bricks, so that he could fire on hearing the noise of the bricks being knocked down. It did not seem very likely but the fact remains that somebody took the trouble to pile up those bricks every evening. However, after a time the game ceased and the bricks disappeared.

Bit by bit I got to know our trenches and the various important points in the German lines. Our trenches when we took them over from the French were in a very poor condition. They were shallow, with very little wire in front.

Account from 'Nine Lives' by Richard Hilton (Major-General) then Subaltern, later RFC

I was fortunate enough to have been given the job of permanent FOO (forward observation officer) for the battery in all these battles of 1915, possibly because I had a good head for heights, and did not mind clambering about trees or winding-towers. So it fell to my lot to get a front-row view of this historic battle. We were placed in support of the 15th (Scottish) Division in this their first battle of the war. Twenty-nine years later I was destined to participate once more with that famous division in its first battle of the Second World War – i.e. the capture of the River Odon crossing near Caen. I believe myself to be the only person who can claim that unique distinction. Old soldiers will understand that I am very proud of that honour.

A remarkable feature of the battlefield of Loos was an enormous double winding-tower belonging to a colliery on the eastern edge of the village. This mine (Puits 15) had two shafts very close together, which required two winding-towers for the cages. The two towers had been combined into one massive steel girderwork construction which rose high above the village and its surrounding undulations and dominated both the British and German trenches for many miles to north and south. It was an obvious place for artillery observation posts to establish themselves, and many FOOs made a bee-line for it as soon as its base was overrun by our infantry. For my part I was certain that it was the right place for me, so I sent my telephonists directly to it with orders to get busy with communications. But, rather foolishly perhaps, I decided to go forward myself to the top of Hill 70 with the infantry, in order to find out the true situation at first hand before installing myself in the tower.

Hill 70 lay just to the east of the great tower, and was overlooked by it just as though the round hill was a flat plate. It was a grim place when I got there. Very little cover was to be found on its bare slopes except what was provided by shell craters and a few unfinished German trenches. The main road from La Bassée to Lens ran across it. Otherwise it was featureless except for the ruins of a little red house, shown as 'Maison Isolée' on our French maps.

I quickly discovered that the hill was no place from which to conduct artillery observation. The only way to remain alive was to lie low in a shell crater or, if one had to move, to do so by crawling like a worm. Any attempt to raise the head for a look-round instantly drew machine-gun fire from the slag heaps and pit-heads to our right. I contacted one or two Scottish officers, and found out what they wanted us to do if we had enough ammunition to do it. Then I wormed my way back to the twin towers and found my telephonists.

Unfortunately for me many other FOOs had installed themselves already in the best seats, so I had to take what was left. Being fond of mountain climbing I have never been bothered by dizziness, so I managed to find an enormous horizontal girder of 'L' section, which spanned the twin towers quite near the top.

As a vantage point for the battle it was hard to beat. Not only could I see every movement of our own infantry, though they were in fact pinned to the ground and did not move much, but from my lofty pinnacle I could see well beyond them and to their flanks, and thus could deal fairly effectively with any hostile movements behind the industrial buildings of Cité St Auguste. Up to the limits of our meagre ammunition supply we did our best to crush the machine-guns which were lacerating the bare slopes of Hill 70.

The value of 'Tower Bridge' as an observation post must have been just as clear to the Germans as to us. It had not been in our hands for long before it became the target for every kind of artillery fire from their eight-inch howitzers down to the 77-millimetre 'pipsqueak'. This bombardment never ceased till the towers finally collapsed – a tangled mass of twisted girders – over three months later.

Fortunately for the occupants on 25th September the French Engineers, who designed and built the towers, had put no shoddy stuff into their work. The great girders were as good as armour plate against all but the heaviest shells, and for some time only a few of the big shells hit the tower. But considerable damage was caused to the lighter steel-work, such as the open staircase by which one ascended to the wheels. A large section of this staircase was blown away altogether, leaving a gap in my line of retreat which almost proved fatal to me.

After I had sat in my 'L' girder for an hour or two, plugging away at targets and thoroughly enjoying life, another FOO near me shouted a warning that we must all clear out quickly, because the enemy had counter-attacked from the north and had recaptured the village of Loos behind us. This gloomy news subsequently proved to be slightly exaggerated, but 'at the time it seemed all too true. I glanced down the tower and saw all the others scrambling down as quickly as they could, leaving their telephones and wire behind them.

I now began to regret my choice of position. It was all very well to have crawled along the girder, but my return journey to the top of the steps had to be taken cautiously and very slowly.

To make matters worse I discovered the big gap in the stairs. By the time I had negotiated this and reached ground level I was quite alone, as I had naturally ordered my signallers not to wait for me. I peered discreetly out of the door into the dingy little side street.

There was nobody in sight. From the village behind me came sounds of brisk infantry fighting – small-arms fire and explosions of grenades. Picking my way through the rubble of the mine buildings I emerged through a hole in the wall on to the main street. Almost at once there were shouts, and a few bullets cracked past me. Glancing in the direction of the shouts I saw a small body of German infantry not more than about a hundred yards from me, advancing rapidly down the street. I ran like a hare toward the centre of the village, 'jinking' from side to side. Luckily they were not expert shots and I soon turned a corner, but I could still hear them hurrying after me.

To make matters worse for me there were sounds of brisk fighting ahead, showing that there must be more Germans between me and own own chaps.

It was as well for me that the village was honeycombed with German communication trenches, which meandered among the shattered houses. There was plenty of cover for one man by himself, and so, very cautiously, I wriggled my way through the small parties of enemy back to our own troops, who were still holding the western part of the village. Even now the situation remained vague for a while, but eventually we grenaded the streets and buildings clear of Germans and reopened contact with Hill 70. To this day it has never been certain whether this German effort was a true counter-attack or an attempt by isolated pockets of enemy, trapped in the cellars of Loos, to break through to freedom. Whichever it was, it was remarkably well co-ordinated, and caused us an anxious half-hour or more.

Late that same evening, on my way home to the battery on relief from the OP a sudden shower of shells forced me to dive into a communication trench. The trench was full of gas (our own, this being the first time that we had used it) and I got a strong whiff down my throat before I could put on my mask. I was violently sick for some hours, but suffered no permanent damage.

So ended 25th September 1915, first day of the Battle of Loos, a day on which more soldiers are reputed to have been killed than during the entire South African War.

The fighting rumbled on for a few weeks before settling down to the stagnation of winter trench warfare. Particularly active days were 8th and 13th October, the former for a large-scale German counter-attack, which was unsuccessful, and the latter for our equally unsuccessful attempt to capture the village of Hulluch, to widen the Loos salient. On each of these days I had quite exciting adventures.

During the big German counter-attack I was buried by the burst of a 5.9 inch shell within about a yard of me. It was the only occasion in my life that I have actually *seen* a shell coming toward me, an unusual phenomenon, only possible if the observer is directly in the path of the projectile! I was going along 'Railway Alley', an old German communication trench that crossed the bare slopes west of Loos. When I saw the large black spot rushing toward me, I threw myself flat on the floor of the trench. Some time later I came to, and found myself pinned under a huge pile of chalk and revetments. Luckily my head was free, though my arms and legs were not. The German bombardment was still at full blast all round. I was distinctly consoled by the old gunner saying that no two shells fall in exactly the same place for some long time. It would be quite a while, I told myself, before another came as close to me as the one that had pushed the trench on me. After a fairly long wait the bombardment subsided, and presently a working party came along 'Railway Alley' and dug me out.

On 13th October our battery was supporting the 1st Division, who made the attack on Hulluch. As FOO it was my job to go forward on to the objective with the leading infantry. I did so, but soon found myself out of touch with the battery because the telephone wires behind me were continually being cut by the German shell-fire. I forget how many signallers were working as linesmen for me that day, trying to keep the telephone wires mended – an unusually large number certainly – but in spite of their hard work interruptions were frequent.

During one of these I pushed ahead over the La Bassée and Lens main road into the village of Hulluch, telling my party of signallers to extend my line to the church and meet me there.

As I entered the village I saw some of our own infantry, between one and two hundred, working their way through the village ahead of me. I took temporary cover, waiting for them to clear the way, and then followed them step by step from house to house, guided more by the sounds of their grenade explosions than by sight of them, because there was a great deal of smoke in the village and our men naturally advanced under cover as much as possible.

I got as far as the main square by the church, then paused under cover to study the situation. It was rather queer. The sounds of grenade explosions had ceased. There were plenty of shell explosions, but it was hard to say from which side they came. After waiting for some time without sight or sound of our own infantry I nipped up to the first floor of an *estaminet* which overlooked the square to get a better view of what lay ahead of me. For about sixty seconds I saw nothing at all. Then three Germans came into sight, creeping along the cemetery wall and coming in my direction. They were moving slowly and cautiously, pausing every few paces to heave a grenade over the wall.

It was clear that I was a little too far in advance of our own infantry. What had become of those in front of me I could only guess. They must have been reduced by casualties to a mere handful, pinned down somewhere among the ruined buildings. My hopes of establishing an OP in Hulluch church would have to be postponed. It was high time for me to get back to my signallers and stop them from walking blissfully into the hands of the enemy. Luckily repairs and line-laying had delayed them enough for me to be able to intercept them outside the village and turn them back.

That night I was summoned to 1st Division Headquarters to report personally to Major-General Holland, the divisional commander. He had been commandant of the 'Shop'* during my time there, and had the reputation of being a ferocious martinet. I was rather alarmed at the coming interview, feeling that I had really nothing of importance to tell this fire-eating old gunner, and that I ought perhaps to have done much more to elucidate the situation before withdrawing from Hulluch. But the great man received me very cordially and seemed keenly interested in my narrative. His staff told me that nearly an entire company was missing. They had last been seen entering the village of Hulluch, but none had come back. I must have been about the last person to see anything of them and come back to tell the tale.

One of the advantages of our great howitzers with their ease of traverse and long range was that we could apply our fire along the whole frontage of the Loos salient without moving the battery position. In another way it was not so good for us, however, because it meant that we had to maintain a large number of observation posts to cover every divisional front. At one time during the Loos fighting we had more than thirty-two miles of telephone wire in use! The work which this entailed for that gallant band of men, our battery signallers, can only be partly visualized by those who never saw the Western Front. Many miles of this wire had to be laid along narrow communication trenches, where every yard of wire had to be carefully fastened so as not to entangle itself with the feet of the endless streams of men who passed up and down the trenches.

After the Hulluch offensive we were put in support of the 47th (London) Division, Territorials, who held a sector to the right or south of Loos. Opposite them lay the mining town of Lens itself, and in the German front line stood the Double Crassier of evil memory, a long slag heap which the enemy had honeycombed with tunnels and galleries and turned into a nest of machine-guns.

On our side of the lines lay the village of Maroc, in which stood two more steel winding-towers. One of these, known as 'Siège 11' became our new observation post. In some ways it was a very good one. Maroc had till recently been held by the French, who believed very sensibly, in a policy of 'live and let live' on unimportant sectors of the front. Consequently, till the British took over, this was a peaceful backwater. The great tower of 'Siége 11' had never been used by the French, because it was far too exposed to view from the German trenches only five hundred yards away. It was impossible to ascend this tower in daylight without being seen by the enemy.

By now the Germans were convinced that the French were not using the tower, so they did not bother to shoot at it.

*Royal Military Academy, Woolwich.

To our way of thinking it was too good an OP to waste, but we decided not to be silly about it. In order to keep up the illusion that nobody was up there, strict orders were issued that the tower must only be climbed or descended during darkness. It was rather a nuisance, because we had to run a system of twenty-four-hour reliefs, each party taking with them 'picnic' food for twenty-four hours, as of course no cooking could be done up the tower, not even the making of tea.

The openwork staircase was in full view of the enemy. But once ensconced among the winding-wheels, an observer was entirely hidden, and enjoyed a most valuable view far behind the German lines; even commanding some of the streets in the very centre of Lens.

One day, after we had used the tower successfully for some weeks, I heard my signaller NCO at the foot of the tower remonstrating politely but firmly with a party of British staff officers, who had just arrived in a car. At that time I was aloft among the girders, but all my telephonists worked in a dug-out at the foot, in order to minimize activity on the tower. We had notices in English and French on all the approaches, requesting people not to come near the tower lest they should draw fire. However, in spite of all entreaties, the whole party of 'brass hats' came chattering up the exposed stairway, and stood for some moments in full view of the enemy, conducting a map-reading exercise over the German lines from La Bassée to Notre Dame de Lorette. At last they refolded their nice new maps, which they had been flourishing like signalling flags during their deliberations, and drove away in their car just in time to avoid the inevitable 'strafe' which fell upon us. 'Siége 11' was never quite the same peaceful resort that it had been before their visit.

It was stupid little incidents such as this which prompted my restless temperament to search for fresh fields of activity. The excitement of Loos had been exhilarating, but the routine of stagnant trench warfare that followed was not very interesting. We were drastically restricted in ammunition, so that OP work became a matter of watching the front for hours on end, recording every trivial movement of the enemy in a log-book, but never firing a round. No doubt this record of German activities may have been extremely valuable to our intelligence branch, but the work became monotonous in the extreme.

As I sat uncomfortably among the steel girders of 'Siège 11' I began to envy the aviators who droned up and down the front far above my perch. What a wonderful view they must have of German movements, I thought, and in what comfort too! Even the black puffs of anti-aircraft fire that clustered round our machines whenever they approached the German lines – even these did not seem to me in my ignorance to be detracting from the fun of flying. In those early days it was rare indeed to see an aeroplane hit by Archie.*

Fights too were extremely rare in those days, and from the ground they looked good clean harmless fun. A couple of machines would occasionally circle round one another in a sort of stately aerial dance. In due course the rattle of their machine-guns would reach us far below. It looked rather like an old-fashioned duel – dignified, devoid of unmannerly anger, and usually without lethal results.

The Royal Flying Corps was, I knew, inviting applications for the job of observer so I set to work to talk my battery into letting me volunteer.

Letter from H. Spear (then Gunner Spear 34th Siege Batteries)
I was an artilleryman, landed in France September 10th 1915, proceeded by road with the guns to Gorre Wood where we mounted and manned the guns without delay, we bombarded the enemy lines at Loos day and night for three consecutive days, owing to shortage of ammunition we used the artillery method of harassing fire, one round every 10 minutes, after 3 days and nights non-stop in which I obtained a burst ear drum, (not bad enough to go sick) we moved in the dead of night to a placed called Vermelles where we continued our bombardment, no wash, scraps of food when available, for days and days all this was between 10th and 20th of September 1915.

Later we moved to a place called Beauvry where we continued our bombarding until we moved to a place called Vieille-Chappelle, where we spent the next period still bombarding, until the Somme offensive 1916. I remained with the same battery through the Somme, Passchendaele, Cambrai and through to Charleroi, Maubeuge, Lille, Namur, to the banks of the River Meuse, Belgium, when I was sent back home February 1919, to form a draft going to India as a Mountain Gunner. You see I was a regular soldier. This little anecdote is not intended to be in any way bombastic, nothing more than what all our lovely servicemen did and went through in the world's worst war.

We could not remember dates or days really, not that we were devoid, but everything seemed to be yes or no, I can hardly find words to describe things as they were.

I remember seeing the Prince of Wales get out of his car in Vermelles, where his Chauffeur was killed. I saw him again later in 1916 in Carnoy Valley on the Somme; he was a Captain in the Grenadier Guards, a Pukka soldier, or good soldier.

*Anti-Aircraft fire.

Letter from W. J. Kemp

In reply to your letter in the *Daily Telegraph* of today's date I am pleased to add a few notes on this battle in which I was engaged, entirely as a telephonist.

My battery, No 59 Siege Battery Royal Garrison Artillery, was a regular battery and at the outbreak of the war, were serving at Roorkee, India, as a Siege Battery. There were three RGA Batteries stationed at Roorkee, two of which were trained as Siege Batteries; the other Battery was armed with a 5-inch gun. When going to camp, and for training during the winter, we were allotted bullock for the means of locomotion . . . about 8 bullocks per gun I think.

Our 6-inch Hows.* 25 cwt. which we had at Loos, were anchored to a platform by a bulk holdfast and a volute spring. The platform was double deck planks about 8–10 ft. long, which took several hours to put down . . . exactly square to get it to fit and level. The bulk holdfast was sunk about 2 ft. deep in front. Range of this How. (or gun, as used in conversation on parade) was about 6,000 yds. Spring recuperators.

With the introduction of the 26 cwt How. with its air recuperator, there was no need for this double decked platform and the gun was quickly moved from the firing position to the loading position by means of a lever.

I do not know the date the battery got these Hows. I met them when I returned to France in October 1916.

For the battle of Loos, the Battery was in position behind Vermelles and our front line was in front of Hulloch, which position you can easily see on the Michelin Map No 51 and also Le Rutoire Farm, leading into the Béthune–Lens Road.

Our Battery fired for four days, 21st, 22nd, 23rd and 24th, firing about 100 per gun per day; just at what target I cannot say, but at hostile batteries, as we had a plane to register and rang the guns on the targets. The infantry went over on the morning of 25th September, I was employed as a 'runner' that day to repair the telephone lines between the battery and our OP. All telephone lines at that time were Earth Returns and to tap in our line which was labelled to distinguish it from a dozen others which may or may not have been on the same 'route' and lined up with it, we had a D/3 telephone, a short wire for the 'line' with a safety pin attached to pierce the battery line – you hoped it was your own line and that it was not cut in any other place – and for the Earth we had a short wire a .303 bullet and so we made contact with our battery or the OP. All lines were labelled by units but it was found that a unit was

*Howitzers, guns which fired at a high angle and were thus suitable for trench warfare.

not above nipping a bit of your line to mend their own, leaving our labels still on the line; this confusion I'll leave you to sort out.

I do not now remember if the battery had a target that day, as I left the battery early to join the OP party, so that I could work on the lines both from the OP and from the battery to the front.

I do not remember anything particular during the morning. The first I saw was the battery with all four guns, horse drawn in No-Man's-Land that was coming into action; I was very near to them and the first thing I saw in No-Man's-Land was that it was full of dead, dying and wounded, we carried some of them out on to the road as some waved to us when they saw we were going to open fire. They had not got far out of their front line trenches before being struck down and all this after four days of bombardment, *so what the hell were the Arty firing at for four days? no wonder French got sent home.*

We fired a few rounds from the position in No-Man's-Land and then Brigade Headquarters told us to get in position in Le Rutoire Farm, which we did before dark. Whilst in this position I was skipped for corporal, as I had been found out of bounds and in a pub, by the Military Police. I was off duty and was out to get bread, but that did not matter, I got the Long S ervice and Good Conduct Medal after 18 years' service so my crime was not entered on my Good Conduct Sheets.

From the 25th till the night of the 29th I was working the wire from battery to OP in the front line. Not that we could see anything or do any good but we just had a line kept busy. I survived the shell fire we underwent but many of the Signallers got wounded, also an officer.

On the 29th, my last day with the battery, I ran the line out and kept it going, it was difficult to peg down, once loose where the hell would it finish? I got back to the front line in front of Hullock a few hundred yards from the road when Jerry bombarded the front line and blew several 100 yards away. I had lost my officer so waited till the firing had finished and then went to look for him as he might have been wounded.

Jerry then decided to come over for a few prisoners. We had different ideas about who should use our trench and lined up and let him have it. I got a rifle and ammo and joined in the fun. All new to me, a siege artilleryman in the front line, having a 'go' in the semi-darkness, but I could just see them creeping over. They got in the trench and there was a rush back so we got out on the top of the trench so that we could see them better. I did not think that they could also see me better down on one knee instead of prone like the Infy man nearby. I got it through the lobe of the left ear, out at the middle line of the neck, got out by a communication trench. Otherwise I should have been there still. Got to Le Rutoire Farm and they got me away.

I woke up in Nottingham Hospital where the Nurse said. 'When did you have your last stool' which meant nothing to me except it was for sitting on when 'op pickin like'? She explained, and said the Battle of Loos. She said when was that, I said the 25th September, she replied, 'Good eck, it's now the 4th of October.' As if I knew or cared what date it was.

The rest of the story you know, I have still some ill effects of the wound but stuck it out in order to serve for pension, which I did, now £8.20 nett.

Please ask me any questions as there is so little here that is of any use to you. I was born on 8th October 1889, so am 85 plus a-bit.

Firing at Jerry at close range did not mean a thing to me. It was like being on the Rifle range again in Roorkee, besides I just didn't care a damn. Awarded DCM for work under fire.

7

47th Division

Letter from W. J. Larcombe, 1/20 London Regiment
I am afraid I have now no diaries etc., which might be of use to you, but at 22 years of age I took part as an infantryman in the first line of attack, and remained in action for the four days or so of the battle – and although I am now 82, I have very vivid memories of 25th September, 1915.

I served there in the 20th London Regiment in the Brigade made up of the 17th-18th (London Irish) 19th and ourselves; and commanded by Sir William Thwaites and formed part of the 47th Division commanded by General Barter.

At 5.30 a.m. we fitted our recently delivered gas masks – P.H. Helmets – flannel bags impregnated with a foul smelling solution and supplied with a mouth tube, a nose clip and a pair of glass eyepieces.

Very soon after we were over the top, I realised that my glasses were steamed up so much that I was unable to see through them – in some desperation I took my mask off and then realised that our gas had blown back on us, but as the gas was heavy and low flying, I was able to breathe fairly normally.

Our company plan was to attack a chalk pit which contained two German field guns – we lost a number of men on the way over, but found very little trouble when we reached the chalk-pit.

We put the guns out of action and then established ourselves at the point overlooking the road to Loos: this was intended to be the starting off point of the great breakthrough which did not happen.

The two guns were soon taken back into our lines by a gun carriage sent up by the supporting field batteries and put on display at the Horse Guards Parade eventually – as a form of recruitment drive no doubt.

In searching the gunners' dug out, we found a set of very interesting Loos photographs – taken by the gunners and showing intimate little scenes in the town – I recall one which showed a German soldier sharing a potato peeling session with a local woman – these pictures eventually reached the London press and caused quite an interested stir.

I recall, too, seeing at an angle from our position, the London Scottish in action – some hour or so of surging backward and forward to the German slag heap twin tower position, and then the arrival in our lines of dismounted cavalry who had been massed behind us nearly for a cavalry breakthrough which never happened – and again the arrival (on the 27th) of the new, untried 24th division (containing Guards units) – who came up in dangerous blocks of platoons, in the open and badly shelled by heavy artillery armour – a part of the action which once again came to nothing.

Letter from C. Arthur, 1/18 London Regiment
I was with the 18th Battalion London Regiment, London Irish Rifles. On the night of the 24th/25th September we marched up from our billets in the village of Maroc and were in the front trenches well before dawn. I was with No 7 Platoon 'B' Company. The guns were banging away and the RE personnel were standing by the gas cylinder ready to release at the proper time. Unfortunately there was very little wind and when the gas was eventually released a little before 6 a.m. it hung about in a bank only a few yards in front of the trenches so that when we went over the top we soon passed through the gas into the clear air beyond. It was an awe inspiring sight – the ground sloped down towards the German front line, with the village of Loos beyond on the sky line the pit winding towers very distinctive – known to us as the Tower Bridges. On the right was the Double Crassier.

There was very little German shelling but the machine guns were active and we had a lot of casualties. The German front line was about 400 yards from our front line and it seemed ages crossing the interval. By this time the gas was well behind us. In reaching the German front line we found the troops in the act of relief and so crowded they couldn't use their rifles properly so we had an easy time standing on their parapet and shooting down into their trench – the slaughter was pretty awful. My platoon's objective was the reserve line but meeting no opposition we pushed into Loos village and settled ourselves in the cemetery, the vaults made good dug outs.

The next day the Germans started to counter-attack which was just beyond the village. In the afternoon we saw an amazing sight, the Guards marching up the Loos road complete with cookers steaming until they came under shrapnel fire from the rocket artillery. Then they went into extended order pretty smartly. We also saw some stragglers from the hapless 21st and 24th divisions who had been marching all night from their billets miles behind the front line. They were only partly trained troops, had never been under fire before, and had no food for many hours. They were, of course, demoralised – poor devils. Loos was a sad story of muddle and bad management, not enough gas and the artillery short of shells. By the way, our divisional artillery (47th Division) were armed with Boer War 15 pounders and each battalion had only two maxim guns each. Haig did not believe in machine guns – idiot.

Letter from Reverend W. Vellam Pitts, 1/23 London Regiment
I was in the battle of Loos as an infantry soldier serving with the 23rd London Territorials. My regimental number was 2820. I went to France to reinforce the 1st battalion in March 1915 and was in the front line on and off for the whole of that six months. Sometimes we were in the front line trenches for four weeks and had to resort to shaving in cups of tea. The manning of the line was very thin for quite often I was on sentry duty covering two bays in the trenches.

My father wrote out the accounts of the fighting in my letters and I still have those records. Here is the account :

We came back from our rest on the last day of August and did three days night working party, then to the trenches at Bully Grenay for 20 days including three days of British bombardment. Then we came out and did a working party and that same night marched through a communication trench to Les Brebis arriving there about 5 a.m. absolutely whacked and wet through, thick with mud having rained hard the previous day. We had not had a night's rest since August 29th and we dropped in our billets asleep till 10.30 when we had breakfast. Afterwards had a bath and cleaned up and did other jobs.

We slept a little that night but turned out at 2 a.m. the next morning to man the third line of defence at Les Brebis. The bombardment was terrific and effective, nearly all high explosives. There were 9.2 and 12.4 guns on the job. The Germans replied but only in the minority, they put liquid fire over. When the boys advanced we used smoke bombs and gas, both of which were effective. Unfortunately the wind shifted a bit and some of our own gas caught us but with the smoke helmet did not do much harm.

After the advance we took up our position in the old German front line which was smashed to pieces. Then we reversed the trench, buried and salvaged the dead of which there were a good many. Our last meal was Saturday morning and we had nothing brought up until Sunday morning and it rained all Saturday night. Sunday morning they put over gas in the form of shells so we put on our smoke helmets which saved us. After that we were rushed up to our new second line in open order under shrapnel and rifle fire. We got there in safety and began to reverse the trench. All the spare ammunition was loose cartridges in a box without clips.

In the evening the Dragoon Guards and the Royal Dragoons came across in open order to reinforce the advanced position. It was a fine sight to see them. They were a fine body of men. The following day, Monday, we were lucky enough to get some breakfast which was brought up under machine gun fire. Soon after that we were called out to reinforce the 20th battalion. When we arrived there about 5 o'clock the order was to fix bayonets and with that we went for the enemy. I remember having to cross a road which was covered by a German machine gun. I crossed but soon after received a wound in the head from a grenade. My shirt was soon covered in blood and after a field dressing was applied, I made my way back to a dressing station. I was moved to Etaples where the nurse told me I was one of the lucky ones, she said, 'It was someone's little prayer in England that brought me through.'

Account by Captain W. M. Escombe, 1/20 London Regiment
Well we're for it at last – I feel sure we shall do well. I had the company out this morning for the last time and practised the advance – they are all right. They got off the mark together and extended beautifully, getting their distance to a yard and keeping it. Their morale is grand. If only our guns have done their job we shall make a good thing of it. I expect we shall lose half the battalion, but how better. It's the Double Crassier and that second line of wire that bother me. If they've got some hidden machine guns along the north side the *crassier*, we shall get hell, unless the 140th brigade gets along the top quickly. Then there's that damned second line of wire. We must make sure and get through at the near end – our guns have hardly touched it farther up, and it's clean enfiladed from the eastern end of the Double Crassier. The 'Tennis Courts' don't worry me much. We must keep to the left of them. However, a few hours will decide everything. If only we can get through. The cavalry have had their advanced parties up this afternoon pegging out their bivouac ground. I have been up on the slag heap and watched the bombardment. It's grand – the 'Tower Bridge' is completely hidden in smoke at times. I expect 'Granny' is giving it a dose. The batteries on Maroc plateau are going like machine guns, and hardly anything seems to be coming back. That's the surprising part. Matthews who has been up again recon-

noitring says that observation posts haven't been touched. Have we outed their guns? Are they saving up their ammunition? Or haven't they got the guns there?

Everyone is quietly but terribly excited. The men had a great time in the *estaminets* last night, but today we have been very busy issuing articles of extra equipment – picks, shovels, periscopes, sand-bag, discs etc. and they haven't had much time off.

This morning the CO told the battalion what is going to happen, though of course all the men knew before except for the important details. The push will be launched from Ypres to the Swiss frontier. Our division has one of the stiffest jobs, and we and the 19th have the longest advance to make in the division – about 2,000 yards : and the guns, bless 'em, we've got best part of a hundred on our divisional front alone. Gee! It will be some shemozzle.

I parade the Company at 8.15 p.m. It's just getting dark. There they are, formed up in column of fours on the branch road off the Route Nationale. They are on the top of their for m– as fine as any troops in France, surely. What can I say to them? I shall never parade them again. We've lived, fought, marched, worked, groused and laughed together for five months – or is it years? I've tried to be a father to them though our ages are mostly much the same. I could talk to them for hours but there's not time. I could go on thanking them and bucking them up to the skies till my throat was dry, but we must move off to the battalion parade – 'Boys remember there's just one thing – your job comes first above everything – Slope Arms – Quick march.'

Ball's company is there, standing or lying at the side of the road. Here and there a cigarette glowing and little bunches of men singing softly their old popular songs. I put my company in rear of 'C' and Williams and Dolphin comes in in my rear. Norman rides up and gives me some final instructions for the march and a large scale map of Loos, which I stuff into my bulging haversack – pray God I use it.

The Colonel comes up, his voice a bit shaky with excitement and emotion. 'Good luck, I've put you in for a mention for your work in the Keeps. Everything all right?'

'Yes Sir, thank you. Good luck Sir.'

He passes on and a few minutes later on the stroke of time moves off with headquarters. Ball's company following by platoons at a 100 yards interval. His last platoon is under way and my connecting files move out. I count the paces 96, 97, 98; I turn to Colin Hooper. 'Carry on'. 'Number seven platoon quick march.' The inhabitants stand and watch us. *'Bon soir M'sieur, bonne chance mon capitaine.'* We wheel round to the left into the open on to the road for Les Brebis. Near ahead lie the slag heaps and beyond the distant ridge, twinkling with bursting shells – Loos.

It's a warm night, and though cloudy it is fairly light owing to the moon. I wonder where we shall be tomorrow night – consolidating the shattered remains of the 'Garden City' whilst the battle rages on eastwards past Haisnes, Hulluch and on to Lille – or perhaps summoning our last remaining strength to ward off the furious Boche counter-attacks – unpleasant thought of long hours of desperate street fighting, where each house has its own bloody battle and death from friend or foe threatens one many times a minute – or, and my thoughts go back to those days at Givenchy, to those little tumbled heaps of khaki lying out in the grass with rifles sticking up at uncanny angles, whilst now and then a moan drifts over the parapet. What of the folk at home; our thoughts turn to them continually but thank heavens the excitement of the coming struggle seems to lull one's apprehensions. Life is dearer to no one than to me.

Last Sunday I arrived back at Nouex-les-mines at 5 a.m. with the company and the rest of the battalion after digging all night. I turned into my billet at 24 Route Nationale where I had a lovely bed with sheets, but the sun was just starting to create a perfect day. At 7 I could stand it no longer. This might be my last Sunday. I dressed and bicycled over to Houchin, saddled my mare and rode out into the country over the glorious fields. I rode west towards Hesdigneul.

Behind me was the tumult of war – Souchez and Notre Dame de Lorette – ahead was the peaceful country beyond the highwater mark of the battle tide. Troops there were everywhere, long strings of gunner horses out for exercise, their bay coats shimmering in the sun; aeroplanes humming off from their neighbouring aerodrome for their morning reconnaissance; motor cycles and cars rushing along the great paved roads raising clouds of dust; but there were no shell holes, no torn trees or broken homes. The shady slopes of the Bois des Dames lay shrouded in the misty bloom of a perfect autumn morning; the little red roofed villages gleamed among the scattered clumps of trees in the plain; and even the gaunt hideous mine heads with their attendant slag heaps were softened in the shimmering haze. The larks sung overhead and the partridges glided away over the glistening stubble. The notes of a church bell came and went on the breeze.

That was six days ago. Where shall I be next Sunday? Little do I imagine that I shall be once more away from the noise of battle and resting quietly by the Bois des Dames listening once more to a church bell on another perfect day.

Just before reaching Les Brebis the battalion moves into a field and halts in mass. We soon lie down and some drop off to sleep for we must get all the rest we can. There is a howitzer battery a few hundred yards behind, and though it opens fire with a blinding flash and a piercing bang it fails to disturb us, and we just bless the shrieking shells as they rush overhead and may they each take a good scoop out of the wire or bag their full tally of Boches.

Half an hour later we are on the move again. We have left our horses behind. Up we go through the quiet familiar streets – past the solitary intact church in its open square and out on to the Maroc plateau. Here the ceaseless batteries bark and spit their shells over our heads but nothing comes back. Near the crumbling remains of a church we turn aside into the trampled cottage gardens and here our cookers are waiting with a hot meal – a sort of last supper. The boys quickly break up into their usual little parties. I move among them. They all seem quite happy and not in the least worried. Someone finds me a barrel for a table and an old chair and I am soon at work on some hot stew and tea and rum. Colin Hooper and Grant join me and later Alan Young. He has been out in front earlier in the night (it's now 1 a.m.) and reached the 'Tennis Courts'. He says they are not held or wired so that's all right. The CO calls us up for final instructions and at 1.15 we move off for the trenches. As we file in, Thwaites is there. He shakes hands with the officers and says cheery words to the men. As long as he's behind us we shall be all right. Then we slowly move along the communication trench to our positions. All is quiet; only an occasional shot from our guns – the final lull before the storm breaks.

It takes about an hour to get the whole battalion into position in the various lines, for although the men move in without any hitch, the progress is necessarily slow owing to the narrowness of the trenches and the bulky equipment the men are carrying. I am with my last platoon – No 8. Colin Hooper is in the front line with No 7, and Grant and Sergeant McDonald with 6 and 5 are in the supernumerary second line. Having seen No 8 disposed at the four saps leading from the second line, I make my way laboriously up to the front. I squeeze along the line talking to the men as I pass. The special REs with their green, red and white armlets are busy getting the gas and smoke cylinders ready. We saw the Irish carry these up at dead of night about a week ago. Everything was done with the utmost secrecy. The cylinders arrived at the advanced RE dump near Maroc mine in GS waggons with muffled wheels.

Here they were unpacked and each slung on a pole between two men. The men were formed into parties, all the men in each party having a large white patch on their back with a black number which corresponded to the number of the bay in the front line to which they were to carry the cylinders. Each party headed by its guide moved off slowly through the darkness, following the rows of houses and finally descending into the various communication trenches. The only sound was the creaking of the slings and the grunts and muttered oaths of the men, for the cylinders weighed about 200 lbs. each and constant halts were necessary. We were up digging that night and though we cursed because we were kept in late owing to all the trenches being blocked with these parties, yet we wouldn't have swopped jobs for a good deal.

I satisfy myself that all my platoons are in position and then retire to my place in the second line. There is nothing to do now but wait as calmly as possible. The guns are not very busy and a drizzle is falling so I select a spacious fire-step, get under my waterproof sheet and doze off into a light sleep, waking every now and then to see if anything is happening. The faithful Andy is close by sharing the same step. The rain soon makes the ground sticky and the men lying or sitting about are already covered with patches of chalky mud. It is very chilly in these early morning hours and one gets stiff and cramped as there is little space to move in. We have been told that the gas attack will probably start at 4.50 a.m. so at 4.30, no orders having reached me I squeeze my way to Battalion Headquarters.

Here I learn that the runner has missed me with a message that the attack is delayed for an hour and the gas will be liberated at 5.50. That means that the assault will start at 6.30 with the Irish. Our first line will go at 6.35, the second at 6.36, the third at 6.36/50, and the fourth with me in it at 6.37. It is just on 5.0 now and a cold cheerless dawn. The guns are going again pretty briskly, but as usual nothing comes back to worry us. Once more I make my way round my platoons and warn them of the delayed attack; they are in excellent spirits.

At last the moment that we have waited for for six weeks arrives. We adjust our smoke helmets ready to pull down at a moment's notice. Suddenly the word comes, 'It's started'. A hasty glance over the parapet shows a thick brown cloud emerging from the front line. The next moment there is the crack of a Boche rifle, then another and another, then dozens, then hundreds and machine guns as well. The bullets crackle and whistle over our heads in a storm. Up go the rockets and star shells and then the Boche guns start. With a shriek and a roar the shells arrive. Faster and faster they come. HE shrapnel, big stuff, small stuff, pip-squeaks, 77s, 5.9s, tearing the air to ribbons, scattering the earth in clouds, smothering the atmosphere with fumes, dust and flying fragments. One

PASS

Period during which available.

1st March.

30th April.

person named below is permitted to pass
the area occupied by the British Army
without a motor cycle or car during the
stated hereon.

Pass is not to be accepted if the name
ly entered on it is erased and another
substituted.

LAISSER-PASSER

Valable du 1er Mars.

au 30e Avril.

La personne nommée ci-dessous est autorisée
à circuler dans la zone occupée par l'Armée
Britannique avec ou sans motocyclette ou voiture
automobile pendant la période spécifiée ci-dessus.

Cette carte cesse d'être valable au cas où le
nom du porteur serait effacé et remplacé par un
autre nom.

Brig. Gen. M. G. Wilkinson. M.V.O

Commdg 44th Brigade. 15th Division.

ture and
o of
g Officer.

W. V. Beatty Major

A.P.M. 15th Division

A.P.M.
PASS
No. 8624
Date 1/3/16

Pass issued to Brigadier General Wilkinson. His widow kindly lent his scrap book from which
many of the illustrations in this book are taken.

Armentières 1915

Sir John French with King George V

Tower Bridge

A

44th Brigade Preliminary Operation Order No. 10.

13th September 1915

1/10,000
ap Sheet
. ×35. 1. S.W

1. The Brigade is to take a principal part in an attack on the German positions -

2. The objectives assigned to the 44th Brigade are as follows :-

1st German front trench from point of salient at G.34.a.4.9. to the little cross trench at G.28.c.9.6 - and support trench behind this line.

2nd Second line trench from G.35.a.6.3. to G.29.c.4.5. (i.e. in line with the cross roads at G.29.c.9.3.)

3rd Loos Village.

4th. Puits No. 15

5th German work in H.31.d.

3. In order to form a defensive flank southwards to cover our advance the 47th Division will attack with the following objectives :-

(a) Double Crassier

(b) German trenches M.4.C.3.9. to G.34.a.6.5.

(c) German 2nd line trenches from M.4.d.8.8. to the cemetery in G.35.a.

(d) Enclosure in G.35.d.

(e) Fosse in G.36

On our left the 46th Brigade will attack simultaneously on

(a) German front trench from G.28.d.0.7. to VERMELLES - LOOS Road, and communicating trenches behind it -

(b) Second line trench from left of 44 Brigade's second objective to the sunken road at G.29.b.2.6.

(c) Trenches behind this to the third line from G.29.d.7.a. to G.30.a.2.7.

(d) Road from G.30.c.4.2. to G.30.b.4.2.

(e) Line from H.31. central to PUITS No. 14. bis (exclusive)

The German trench running from G.35.a.6.3. to G.34. central is allotted to the 47th Division who will deal with it - This trench exclusive will be the boundary of the 44th Infy Bde attack -

4. The attack will commence by a steady bombardment by all available guns day and night for 4 days up to the moment of the infantry assault on the 5th day. This bombardment will be distributed over the whole front of the 1st & 4th Corps -

5. Further details as to the actual date and hour of the assault will be issued later -

6. The attack of the Brigade must be pushed home to the full extent of its power -

7. The positions of the Battalions at the commencement of the bombardment will be as follows -

(a) In formed trench lines - 10th Gordon Highlanders

In GRENAY - VERMELLES branch line of trenches - 7th Cameron Highlanders

In GRENAY - VERMELLES main line - 8th Seaforth Highrs.

In Mazingarbe - 9th Black Watch -

Operation order, written in pencil

a) EQUIPMENT TO BE CARRIED. (i) Packs + great coats will not be taken to the forming up positions on the night preceding the assault, but will be labelled and left under guard in selected houses or dug outs.

Every man will carry – Rifle + equipment (less pack)

2 Bandoliers of S.A.A. in addition to equipment ammunition (220 rounds in all).

1 Iron ration + unexpired portion of day's ration.

2 Sandbags in belt (Pioneers 6 sandbags).

Smoke helmet.

Note – The haversack will be carried on the back.

Grenadiers will carry equipment ammunition only (no bandoliers).

(ii) 10 selected men per platoon throughout the Brigade will carry wire cutters (attached to a lanyard).

(iii) 8 selected men per platoon in the two leading Companies will carry bill hooks for destroying wire. These men, and men with wire cutters will be supplied with hedging gloves.

(iv) Yellow flags will be issued as detailed in Instructions S.33.

The 47th Division will carry yellow flags with a black Cross.

The 1st Division red flags with a white stripe.

(b) GRENADES. 500 grenades packed in boxes (which can be carried by one man) will be stored in two forward trench depots.

These depots will be kept full during the action.

Grenades for bringing the equipment of grenadiers in the attack up to the full amount will be issued direct to bombing squads of battalions who will attend to draw them when ordered.

(c) S.A AMMUNITION. Two trench depots for S.A.A. are being prepared each to hold 100,000 rounds S.A.A. near grenade depots.

Boxes of Ammunition will also be placed in each bay which are to be used for any firing at night so as to keep the amount of 220 rounds on the man intact.

(d) R.E. STORES 1. An advanced R.E. Store is established in Trench 27 at a point 125 yds from the junction of 27 + 7 towards 8. This store will contain sandbags in double bundles of 25 for slinging, picks, shovels, crowbars wire cutters, tracing tapes, coils of rope coils of plain wire, billhooks + axes –

(e) WATER. Tanks of water have been placed in the support trenches at intervals. Sentries will be posted to see no water is touched before the attack takes place.

(f) M officers of Battalions have been instructed regarding advanced Dressing Stations

There will also be an advanced dressing station just behind FOSSE 7 and in the BREWERY at LE PHILOSOPHE.

Operation order, written out in pencil for Brigadier-General Wilkinson

General de Castelnau (commanding the French 2nd Army), Marshal Joffre Commander-in-Chief of the French armies on the Western Front and General Pau (commanding the Army of Alsace)

(*Below*) Les Brébis as seen from the trench

The battlefield from the air

The battlefield from the air

gun or battery in particular persistently puts HE's about 50 yards beyond my bit of trench showering us with dirt each time, and incidentally I imagine going pretty close to headquarters. A bit of spent shrapnel hits me thud on the shoulder but has not the force to go through my clothing. Then a bit of dirt hits the rim of my goggles as I hold them in my hand and knocks the glass out – a serious accident this, but with Andy's help I am able to replace it. Our own guns have now worked themselves into a frenzy, and the din is awful.

I glance constantly at my watch. It seems impossible for anyone to get out on top and live, but my mind goes back to accounts of previous battles. How often is that phrase used; and yet men do get through, so why shouldn't some of us?

Six-thirty at last. 'They're off' the news flashes along the line. I glance over the top and there in the dense smoke are the Irish advancing in line. Weird and uncanny they look – mere shadows in the curling yellow fog – but they never hesitate; each line adjusts itself and disappears. Here indeed is borne the fruit of all that training at Hatfield, St Albans, and in our days of 'rest' behind the line; for nothing but the absolute habit of moving in line at five paces interval could enable men to do so under these hellish conditions.

There goes our front line, now the second and third – our turn next. We scramble over the parapet and out of the saps, stumble through a few strands of wire and throw ourselves down for a brief pause. Then up and we double forward as fast as we can, jumping our supernumerary and front lines or crossing them by the bridges placed there by our men before they left. We must get clear of our lines as quickly as possible as that is where the shells are falling thickest. My helmet hampers my breathing considerably and once clear of the front line I am glad to break into quick time. I can see Andy beside me but we have to shout to make each other hear. It is impossible to recognise men at a few yards owing to their helmets and the smoke. The air seems to whizz past me with bullets, but I hardly notice anyone falling.

Suddenly my outlet valve becomes choked and refuses to work. I can't get my breath fast enough; in vain I gasp – my lungs are empty. But for Andy I should fall. I feel I must drop just where I am and rest, but he clutches my arm. My only hope is to raise my helmet and chance the gas. I can see others doing it and tear mine off. A few deep breaths of cool air revive me and as there is no gas to hurt I can push on. Now I find myself in the Boche wire, but luckily I strike an easy place and get through without trouble, though I can see men dropping all round. A grenade pitches amongst a group of men on my left. I can see the hole it blows in the ground. The men seem to hesitate and then fall, but I hear no sound – the general roar of battle drowns everything. The Boche front line at last – I hurl myself over it but the parados gives and I slip back. There is a dug-out behind me into which the Irish have driven some Germans.

I take a chance shot down the entrance before willing hands heave me up again and Andy pulls me to my feet and on we go. It is still impossible to see more than a few hundred yards.

I try to find the 'Tower Bridge' or *crassier* to check my position, but I cannot see them, so I drop down and take a compass bearing – we are too far left. Now we cross a track and reach a communication trench. I rack my brains to think where they come in on the map. A Boche is located in this trench, but the lines sweep on. Here I recognise some of my men, P. C. Litten amongst them.

Again I drop down to take a bearing and then thud – something hits me a stinging blow on the right arm just below the shoulder. I am hit, I tell Andy but get up. He helps me into a trench and rips up my sleeve. My arm is bleeding a bit but he soon binds it up and it doesn't hurt much. I have a drink of water and after a few minutes I feel better though a bit shaky. We move along the trench a bit and then climb out. Andy wants me to go back, but I must get to the Garden City and find the Company. He takes my arm and tries to make me go back with him – I think he thinks I am worse than I really am – but I order him to come with me, and then guided by the Tower Bridge which now shows up, we make for the Garden City. We were too far left as I thought and as there seems to be a good deal of fire coming from Loos we follow a communication trench past the second line.

We can see our men in the City and after about ten minutes we join them. They have practically cleared the whole place out and are now working through the neighbouring trenches and consolidating. Bell has got a platoon, or rather, what remains of it on the *crassier* on the left, exactly as arranged, and 'A' Company has pushed on about a quarter of a mile up the slope of hill 70 and is digging in. The line is very thin though.

I soon find the remains of my company in the NW corner of the 'city' and with them Major Matthews. There are still one or two Boches in the cellars and there is also a cellar full of French women and children. These are sent back to Maroc under escort and also a few more prisoners which we get. The latter are mostly miserable specimens and in a frightful state of funk. They all seem to think that they are going to be shot at once and grovel on the ground for mercy, whimpering like children. We set to work to loophole the forward houses, and by this time some Boche shrapnel is coming over, but only about one shell a minute. I find the CO with Norman and Clout in a trench on the east side of the City. He is anxiously awaiting reinforcements and tells me he has already sent back some messages for them to the Brigade. Our men are also disposed along a trench running half right towards the copse and I work along this trench to see how far they extend. I find several of No 5 Platoon here. About three hundred yards from the City they have erected a barricade. There is very little rifle shooting around here and no shelling. I rejoin the CO and he sends me up to Bell on the *crassier*. He has got a disc there but very few men. Below to the left are the 15th division pushing well on but their front line appears to be coming under the fire of our own guns.

So far there is no sign of the enemy massing for a counter attack, and leaving Bell I return to the City by the paths running down by the side of the *crassier*. Afterwards many men were sniped on this path. Shortly after I reach the City again Bell is led in by two orderlies. He has suddenly broken down completely and having lost his glasses cannot see. I give him some brandy and meat lozenges and install him in a room. A little later I rejoin the CO and find him there pulled together a good deal. Still no reinforcements and we scan the crest in rear anxiously. At length the CO orders me to make my way back and explain the situation to Brigadier, so with Andy and a prisoner who has just been brought in – a big hefty chap – I start off. We move by a trench for the shrapnel is still buzzing about and about 400 yards ahead some heavy HEs are pitching pretty regularly, so we bear off to the left a bit to give them a miss. We pass through the Boche second line now filled with the Irish and reach the first. Here I find Colonel Tredinnick and Hamilton, the latter slightly wounded in the leg. After this we take to the open. The Boche wire is a nasty sight. They had machine guns and rifle grenades playing on this and many of our fellows were stopped. I talk to some as I pass and give them water and cigarettes. I tell them they will shortly see the Guards advance, for before the action we were told that they would come through us and we were now eagerly expecting them. We now move along the Loos–Maroc Road, and I overtake Trinder who has got a jammy one in the thigh but who says he is all right and has got all the help he requires. The Boches are now strafing our front line with HE so we sheer off to the left to avoid them. I watch the effect on our prisoner of his own frightfulness, but it does not seem to worry him much. We reach our front line at sap 6 and proceed up it to Brigade Headquarters, closely attended by the HEs which shower us with dirt. Here

I meet Ronny Grant who, having been slightly gassed, is rejoining the battalion.

We emerge at Maroc and hand over our prisoner to the police. The place has suffered little from shell fire. I report to the general and tell him the situation. He tells me he has sent up a company of the 17th, and that is all he can spare at present. Danby gives me a whisky and soda – the best I have ever had – and I proceed to the dressing station. Here everyone is very busy for many casualties are coming in. A large padre whom I don't remember having seen before sticks a cigarette into each newcomer's mouth which is empty.

Steels, my QM Sergeant, brings me a cup of hot tea which is refreshing. Our brigade Padre Wood is there and he chats to me for a bit. After some time I get my wound dressed. It doesn't hurt much as the bullet has gone clean through without touching the bone. I am put into a Ford Ambulance and saying goodbye to the faithful Andy I am whirled away to Noeux-les-Mines. There the RAMC are also very busy and can't keep pace with the constant stream of ambulances which roll up. All day and far on into the night the Doctors and orderlies work quietly and quickly. One hardly ever hears an order given yet the work is going on smoothly and rapidly all the while. Ball is there with a shattered forearm. He was shot at close quarters by a Boche but shot the blighter dead with his revolver in his left hand.

In the afternoon Colin Hooper is brought in. His left leg is badly smashed and he has lost a lot of blood. He was hit in the Boche wire. He is very white and weak and I sit by him for some time holding his hand and telling him how splendidly everything has gone to buck him up. They carry him away in the evening – 'So long old boy,' I call, 'see you later', but he died a few days later at Le Treport. About five a.m. several of us are woken up and taken by motor to Lapugnoy, arriving there an hour later. We gather round the cookhouse fire and drink hot tea, for it is very cold in the early morning air. We are attended by a real English female nurse – very comforting.

It is Sunday morning – just a week since I went for my ride – and here I am eating breakfast in the open with the green woods rising above the quiet little village and a church bell ringing. Faintly through the calm air comes the far away rumble of guns, where the remnant of my devoted regiment is still carrying on the struggle. A squadron of cavalry moves along the dusty road. At midday the long hospital train moves slowly out of the siding and I am on it. Many are the encouraging rumours that have reached us and our spirits are high – for surely we have got through this time. Not till we reach England some two days later do we begin to learn how once more we have failed. Not through any fault of the 47th Division though.

Letter from F. J. Drew, 1/5 London (Civil Service Rifles)
I was in that cock up as an infantry soldier and as such had a good bird's eye view of what transpired although I cannot pretend that I, or anyone else for that matter, had any idea of what it was all about and what we were doing. I have two friends who were in the same regiment and we still meet, although in our eighties, and I am sure that between us we might be able to give you some information.

It happened that this was the only battle in which we were involved. My two friends were both wounded and were not sent overseas again. I was transferred to a technical branch in November 1915 and said goodbye to the front line with no regret whatever.

Letter from F. E. Heninghem, 1/23 London Regiment
September 25th 1915 was the Battle of Loos. Our battalion, the 1/23rd London Regiment with the rest of the 142 Brigade of the 47th London Division, went over the top just in front of the 'Garden City of Maroc' a mile or two from Les Brebis.

We met with little opposition and took the 1st and 2nd German line of trenches with very few casualties.

It was grand to be out in open country and the tree lined cobble road to Loos we could see the Double Crassier of Loos and the Slag heaps on our right. We came across a house on the corner of the Loos Hulloch road, here there had been heavy fighting and many dead British and German laid inside and outside.

We halted here and looking back saw 2, 18 pounder guns of the Royal Horse Artillery gallop into action under heavy shell fire along the cobbled tree lined road, sparks flying from the horses hooves, the drivers with whip and spurs urging their mounts on; they swung round a few yards from us and fired a few rounds.

We carried on and reached the German trench a few yards from Loos.

Next day looking back towards the British line we saw the Brigade of Guards coming towards us. Our Officer, Lieutenant Clinton, went out and cut the German wire. We put trench boards across the trench for them to cross. Meanwhile the Germans had spotted them and were putting shells into them. This was the first time the Welsh Guards had been into action. They made a grand sight as they advanced with fixed bayonets and disappeared into the village and so to Hill 70 and some even got into Lens.

Being a machine gunner I was detailed to hold the crest until the French, who were going to relieve us, arrived. During the take-over I rescued a French officer and was mentioned for the Croix de Guerre but never received it. I suppose the officer concerned was killed. We had been in action eight days and marched back four or five miles to a corn field and laid down exhausted.

Transferred to the Machine Gun Corps in 1916 as a driver and was in action at Ypres, Arras, Somme Retreat 1918, and final advance to victory November 1918.

Lieutenant Colonel J. J. Sheppard, 1/19 London Regiment
Came the dawn of 25th September. Zero was at 5.30 a.m. when gas was released from our forward trench and drifted toward the German lines, but, unfortunately the wind also took it across the front of the 15th Division on our immediate left.

We went forward in attack at 6.30 a.m. and as Signal Sergeant I followed the attack in order to lay telephone lines and maintain communications between the forward area and the original British lines.

When arriving at the German front line I found 'Mopping up' in progress, but we had suffered many casualties during the advance, and in consequence few men were available for this purpose. There were some deep dugouts in which the enemy were still sheltering, and I stayed to assist in winkling them out. When they eventually came up into the trench a small number were wounded and I saw two Germans with white handkerchiefs tied round their arms with a Red Cross crudely made in human blood. They were directed back to the British lines without escort as every available man was required to consolidate the captured trench.

I subsequently went to the German Second Line – enemy shell fire was heavy and many were lying dead and wounded.

Two incidents at this time stand out in my memory – a Scottish soldier of the 15th Division standing astride a German on the ground and with his rifle upturned was sticking his bayonet into him and shouting, 'Here's one for Jock, now one for Andy' etc. I felt sick but could not interfere as it was obvious the Scot was temporarily out of his mind.

The second incident was seeing a HP shell burst at the feet of an advancing soldier which had the effect of blowing off both legs cleanly at the knees exposing both knee joints.

The CO of my battalion (19th London's) was killed during the advance and my Signalling Officer (Lieutenant de Fontaine) was severely wounded which left me to take over the responsibility of maintaining communication between Battalion HQ and Brigade HQ. I discovered that the CO of the 20th London's had assumed command of my Battalion and found his Headquarters in a cellar on the outskirts of the village, and set up a Signal Station with operators and linesmen to keep the line to Brigade HQ intact. When this had been done I was free to roam about the village in search of any German signalling equipment. I entered a court-yard off the Main Street and saw in a corner an entrance with the words *Gott strafe England* in German text printed in white chalk above. On entering I found hot soup in boilers, also food including large coils of sausages, potatoes, and tins of various sorts. In one room was a large cupboard containing bundles of cigars and flat packets of 10 cigarettes. These cigarette packets were printed in English 'Cycle Brand' Virginia Cigarettes made in USA with a picture of a lady in bloomers standing beside a cycle – I carried as many as possible to the position on Hill 70 where the 19th Battalion were digging a trench and distributed them along the line.

On my way back from the old British line after collecting some equip-ment I was hailed by our Lewis Gun Officer Lieutenant L. Pollak who asked me to direct him to the front line as he wanted to bring up an ammunition party.

As we were passing through the enclosure near the 'Tower Bridge' (Pylons) we heard someone call Leslie! Leslie! and noticed about 30 yards away by a wall a German Stretcher Bearer with a German Officer on a stretcher. Lieutenant Pollak asked me to wait and went across to investigate – he came back and told me the officer who called was his cousin who was badly wounded and had asked for his help in getting him down to the Casualty Clearing Station. He asked me what I sug-gested he should do. I said it was a matter entirely for him to decide. He thereupon returned to the German and told him that when all our own wounded were dealt with he might then receive attention. (I would men-tion here that the 19th London's had some officers of Jewish extraction who were sons of naturalised German Jews and probably had family connections in Germany.)

During the afternoon the intensity of the fighting died down and some civilians who had stayed in shelters in cellars in the Village were evacuated to the British lines.

A thrilling sight was the arrival of a battery of Royal Horse Artillery dashing down the cobbled Lens–Bethune Road and when about 500 yards from the village of Loos, suddenly pulled off the road, swing the guns round to face the enemy, unlimber, and gallop back. Sadly however before the gunners could really get into action, the whole battery was wiped out by German guns firing at them over open sights. Some time later with two of my signallers I visited this battery and found a large reel of red covered cable (D3) undamaged which was useful in establishing a more permanent line back to the old British Sector and Brigade HQ.

An impressive sight of the 27th September was the counter attack made by the 3rd Guards Brigade which advanced across the open territory in artillery formation of platoons, and in so doing suffered many casualties – as shells burst near platoons the guardsmen closed ranks and continued their advance. When they reached the Loos village they sloped arms, formed columns of fours, and marched through the village and on reaching the other side opened out into extended order and advanced to attack and consolidate our position on Hill 70.

Contemporary account from A Company, 20th London
Since the very early hours of Saturday morning before dawn signalled the start of the greatest onslaught since the Battle of the Marne until after dusk on Tuesday night, this battalion was in the thick of the fighting, so you can now guess I have a story to tell. Before going further I must mention that our battalion has by sheer British grit gained fame that will live for ever.

To start from the beginning. For weeks we had prepared for the advance. We knew exactly what was wanted of us when we went over the parapets. We had practised the charge, and taking the village several times days beforehand. As we had nearly — guns behind our part of the line you can tell what kind of a furious bombardment the Boche were subjected to. For days our guns pounded the German lines, and paved the way for our boys.

Leaving billets in a town a few miles behind the lines after dusk on Friday, our battalion moved to the trenches in easy stages. We were in the firing line at about three o'clock on Saturday morning, and then came an anxious wait, for the charge was not to commence until after dawn.

Joys of the Charge
Just before dawn our guns cut loose again, and the Boche's artillery responded strongly, the din being terrific. We shivered with the cold and the rain, but if the boys felt at all nervy they did not show it; indeed, everyone seemed cheerful. It was a tremendous trial for our nerves, and we were all glad when the order to fix bayonets and don smoke helmets came through.

Then came the sound of much heavy rifle and machine-gun fire, as one battalion of our brigade went over the top. Their objective was the first two lines of German trenches. They went over in gallant style. Then came our turn. Dashing over the top without the slightest hesitation, our boys soon got into some kind of order. Our smoke helmets were pulled up and used as headgear, to be handy in case they were wanted.

Once out in open country the din was awful – shrapnel bursting all round, and men dropping, some never to rise again, at every moment. Yet I must say it seemed a great relief and a pure joy to be out in the open. Our battalion went forward quickly towards our objective, which was more than two thousand yards away. We jumped over the first line of German trenches, wherein the battalion were slaying the Boche opposing them. Then over the second line after cutting through barbed wire, and here again the battalion were fighting hard. Our artillery was perfect; the guns backed us up as no infantry has even been supported. Always were we nicely covered.

The First Check

My company now bore off to the right, and barbed wire caused our first slight check. We lay on our stomachs as the party in front of us got over glad indeed of a few minutes rest. Many of us lit cigarettes, and had a slight check. We lay on our stomachs as the party in front of us got over, that wire – it was only in few parts that our artillery had managed to sever it – we lined up as though doing extended order on the parade ground, and went forward smilingly and quickly. None of us seemed to care a hang, although rifle bullets crashed round us like a hundred circus whips being wielded at once, and shrapnel bursts sounded like tons of coal being slipped down an area grating. We continued in perfect order, reaching houses at the end of a village, the best part of which our battalion captured by the aid of bombs. We settled a few Germans in outstanding houses, and reached another line of trenches. But the Boche had retreated further back and on we went.

Finally our company had to halt at the top of a ridge in front of which the Boche stood tight in a copse and barbed wire entanglements prevented us getting at them. We got down on our stomachs and potted at the Boche in the copse.

Digging ourselves in, we remained on that ridge from something like nine o'clock until two in the afternoon, when we received orders to crawl back to the trench just behind us. This trench was a long German communication line and a long way beyond the second line of German trenches, which the battalion were now consolidating. Here, as we straightened our position, we learned that the village just a little way to our right, had been cleared of Boche. It was a significant advance. Nearly all the boys were saying, 'This is grand sport,' and all were as keen as mustard. But the aftermath was horrible. Poor old Jimmy! poor old G – ! All of us lost pals.

As a result of our charge the battalion, in addition, took ground far in advance. (Our lads captured a couple of field guns, which will one day be removed as souvenirs to our headquarters). Our casualties were not so great when one considered the hundreds of German dead, and our prisoners were very numerous.

When we settled down and consolidated the ground we had taken, many of us were really surprised at the extent of our advance. We were always ready for any German counter-attack, but the Boche had had enough of us.

Trying Moments

We had many trying moments from that Saturday afternoon until when we were relieved, but we held on to our captured positions. At times it was hellish; I cannot express the feelings that came over one. All around us were German dead; indeed, in the copse which our brigade subsequently captured I counted over one hundred dead as I walked through part of it. As time wore on the smell of these Germans became oppressive. Much rain fell during the time we were holding on, and with no sleep, no hot food, and much shell fire it.was a terrific test. German kit lay scattered about all over the place in the trenches I was in, and we smoked many German cigars during those remarkable days.

On the night our relief turned up rain fell in torrents, and we were drenched to the skin when we filed slowly out through open country to a village behind the lines, wherein we billeted. As we marched through the darkness one felt almost sad as though everything had been a failure, and most of us were quite bucked when a voice called out : 'Who are you?' 'The – th.' 'Bravo the – th.' It was an artilleryman.

As we lined up this morning to be congratulated by our Brigadier – we are now some miles behind the lines re-equipping, etc. – some artillery passed us, and the Colonel at the head of the column said as he passed : 'Well played'. In a few days we are to be back in the fray. Already we had had experiences that will never be forgotten, but there are still more Boche left.

In conclusion I must mention that the whole of our division has been highly commended by those in the highest authority. I have mentioned what our battalion has done, but I know that all the other battalions in the division did their work just as well as our boys. The Terriers scored a tremendous success, and those at home must know that those poor fellows who have fallen the fortune of war were avenged, for the battlefield was covered with German dead.

I hope you can make this yarn read sense. The strain of the last few days has been very great indeed and one's memory gets very rusty.

Sergeant S. Stadler (now Sir Sydney Stadler) 1/18 London Regiment
My first visit to the front line
Since my platoon had never been allotted an officer, I received instructions to proceed to the front line for 36 hours, together with Sergeant Signaller Jones and Brigadier General Hugent's galloper, a subaltern named Neville from the 19th London Regiment. However, my colleague, Sergeant Jimmy James, begged me to intervene with Captain Trinder; I obtained permission for Jimmy to accompany the party. Again the London Omnibus was helpful and carried us to a point where we had to foot it. A guide met us and we started on an eerie tramp at dusk through shell-swept and deserted villages. As we entered a communication trench, we were informed we were approaching the battle front of Neuve Chapelle. The South Wales Borderers were being relieved by the 1st Gloucesters.

Now this district was marsh, similar to Festubert. Trenches were out of the question, sandbag breastworks comprising the only protection with a shallow breastwork behind. At 'dawn-stand-to', we had our first experience of the ravages of war. Apparently, the Indian Division had attacked at this point and there had been terrible slaughter. It seemed that there was no hope of decent burial of the dead, as the corpses were only partly covered with soil. There were dozens of dead, in all sorts of frightful attitudes and conditions.

The next move was to mix the regiment with seasoned troops. We moved to a sector, where forty-eight hours quickly passed with the novelty. The sector was the Brickfields at Cambrin Quincy; the enemy held the Brickfields. As they used stacks of bricks for machine gun shelters – quite formidable shelters – we were unable to dislodge them, as intense bombardment was necessary, and unfortunately we were very short of shells and armament. When life on active service began, home soon faded beyond the horizon. To come back from the line into rest billets was to feel an intense joy at merely being alive. We platoon sergeants were to discover in due course that one part of the job at the front would be to carry out platoons through spells of the most mind-numbing and heart-breaking boredom and misery ever conceivable. We were also to learn that demoralised men can be brought back into prime condition by a good hard spell on the square with a liberal ration of food and sleep, although we Irishmen and Cockneys often cursed our luck.

Festubert came next, sandbagged breastworks, not any shelter behind, similar to Neuve Chapelle. The first casualty in my platoon was a fine fellow named Bennett, who fell victim to a sniper's bullet.

Givenchy

A death trap. There was a network of trenches named after all the thoroughfares around Whitehall, enemy bombardments were frequent and heavy. One of their specialities was the coal box (high explosives). We were rationed with nine shells a day for the light field guns, the Ministry of Munitions had not yet been created. It was so bad on my trench – a reserve trench thirty yards from the front line – that word was passed to me to withdraw my platoon.

This was done, and I dodged back for the final check; as I was returning a shell dropped behind me. I heard a groan – it was young Lightfoot, hit in the spine with a fragment of shell. He was dead. He had returned for a food parcel. He probably saved my life. The same day, at 2 p.m., I received an order to collect my platoon and report to Captain Hobbs, of A Company, the rendezvous being at the left flank of the battalion's front line; there also, was A Company waiting to assist in the job described below.

It was explained that the enemy were in possession of a strategic piece of trench, that the 23rd Surrey Regiment (6th Brigade) were to attack and A Company and my platoon sixteen were to join in the fun. We were warned that the enemy were using flamethrowers; this last piece of information was comforting. Glancing over my men, they, and no doubt I also, had a tense look, for there were no complaints. Bomber Rose was there with a string of 'Batty Bombs,' made out of jam tins. (This was before the Mills). However, we were not kept in suspense. The attack was cancelled and everybody appeared to look casual. At the entrance to the Givenchy sector at the cross roads, (it was called 'Windy Corner') on the farther corner, there were straw-covered dugout shelters sufficient for one company. D Company occupied these on two occasions for 48 hours. There occurred two incidents, one the death of a fine soldier our Brigadier, Colonel Nugent. He was sniped at dawn and was buried at Bethune. The second, the arrival of the remnants of the Canadian Division, after being gassed at Ypres. They took over our dugout billets.

Vermilles

We took over the sector from the French. I recall many happy times billeted in this practically deserted town, and our sojourns in the trenches.

Loos

The preparations for this offensive were detailed and minute, very fine staff work. And finally, the hour approached. The incessant bombardment had continued for fifteen days. It was Sunday, 24th of September, parade was for 10.00 p.m. I entered an *estaminet* for a final talk with my elder brother, Edward. We talked soberly of the coming attack and the future; we parted at 9 p.m. I never saw him again.

The Regiment moved up, the leading platoon of each company to the line, Nos 1, 5, 9, 13, the next in rotation, to the second assault trench and two platoons of each company in a reserve trench. At midnight all watches were set. The attack was for 6.30 a.m., followed by waves at three-quarter minute intervals. At 6 a.m., the gas was to be turned on, at 6.15 a.m., smoke bombs – brown and green smoke – began to be shot over. At 6.30 a.m., over went the first wave, and then the second, and so on. Nos 4, 5, 12 and 16 followed up communication trenches to our allotted assault trenches. Wooden ladders were placed at intervals; there were ten to the platoon, five or six men to each.

Up I went, in the middle of a heavy September ground mist, added to which there were smoke bombs, and gas, and a hellish machine-gun fire. As there were no steel helmets, we had to wear those inadequate smoke helmets. I rolled up my flannel mask to see, risking death from the gas. I can verily say that I stood on the brink of hell!

Around me I saw piles of barbed wires torn in heaps, unexploded shells, dead and dying, there was Bomber Miller dead, another tearing at the soil in his death agony. It was an appropriate moment for the words, 'If you can keep your head . . .'

Whilst I was urging or cursing my men to hurry up the ladders, a voice called, 'Lie down, you bloody fool.' I decided to be a BF, this was not a text-book operation, standing was the only means of controlling my platoon, besides by the spurts of chalk and earth all around me and in front – a machine-gun was doing its work – I would have received a dozen bullet wounds, had I attempted to lie down. It must be recorded here that I felt no fear, whether it was the responsibility or the novelty of the situation, it cannot be explained. In retrospect, it must have been an absolute miracle which enabled me to come out of it to speak and write the story.

So, with the lads on top – their average age was 24 – I blew my whistle, and on we moved into the unknown. It was something like a London fog. The enemy's front line at this point had been blown in, it was a walk-over. The target, 2,000 yards away, was the Cemetery of Loos. We were to be guided by the Pylons of Loos, but in the mist everything became hidden and we had to wander on. Behind us, we were not aware of the casualties on both sides.

Apparently, the enemy's front line was heavily manned, but they were all sheltering in dugouts. The hand-to-hand combat was missed by us, and we pushed on to the cemetery, 2,000 yards away. Suddenly, the mist cleared, and there were the Pylons.

We passed four days consolidating and resisting counter attacks, until at last we were relieved by the promised Scots Guards, late four days through no fault of their own. It should be mentioned here that General Headquarters had promised that an Army Corps would pass through our lines within an hour. It never came. If that had happened – so it was said – the war would have been shortened by many months. It was through this that the Press published the report that the London Irish Rifles had saved an Army Corps.

Through an inferno of death and desolation, the remnants of the Battalion staggered back through Maroc to Les Brebis, to billets and sleep. I recall being awakened at 9 a.m. by the Company Sergeants' mess orderly. The eggs and bacon appeared to me the best meal I had ever eaten. From here, we were moved back for three days to reorganise; there was a regimental parade, the Brigadier Thwaites, a remarkable soldier, gave us a pep talk, and then we moved up in reserve for the Battle of Hulloch, to Massingarbe, I believe. It should be mentioned that Regimental strength before the battle was 900 odd; at roll call, five days later, 360 were present.

It is not easy to visualise today that mechanical transport was non-existent and that all transport depended on horses and mules, springless wagons and limbers with drivers handling difficult horses. Each regiment had its own transport. Each company was allotted two ammunition mules, huge unruly creatures. It was a common sight to see these sons of Satan rolling on their backs attempting to throw off the two small arms ammunition boxes, and, usually, a small rifleman who had been a naughty boy and who was endeavouring to calm the brutes. There were no volunteers for this unpleasant job. As to casualties, penicillin, anti-biotics and blood transfusions did not exist; if they had, many thousands of lives would have been saved.

Hill 70

Around October 10th, 1915. We moved up to this sector, chalk formation, hopeless for barbed wire defence. The dead remnants of a company of the Munsters were lying in a bombarded trench. It was decided to fill in this stretch, by-pass it, and cut another section. I never took over a trench without sandbagging, and on this occasion decided to re-bag fire bays, parapets and traverses, despite the curses of my boys.

I should not forget to mention that in the trenches we slept, oftener than not in soaking clothes with boots full of water, drank rain with our tea, ate mud with our 'bully' and endured it all with the philosophy of 'grin and bear it,' laughing in our dare-devil way. It was so bad in some parts of the line during the storms of November 1915, that whole sections of trench collapsed into a chaos of slime and ooze. It was the frost as well as the rain (plus the bombardment) which caused the ruin, making the earthworks sink under the weight of sandbags.

Three nights after we had re-bagged, we were standing-to at 7 p.m., away on the left, there was heavy artillery fire. It was a fifth of November night. The Battalion signals were in the front line, between my platoon and fifteen platoon.

Corporal Forsyth, who was in charge, spotted me as I patrolled my section.

'Sergeant', he exclaimed, 'run and pack up, the order has just come through for you to go on leave. Not a word, pack up and be ready.'

Within five minutes Captain Lane appeared. 'Sergeant Stadler, you are to go on leave, report to Battalion headquarters, goodbye and good luck.'

Needless to say, on reaching the shallow communication trench which led to the cobble road, I decided to keep very low. The night we entered Lieutenant Bateman was hit very badly, so I was not taking any chances. On reaching the road I met two more sergeants. One, I believe, was Mildred. He had been a Corporal of Signals, red-headed, an old-timer and a contemporary of mine. It was unanimously decided to take to the ditch and crawl to headquarters. On arrival, we met our Adjutant, Major Hamilton; he told us to report to Brigade Headquarters for instructions and passes and loaned us 25 Francs each. By 11 p.m., we had reached Massingarbe in time to sup with the cooks, gallons of tea and fried bacon. Army cooks do live well, indeed.

Leave, 1915 or Arrested as a Spy

I took St Albans in my stride and also Epping Forest, where I intended to visit two families near High Beech. My late brother's fiancée was a member of one of these families.

From Loughton Station I engaged a fly and proceeded to the King's Oak Hotel. I remember wearing mufti, bowler hat, Malacca cane, rain-coat and German binoculars. My uniform was being deloused. On enter-ng the King's Oak and approaching the bar where I had quenched many a thirst, I found no response. Within seconds, an officer, a Captain of the Artists Rifles appeared. He explained that the hotel had been requisitioned by his regiment; apparently, it was a defensive centre, forming part of London Anti-aircraft Artillery net. I was cross-examined – I mentioned that I was on leave and was about to visit two families in Honey Lane, twenty minutes away. He replied that the people in question did not reside there, although I knew they had for fifteen years. (I have often wondered why these scattered houses and homes of owners and tenants were not recorded, there being not more than twenty-five.) Finally I departed and made my visits, remaining half an hour with each family. The coachman, whom I had left at the hotel, although requested to wait, had departed. It was a question of walking through the Forest by short cuts. On reaching Loughton, I met an Artist Captain with a Ford car. He stopped me to make further enquiries. I produced my paybook and pass, mentioned my late officer chief, an old Artist Volunteer and an Ulsterman. I proceeded to the station, the train was waiting, found a coach and as I began to enjoy the comforts of an easy cushion, the officer appeared once again.

'Step out a moment.' So I did. He then said that I was under arrest.

The time was 12.50; I pleaded that I had a date with two ladies from St Albans for the 2 p.m. matinee at the Coliseum, and to substantiate my claim, I produced the tickets. Unfortunately, it did not work, so I slipped from his grasp and jumped into the compartment and the train moved off.

On reaching Fenchurch Street Station, where I must have been an easy target – blue suit, Burberry on arm, Malacca cane, cropped hair, bowler hat – two heavy city cops met me at the barrier. One said, 'Don't make a scene, and come quietly.' I was conducted to a room on the station premises, produced my paybook, pass, undid my shirt and produced identity disc, and, finally, the Coliseum tickets. The cops said, 'You win,' and off I went.

Upon returning to the sector and reaching Hill 70, Father Lane Fox greeted me with, 'Here's the spy!' I was also taken to see the remains of my shelter, destroyed by a heavy shell the day after my departure. My men volunteered that the sandbagging and traverses had saved them.

Account by Lieutenant Colonel G. A. Brett, 1/23 London Regiment
At the end of August 1915, the 47th Division had taken over the sector from Maroc Puits No 16 Road northwards to the Bethune–Lens Road. Schemes were in hand for an offensive on a grand scale, and the preparations were busily pushed forward. A new front line had to be constructed, and the Divisional History records that over two miles of trenches

were dug in three weeks. A system of 'keeps' was, moreover, completed all along the old support line. Among other devices dummy trenches were dug in front of the forward line, and, for a few days before the attack, there were short bombardments, after which dummy figures showed up in these trenches in the hope that, when the real attack came, the enemy would take it to be no more than the usual morning exhibition of the dummies. Fortunately, the Germans omitted to interfere seriously with our activities and there were amazingly few casualties in the Division.

The 142nd Brigade was not intended for use in the first phases of the attack. It, therefore, held the line for the Division while the other Brigades practised and rested out of the trenches. It was relieved during the night of Septmber 24th, and at 2 a.m. on the 25th the 23rd was at its battle station, sheltering from the cold wind under the slag-heaps of Fosse 6, Les Brebis. There was intense activity throughout the darkness, and at 6.30 a.m. on September 25th the infantry attack, which had been preceded by four days' bombardment, was launched. Four hours later the battalion was ordered to relieve the 17th Battalion so as to enable it to move further forward, and thus came under the orders of 141st Brigade. By noon two companies were in the captured German front trenches and two with headquarters in the old British lines. Gas, used by us for the first time in this battle, still hung in heavy patches over the British trenches, enforcing the wearing of gas-helmets for an hour or more. The helmets then in use were the 'PH' variety – a cloth hood, dosed with chemicals, fitting lightly over the head and with the ends tucked under the collar of the jacket. The goggles rapidly dimmed over, and the air came through in such suffocatingly small quantities as to demand a continuous exercise of will-power on the part of the wearers.

The 141st Brigade was at the moment in a most difficult position. All the battalions had had severe fighting, and yet were compelled to keep on the *qui vive* in case of counter-atack. The left flank was open to a swaying battle of doubtful outcome. The line from Loos Crassier on the left to the spinney on the right was, it was true, intact, but the north of the village lay open, while the west end of the spinney was in German hands. On the 26th the Battalion was moved to the old German support line in the southern outskirts of Loos to protect the left flank. Part of the trench ran through an old cemetery, and the company quartermaster-sergeants coming up that night with the rations were somewhat startled to find on rounding a traverse, a sculptured skull glaring at them in the moonlight.

Things were not going too well with the attack. The 47th Division had gained all its objectives, except Chalk Pit Copse, within a few hours of zero, and was subsequently engaged in keeping what it had won, but elsewhere a complex battle of varying fortunes was being waged. The 26th was a day of rumour and counter-rumour, and, placed where it was, the battalion rendered valuable service in rallying men who had lost their leaders and knew not where to go nor what to do. At one time it had gathered 250 men belonging to a neighbouring division and had put them into a trench covering the western exits from Loos. Here they were kept until a regimental sergeant-major arrived and addressed them with the fluency and imagery traditional in his rank. It was, indeed, only leadership they required, for they followed him back to the line without a moment's hesitation.

The night of the 26th was damp. Headquarters, therefore, sought the shelter of an abandoned tool cart. When in the morning the commanding officer and adjutant had been 'called' effectively by some crumping shells hard by, they found that they had had a night-long but silent companion in the shape of a large dead German.

On the 27th D Company and the Grenadier Platoon were sent forward to the 20th Battalion. From the position held by this battalion they attacked and captured Chalk Pit Copse, the last of the objectives assigned to the 47th Division. A preliminary bombardment had prepared the way, and the assaulting troops, led by the bombers, smothered the garrison in the maze of trenches which had been the centre of an obstinate resistance and a continuous menace for the two previous days. Company Sergeant-Major T. Hammond, DCM, was, to the great regret of the battalion, among those killed, and Second Lieutenant G. A. Ballard, who commanded the bombers, was never seen again.

The advance of the newly-formed Guards Division to attack Hill 70 will be remembered by all 23rd men who took part in the Battle of Loos. Attention was first drawn to them by a sharp increase in the number of German shells passing overhead; then bodies of troops, at whom these shells were directed, were seen advancing over the crest of the high ground about Maroc into the valley. More and more came over the crest by platoons in artillery formation, and the intensity of the shelling increased. Quite quickly the opposite slope took on the appearance of a gigantic chess-board as the platoons approached with intervals between them. The steadiness of their march was impressive, and those who thought that Guardsmen were only ornamental soldiers revised their opinions speedily. So inspiring was the sight that scores of 23rd men of their own accord clambered out of their trenches and, under machine-gun fire, pulled aside wire entanglements and threw duckboard bridges over the ditches to facilitate the way for the Guards when it was seen that they had to pass through their lines. The attack was destined to make considerable headway, but it failed to capture Hill 70.

On September 28th the 2nd Cavalry Brigade, dismounted, were ordered to renew the attack on Hill 70, and the battalion was placed at fifteen minutes' notice to come under the orders of the Cavalry Brigadier should he require support. The companies, therefore, got ready and stood by, expecting at any moment to move up to the dreaded hill. There were several false alarms; in fact, every time a runner was seen approaching headquarters officers and men would tighten their belts or adjust their equipment. When however, after a few hours a motor-cyclist was seen to pass through the machine-gun fire and hand a dispatch to the Adjutant, there was no longer doubt.

Colonel Newman said shortly: 'Come, what is it? When do we move?'

The Adjutant handed him the missive. It came from a branch of the Army more deeply concerned with the custody of stores than the emergencies of battle, and it asked that in future shoemakers' lasts should be indented for through brigades and not as heretofore by battalions direct.

By the evening of the 28th matters had been sufficiently stabilised on the divisional front for the 142nd Brigade to relieve the 141st. In so far as the 23rd was concerned this meant remaining as they were, except that D Company returned from Chalk Pit Copse and went with A Company into the old German front line, B and C Companies remaining near Loos Cemetery. French troops relieved the Division on October 1, and the 23rd moved back to bivouacs at Les Brebis. Although the battalion had been through the whole battle from beginning to end, little more than one company had actually engaged the enemy. Over 70, nevertheless, had been lost – killed, wounded and missing.

After Loos it was found that every man in the battalion had exchanged his long rifle for the new short weapon with which the Regular and service battalions were armed. The long rifles were old and to a large extent inaccurate. They would not, moreover, fire all the manufactures of .303 ammunition then coming into France, and it was, in fact, found necessary a month later to sort out the whole ammunition in a trench so that each rifle might be supplied with that which it could fire. Consequently the men were praised for re-arming themselves with up-to-date and trustworthy weapons, but they had either neglected, or been unable, to provide themselves with the long bayonets. Indents to the Ordnance met only with queries as to why a Territorial unit should ask for that to which it was not entitled. Remonstrance was unavailing, and the battalion was required again to equip itself with the old long rifle.

Some Further Recollections of Loos

The mining village of Loos lay in the bottom of a broad shallow valley, the crests of the hills on the two sides being probably a little over a mile apart. Maroc, another mining village, sprawled over the top of the high ground to the west, and we in the 23rd Londons had been quartered here for some weeks. The front trenches were forward of Maroc a few hundred yards down the slope, and from the village itself we had excellent views of Loos and its two dominating slag-heaps, the Double Crassier and the Loos Crassier.

The 27th September 1915 was my 23rd birthday, and I was Adjutant of the Battalion.

When I was looking over the parapet of one of our forward trenches one day, I saw a man rushing down hill towards us. He had no rifle or equipment, but was in British uniform. As he saw me, he shouted : 'Run ! Get away quick ! Germans are all after me !' and jumped down into the trench. He was in a state of absolute panic, but I persuaded him, with the aid of my pistol, to stop up beside me, look over the parapet and show me the Germans. He calmed down then, and as a Scotsman from the neighbouring division was very ashamed of his breakdown. I handed him over to one of our sergeants with instructions to look after him, and was told later that he had voluntarily gone back to rejoin his unit.

Another day an NCO of our HQ staff came to me and reported that there was a cottage in the village where signalling was taking place through an attic window. He was one of our Regimental Signallers and knew it was not one of their stations. Could it be spies left behind by the Germans? I told him to get half-a-dozen men, and we would go round to investigate. The cottage was in the middle of a block of similar cottages, and I sent two men round to the back, posted two in front and entered the cottage quietly with the remainder. We found ourselves in a largish room with a ladder leading up to a trap-door in the ceiling, and an acute dilemma immediately presented itself to me. I couldn't order the corporal or either of his men up the ladder, because they would be shot, and I stupidly never thought of shouting to whoever was in the attic to come down. Instead I climbed the ladder as quietly as possible, pistol in hand. On poking my head over the edge of the trap-door it was to see a party of three or four men in British uniform very busy in one corner. They turned to be brigade signallers from the Scottish Division next to us, and they were sending messages to their HQ somewhere north of Maroc.

When the Guards Division came through us I vividly remember seeing one officer of the Welsh Guards with his left sleeve tucked through his

Sam Browne belt, he having evidently lost his arm in the fighting of 1914.

Letter from W. R. Ford – about 1st City of London Regiment
My brother was, for a considerable time before the war, a member of the 1st Cadet Battalion Kings' Royal Corps and on the outbreak of War, he with many others joined up and was posted to the 1st Battalion, 6th City of London Rifle Regiment. The Reverend A. E. Wilkinson was Chaplain to the Cadets and was eventually posted to the same Regiment early in September, as Brigade Chaplain with the rank of Captain. He wrote to say the losses were very heavy on that day (the 25th).

The men were buried at the Maroc Military Cemetery, France, Special Memorial 39.

A fellow Corporal who was wounded wrote from hospital at Margate, to say he and Cyril were hit when charging the German trenches, (before the days of tin hats). He added that all NCOs of the rank of Corporal and over were called together two days before the affair and were told in detail all that was to come to pass and were put on their honour to keep all information to themselves.

The following may be of interest: *Palm Sunday, 28/3/15.* About 4 p.m. in firing trench with South Staffords. Firing through loop holes all night. My part of trench 120 yards from Germans. Remainder of section in sap head 6 yards from Germans. About 200 dead Germans lying between trenches. Rotten sight. Have been there about 3 weeks.

29/3/15 Relieved by KRRs.
May 31st. Fairly quiet. In captured trenches. Walking on planks on German dead 3 feet high. Thousands of them.

How little the present generation know of the hardships our men had to endure.

Account (anonymous)
Trench Warfare in Summer Away from Festubert to Loos Sector
Lieutenant Gardiner was killed in No-Man's-Land whither he had gone to help a wounded man. Also killed was the well-liked CSM Rudolfsky, one of the best warrant officers of the battalion. Buried at the POR Cemetery at Festubert, we still honour his memory on our Pilgrimage.

Lieutenant Brooke – brother of Rupert Brooke – was killed.

Out in the tall grass and weeds of the derelict cornfields of No-Man's-Land, in front of La Philosophe, lay many dead. Frenchmen killed in the attack of May 9th. Riflemen went out at night and buried those they could, bringing in letters or personal letters. One of these read 'Dearest

Marie – you tell me you and the children think of me every day – but I, I think of you every moment.'

Loos

On 24th September the Battalion left Noeux Les Mines for its Battle position in trenches facing Double Crassier, in support of the Shiny 7th, and soon, 1 and 2 Companies under Captains Powell and Vince, took their men over – fortunately casualties were slight but success of the whole operation seemed doubtful. The Battle in this sector slowly died down and like many other battles to come, began with a good advance and only continued with success and failures.

After the Battle of Loos

In the trenches before Hulloch – no water available – an Engineer suggested running a pipe across from the nearby village – the 'Gilded Staff' replied, 'No', it would weaken the men's offensive spirit.

This meant a meeting of water carriers at the infamous Lone Tree – the only tree left standing in an open plain. The clinking and jingle of transport horses, etc., soon attracted the attention of German gunners, to this easy target, which with the everlasting fatigues, made the whole period a nightmare for me personally.

Lieutenant De Gaux, our French interpreter, writes of this period, 'The PORs* had as uncomfortable time as it is possible for men to undergo without dying of exposure. No praise of their endurance could be too high.'

As one *who was there – I entirely agree.*

A time-expired Rifleman, going home, invited a couple of pals to a parting drink, but took them on a longer journey, for a shell killed all three at the *estaminet.*

Account re: Post Office Rifles (Anonymous)

I was a very frail child in a secluded, narrow, religious and patriotic family. I naturally, and early, imbibed a real worship of our military heroes, so that when the First World War started and my elder – and only – brother Leonard left with the PORs on 4th August 1914, I was afire with patriotism and trudged the London streets with another 15 year old (Snowball Taylor) to join up.

Of course, nobody would look at us until on 28th December 1914, ten days after my 16th birthday, I directed my steps to Bunhill Row, where to my great joy I was kitted out on the spot in khaki and proudly went

*Post Office Rifles.

home to display my new found glory to Mother, Father and two sisters. Despite their disapproval I refused to be deflated and left, with tremendous pride, to join the 2nd Battalion PORs at Cuckfield.

Then followed six idyllic months playing at soldiers, drilling and marching round the beautiful Sussex country behind a first class band, billeted in a comfortable home with a nice bedroom and with the landlady feeding me like the hungry, growing lad I was.

Still a most innocent and immature 16-year-old, and still full of romantic ideas of charging the enemy with bugles blowing and Union Jack flying, I volunteered for the draft to the 1st Battalion and in June 1915 was off to France without a thought in my silly noddle of what I was letting myself in for.

After moving around the back areas of France our Draft eventually joined the 1st Battalion at Noeux-Les-Mines just as they were about to go up the line in the 2nd stage of the Loos Battle. At this moment I saw Brother Leonard just long enough for him to utter those three immortal and historic English words – 'You Bloody Fool'. This was an unexpected and uneasy start for the next 2 or 3 hours journey up the line in artillery order over the ground captured a day or so before. Now was the moment when the innocent young boy was to be cast from his calm secluded (though not spoilt) and narrow life into the deep waters of the most savage horrors of war ever conceived by man.

First I saw some khaki clad dead soldiers – their ashen faces, and grotesque positions when violent death had suddenly overtaken them, was my initial shock – why had they been left there and not properly buried – nobody seemed to care about them; with my mind already in a turmoil from this first mild encounter with war, it received many more shocks as we trudged on. Now came the many shell holes where the enemy had laid down his barrage and here came the debris of war which I was to know so well, later, on the Somme and Ypres Front, where I barely vouchsafed it a glance; but now with its mutilated bodies and the sudden and fearful realisation that shells were falling around and splinters were whining direct to mutilate me, (as I imagined) I was only too happy to reach the shelter of the communication trench, little dreaming – when a gas cylinder was thrust into my arms for the front line – that this was but the prelude to over 3 weeks martyrdom of non-stop fatigues so graphically described by our French interpreter, Lieutenant De Gaux, in these words: 'The PORs had as uncomfortable a time as possible for men to undergo without dying of exposure. No praise of their endurance could be too high'.

Struggling through a long communication trench, carrying not only one's own kit of some 60 lbs, but also dead weights like gas cylinders – 2 one gallon petrol tins filled with water, boxes of bombs, chunks of duck boards – with constant wire overhead – wire underfoot – shells bursting around – wounded men enviedly going back – bodies lying waiting to be put over the top at dark – was a seething nightmare which seemed to have no connection whatever with those brave charging pith-helmetted soldiers I had so worshipped.

At last we reached our part of the front line; sappers took away our gas cylinders and I just had time to take stock of this ultimate place where – to coin an American phrase – the buck stopped. It was (in the light of later experience) a quite comfortable piece of former German trench, the fire-step of which was being hurriedly moved round. There were, I remember, but three of us in this fairly short bay – the Company Sergeant came round to give us our sentry go times and start us digging the new fire-step and then came the shout, 'Look out, a Minnie'.

Without any prompting I threw myself down with the others, when an almighty crash came showering us with earth – it had fallen in the next bay burying three of the four occupants – the fourth being my young draft friend, Charles Thomas, who walked round into our bay with a minor wound in his left elbow. How I envied him as he walked steadily away to the dressing station, to England, and discharge. It was then I first heard that melancholy cry 'Stretcher Bearers', but we had little time for speculation, it was dig, dig dig, first to fetch out the remains of the two who were killed – this really demoralised me with horror – the third man seemed intact but unconscious.

Then came sentry go – (while the other two were digging away). I have often wondered about the reactions of soldiers on sentry go for the first time in the front line. I still remember mine as being such a mixture compounded mainly of fear, of being suddenly attacked on my own, of bullets, shells and lastly, of dozing off in my present tired condition. Hunger and cold came into it as I gingerly raised my head very carefully and cautiously – not for me the reckless jumping on the top at night time which I frequently saw, later.

The Loos Battle was still on and shells and bullets abounded it seemed everywhere; so I took careful stock. It was a nice night but cold – no moon but star shells in profusion all around me in an arc. What could I see? Nothing but a jumble of earth and odd shapes, then I thought I saw something moving and let off a few rounds which seemed so very feeble in all the din – my fellow diggers rushed and gazed at the still scene, but they were very kind to me, making me feel a real, frightened Rookie.

Rations, including water, were in short supply, mainly I suppose because of inexperience in trench warfare; this situation improved as more knowledge was gained, and later – even in the worst fighting on Some and Ypres – efforts were made to get hot food and drinks up, whereas during all of this period we had but Bully Beef at intervals plus hard tack.*

With hardly a pause, we were then put on completing a sap started out towards the German lines and learnt, for the first time, the Jocks were going over the next day at noon and we were going into the support line to follow them up as support troops for the inevitable counter-attack.

This nearly paralysed me with fear – how could we get out on the top in broad daylight and survive with all stuff whizzing around overhead, I could not imagine. But back we went to the support line and waited in trepidation. I remember taking the only precaution I could think of by hanging my entrenching tool in front rather than behind. But noon came with a crescendo of 18 pounders and it passed without any orders – my first stroke of luck. After a peep through the periscope at the many kilties lying out there I felt more than thankful we had been spared.

No more attacks, fire slackened down, we went back to our front line and relieved what was left of the 15th Scottish Division and normal trench routine took over. But not quite, because the muddle of the Loos Battle involved so much sorting out and movement and replacement of stores, ammunition, etc., that we were faced with never ending ghastly rounds of fatigues described so vividly by Lieutenant De Gaux earlier in this narrative, with struggling up and down on ceaseless carrying parties, dragging tired legs and weary bodies along; without food and sometimes no water, desperate for sleep, cold and wet and in such sheer misery that even sinking into the mud when a shell burst near was a moment's release and rest and indeed when staggering with yet another load from the dump I felt a quick, clean bullet might be a relief.

It was then that my Company Commander, Captain Vince, must have seen I was at the end of my tether and sent me back empty handed. Literally, physically and mentally it took such a load from my shoulders that he could never have imagined.

At long last this nightmare came to a temporary end, but after a few days in a shelled house at Massingarbe, disturbed by rats at night and more fatigues during the day – but compensated by good hot meals and a bath – we return up the line to Hulloch with cold, wet, mud, and all the inevitable struggles to and from Lone Tree of evil repute. The fatigues in themselves, plus the mud, cold and wet, and absence again of any hot food or drink were sufficient to reduce this body of mine to

*A very hard, dry biscuit.

despair, added to which our bit of front received enfilade fire and on sentry go we could hear in the quiet of night the faint pick pick of tunnelling going on beneath us, almost the most hated of all trench hazards, and then came the crowning blow of all time : a raid was being planned – on reaching the enemy trenches we were to work in teams of threes to mop up each bay – two bombers (one as reserve) and the third man the bayonet man to rush round to finish anybody off or capture the prisoner, with me as the bayonet man. I could not believe my ears. Of all the soldiers in the British Army I could think of no one less suitable than me – I was struck dumb with terror. What could I do ! the raid was due for 7.30 a.m., after stand to. I staggered on my fatigues that day with a feeling of absolute despair. I was quite certain I could never do this.

Again my luck held and the raid was called off; but by the time this long spell was nearing completion I was again spotted by Captain Vince who ordered me to the Battalion Dressing Station where the sergeant did an unusual thing by taking my temperature and saw me to the Advanced Field Dressing Station in one of the chalk pits in that area, left me on a stretcher where I remained several days with a very high temperature, and something known then as Trench Fever – which I suppose is analogous to flu.

This was the second kindness done by Captain Vince to somebody he must have known as pretty hopeless. This I have never forgotten. Bewildered and exhausted in mind and body, full of self pity and very ashamed of myself – a kind of Walter Mitty in reverse, I must leave this pitiful toy soldier, cowed with fear, and terror, and crushed with fatigue, with but a small crumb of self respect to cling on to – insofar as being able to keep my fears to myself unlike the windy men who could not do this and thereby were recognised up the Line as menaces who spread their fears and terrors around them like a cloud. Later I will recount how the Toy Soldier recovered his nerve and spirit and on the Somme and Ypres grew so familiar with the sights and sounds of war, including shelling etc. – as to become almost callous – though never coming to terms with fatigues.

The Lone Tree was an enormous flowering cherry that had blossomed during May 1915. At that time it was between the lines.

After the blossom had fallen a young lieutenant of the Seaforth Highlanders had led a night patrol there and climbing to the upper branches had attempted to fasten a Union Jack there. Unfortunately, although successful in this, he had been caught in a flare on the way down and machine-gunned. For several days his body hung there.

Two attempts to recover it on subsequent nights failed and finally Artillery was directed on to the tree in an attempt to bury him. As the days wore on all the branches had been blown off, but the guns never scored a direct hit and the stump remained standing some 15 ft high.

The ground was overrun in the 1st stage of the Loos battle, and Lone Tree then became a notorious and bloody rendezvous for transport and stores going up the Line.

Naturally, the enemy soon registered it with his guns and after many casualties, common sense prevailed and it was abandoned as a rendezvous for the Line. It was reputed to have flowered again in 1920, but in several visits to this area I have never been able to identify it – not surprisingly when all is so changed.

Having a Bath – France 1915–1918

Le Brebis. In the early days, getting a bath was a rather haphazard affair in the PBI (Poor Bloody Infantry) and looking back some sixty years I recall one or two of my baths that were very amusing.

I remember after my first horrible spell up the line in the Loos affair, the battalion were marched to a disused brewery at the Le Brebis. The baths consisted of a row of about ten enormous barrels cut in half, which held about 12 soldiers per barrel – in front of this array there was a long line of small half barrels which held but one soldier per barrel. All barrels were very heavily impregnated with a Jeyes fluid compound, and the single barrels were almost solid with Jeyes. And I remember wondering why these particular men had arranged such favourable treatment, but to my surprise I saw they were all sitting in their tubs with their shirts on and not looking very comfortable. Then the truth dawned on me, these chaps were so infected with lice that their shirts had stuck to their scratched flesh and this was the only hygienic way to get them off. Anyway, I, personally splashed about happily, glad to be cleaned up with Jeyes Fluid or whatever it was.

But the great story, of course, was the apocryphal link with Lord Curzon who when taken to see the British soldiers at this particular ablution spot was reputed to have said: 'Good God – they have got white skins'.

Auchel A mining village in the Bethune area was another bath adventure. The Pit Head bath consisted of an anti-room with an enormously high pointed skylight roof. Around its white tiled walls were a series of numbered hooks on which were tied ropes which stretched up to a pulley on the skylight, over which dangled a small anchor. Each man was allocated his pulley number which he then let down and hung all his clothing on including his tied boots on the anchor.

The scene and the language from an angry crowd of naked soldiers was indescribable when a cloud of insecurely hung socks, shirts, pants, etc. came fluttering off the anchor from high above all over the place. Innumerable altercations happened when retrieving personal articles and I remember I had at least three goes before I got mine to the top in one piece.

By the simple yet terrible fact of those countless graves in France; Britain, and in particular the Post Office, should never forget what their men suffered and did for us all. Please do not regard us veterans in the current Western fashion as a race of old people, apart from the main stream, to be specially cared for. At home I am a part of my family and all of us Post Office Veterans with 40 or 50 years of PO service behind us feel we are a part of the Post Office Family. It is therefore altogether fitting and proper that as a Post Office family we should remember those who protected and saved our family life.

In those far off years we 'didn't have it so good'; but we did have something so lacking now – roots; warm, understanding, deep and time-less. Even now after 60 years, many microcosms of groups of men who formerly shared Post Office life, look forward to their old Office Annual Reunions and love every minute of it.

Perhaps these roots may grow again in the Post Office and the staff will not forget those who had so little of this shared joy.

8

15th (Scottish) Division

Letter from L. J. Hedges

I was a private in the 7th Battalion Royal Scots Fusiliers, No. 17413, C. Company, 15th Division. On the Saturday morning 25th September 1915 at 6 a.m., we went into action as supports to the Black Watch. I believe it was the 8th Battalion of the Black Watch. We suffered along with the Black Watch, I think all our officers were casualties. I was fortunate to survive unhurt although I was wounded twice.

We had severe casualties in the charge for Hill 70 which we captured, but we were driven back, as the supporting division were late in arriving, they did not arrive until Sunday afternoon and we tried to dig ourselves in with our entrenching tools. The weather was appalling, raining all the time and we had no greatcoats. We were eventually relieved by a division, who I believe had no experience and had not been in the trenches.

I am now nearly 80 years and unfortunately nearly blind.

After the battle we were sent back to Bethune. I think the other division who made the attack on the Saturday morning were the 47th London Territorials, and the 1st Division. My memory is as clear today regarding same as it was 60 years ago.

I believe that was the last battle that the then Sir John French, later Earl of Ypres commanded.

I am afraid at great sacrifice it was not a great success.

Letter from C. M. Tain

My regiment was the 7th Battalion Royal Scots Fusiliers, now renamed The Royal Highland Fusiliers.

We embarked in the Spring of 1915 and began marching towards Massingarbe from Boulogne; from there we went straight into the front line trenches to relieve the Sikhs (Indian Soldiers) who had held the line at that time.

At dawn on 25th September we went over the top! we went into action and advanced through the German front line trenches into, and through the village of Loos thereafter we attempted to capture Hill 70, but when going over the crest and half way down the slope the enemy opened fire, there was no shelter of any kind, the Scots division was almost annihilated. I myself received severe wounds resulting in the loss of my left arm and also a severe gunshot wound in my right leg. The firing was so intense and prolonged, consequently it was two days before I was picked up by stretcher bearers. May I mention my age at that time was 18 years in the year 1915.

I am now 78 years of age and have lived a very happy married life with my wife and son and daughter. My son is now a well known professional artist in the art world.

Letter and account from Joseph Wallace, 11th Argylls, 15 (Scottish) Division

Herewith enclosed are a few lines of what my father remembers of Loos. I'm not sure if it is exactly what you require in the way of material for your account of the battle, but I myself was pleased that for some reason or other he produced this in his own hand. The original I enclose, along with an attempted typed copy, in case you were not able to decipher his hand. (My typing is not all that wonderful!) There are only a few minor changes between the original and the typed versions. Perhaps you would let me have them back when you've finished with them?

There was considerable reticence on 'Auld Tam's' past (that is the name by which he is affectionately known in family), to put anything in writing, but I think he surprised even himself after he'd completed it. This took him about three weeks. Of course, I asked him to speak a bit more to me about details – which he did – but he spoke mostly about the humorous aspects.

For example, when they left Hill 70 they were returning through the artillery lines, and 'Tam' had a German helmet on his head, a trophy from the battlefield, marching along, while playing the pipes and an officer rushed out and remonstrated with him about it with the result that 'Tam' had to continue his march with his own military headgear in its proper place! (He was offered a pound – presumably sterling – for this helmet by one of the gunners, but whoever made the offer was told that any number of these articles were to be had, just for the picking up, on Hill 70).

He told me that on the retreat from Hill 70, he had been late back for the first roll call at that time. Apparently, gas had been used by the British, and the wind had tended to blow it back on them. The gas masks used, some type of ill-fitting grey cloth headgear, with a transparent eye shield and part for breathing through, were not really suitable for pipers when they were carrying out their musical duties. Consequently, 'Tam' had his pushed up on his head, with his balmoral perched on top of it, lying on top of Hill 70, with two sandbags behind his head (he was lying on his back, with his canteen in the small of his back) and two sandbags on either side of him, while piping. I expect this was more than slightly uncomfortable. He says his piping was not superb.

Anyway, a fellow soldier, back in time for the first roll call reported that he had seen Piper Wallace, 'blawin his pipes wi' hauf his heid shot off, sur!' My father's gas mask must have been at some rakish angle to give this impression to a fellow Argyll.

Account

After all these years it is a little difficult to really remember, but over the top we went. We were the second wave to go over, but before we got near the village of Loos the amount of dead was awful. However, we struck the cemetery where there was some skirmishing with the Huns. Then we got into the village, got a good drink of water from the heroine Emilienne Moreau. She had been on the roof of some building watching, I think it was the school. She told some officers where ammunition was stored (in a church). Jerry tried to blow this church up, couldn't say whether they managed it or not as we went up to Hill 70 where we dug ourselves in. Lens was on fire, so when the Huns tried to retake the Hill, we could see them, as the fire was at their back. Oh boy, did we give them Hell. They couldn't get over the top of their dead.

Then we had help from the 21st Division, Yorkshires, Lancashires, and Durhams. They went over but couldn't get through the barbed wire. A great many lost their lives there. Our line was so thin that the machine gunners were brought up from the village to assist us. When Dunsire came up, he saw an arm waving in No-Man's-Land, he went and brought him in. While doing so, he saw another wounded and went and brought him in also. He received the VC for that. However, his leg was blown off in a dugout, and he was brought down to hospital where he died. I had the honour of playing the pipes at his funeral. I think it was on 15th January 1916 in Massingarbe cemetery that he was buried.

When we retired off Hill 70, and going back for roll call, we had to pass through the Artillery lines someone shouted, 'Give us a tune, Jock,' 'Give me a lump of ham first.' I got the ham, they got their wish (Scotland The Brave).

I think Dunsire, VC, belonged to the Royal Scots or Fusiliers. Didn't know Piper Laidlaw very well before the war, but when he was stationed in Kirkcaldy, we had a few get-together nights.

Emilienne Moreau was decorated by the French and British Governments. She is dead now, 7 or 8 years.

Eighty-nine thousand casualties for the month. Piper Laidlaw is now dead. There can't be many of the 15th Division left now. I'm almost 88 years of age.

Laidlaw continued playing till his legs were shot from under him, and even a short while afterwards. After leaving the army he became postmaster at the hamlet of Shoresden near Berwick. He died aged 75 and was buried in an unmarked grave but some years afterwards his regiment the KOSB put a tablet in the church at Norham near his grave.

From 5042 Piper T. Wallace, D. Coy., 11th Arg. S.H.
Another correspondent says that Laidlaw was 'the most modest of men'.

Letter from Second Lieutenant Gilbert, Gordons
Just a line to let you know that I'm still quite fit and well, I suppose you've seen in the papers all about the large advance we've made here. Well I came through the whole thing.

We attacked the German lines, captured them all; we then attacked and after a lot of street fighting captured Loos and then we pushed on the Hill 70 (see map in Mon's *Daily Mail*) and I was in command of the Company then. Well I pushed forward captured Hill 70 and went on about 500 yards past it and there I was hit in the arm. Well we hung on there under the most terrible fire, with no cover at all and with the Germans firing from behind loopholed walls for five hours until eventually we had to retire onto Hill 70 again.

During that retreat I was hit four times in the kilt, about six times in my haversack and all my shaving materials, towels, food etc., were all riddled and dropped out of the latter. Anyhow we hung on up there and the Germans killed our wounded which they captured and took off their kilts and bonnets and put them on.

They then attacked us all night, but we were not had on by them and drove them off.

About twelve hours later we were relieved by another brigade and we went back and I had my arm dressed. It was only a scratch through my left arm above the elbow.

Next day we relieved the other brigade again and then we were gassed and I got another cursed bullet in the face this time. This was only a flesh wound but it was rather painful owing to the gas which was hellish.

Anyhow we held on and were again relieved and now we are marching right back again to rest. We are not taking any further part in the attack now as of course we are most terribly cut up. I'm a wee bit dazed, but none the worse for it all but I've lost all my things. Most of them were shot off me as the Boche used explosive bullets (not dum-dums, actual explosives, we captured some unused ones.)

Well I must shut up now, God has protected me and really I escaped by a miracle. The CO was awfully pleased with the work done.

My watch was shattered but I captured one from a Boche, my macintosh was lost. All my washing and shaving things were shattered, my kilt is in ribbons, in short I'm rather a wreck.

Please send parcels *as usual* now! *Also* include a new razor, sponge, soap, soap-box (aluminium), tooth brush and powder. I'll send you details of other things later. The men were simply splendid and stood the slaughter like heroes. There are 70 left out of our company of 250 now. Anyhow we won't be in the trenches again for *ages* and I'll be back *very very* soon.

Letters sent by J. C. Pringle, son of Captain Pringle, killed at Loos.

Narrative of Lieutenant Lovell of D Company 10th Cameronians. (Scottish Rifles)

There was some uncertainty about our attacking as the wind was not right for the use of gas. The men heated up some *Café au lait* in the trenches and had it with some bully beef. The attack was timed for 5 o'clock; it was put off an hour and a half in the hope of the wind changing. It did not change but at 6.30 the expert telephoned down that it was now right and the attack should begin. The wind was actually in our faces.

I was in the 5th line: an officer came along the parapet and gave us the order to get out. We climbed out and doubled off at once over wet grass, not long, fairly good going. My captain, Tronton, was shot thro' the eye and killed almost at once. It was about 300 yards from us to the German trenches. Our orders were to go straight over the top of them and straight on. It was the business of the 12th Highland Light Infantry to clear the Germans out of them. I was hit and fell about five yards from the German Trenches. The grass was wet because it had been raining a good deal the day before and in the night. The rain was adverse to the success of the gas. I believe the gas did some damage to the Germans in the Hohenzollern Redoubt which lay to the North of us.

Our orders were that the first brigade to reach Hill 70 were to hold it. The next was to go on through them and take Cité St Auguste. Hill 70 was between $2\frac{1}{2}$ and 3 miles from us. The second great German line of defence ran over the crest of it with a redoubt projecting. Our battalion took the crest of Hill 70 and passed thus right thro' the German second line.

It was only at night that Captain Grant then in command withdrew them behind it. The Germans then brought up a great number of machine guns and reoccupied it. The 45th Brigade supported us and the 44th on our right came up a short way behind us, but absolutely no reinforcements came up till nightfall and then they had marched twenty miles. This extraordinary blunder about reinforcements alone prevented our successfully piercing the German line.

Duncan, our adjutant, was shot in the evening running back to the telephone. The field telephone people did well to get it there. I know that at least one field gun reached Loos quite early and this involved bridging the German trenches.

Captain Grant had to fall back owing to the retirement of a neighbouring battalion. He and the other second in command of companies were kept back in the morning and went up later.

The Germans fired at us with machine guns at long range: from the moment of leaving our trenches we heard the patter of the bullets.

Captain Pringle was a tremendously strong man: think of his going on after he had been hit 4 or 5 times: he was the kind of man nothing could stop: everyone liked him he was one of the kindest hearted men you could meet.

The men of the battalion could not have behaved better: there was absolutely no hanging back or anything of the kind.

Captain Pringle Dead

The worst fears regarding Captain Arthur Stanley Pringle, of the 10th Cameronians, who had been reported wounded and missing have been realised: news has been received from German sources which make it certain that he fell in the fighting. Thus another old Cantab Rugger Blue has laid down his life for the cause of Right; a gallant man has been lost to our country.

I can recall him when he went to Edinburgh Academy: a healthy-looking youngster, with a towsy shock of dark hair, an utter indifference to whether his stockings were fastened up properly or dangling about his calves, and wearing on a cheery face 'the smile which wouldn't come off' – as the saying goes. Was it any wonder that he was re-christened 'Towsie', and that the name stuck?

Through the smaller teams, from the 'Gytes' upwards, he played and became a line forward, though not quite good enough for national honours. But for Cambridge and the Academicals he did much as a 'hard-working scrummager', who was a lovely dribbler and tackler of the real Raeburn-place type.

When the war broke out Captain Pringle joined the active forces of his country and in Flanders he, foremost of his company fighting, fell.

Captain Pringle leaves a widow and three young children to mourn the memory of one of the cheeriest men who ever lived. Somebody has written of him – 'Stan Pringle was a man; and as in all else he did, when he made friends he made friends heart and soul, and kept them so'.

I like best to remember that frank schoolboy appearance when, beaming with satisfaction, revealing the very joy of life, and with just a little sign of mischief in his eyes, he would take the field for an important scholastic championship match wherein he was sure to do well.

I remember him doing a five mile run at the Academy, and he would have been a good man had he persevered with track work. Which he did not.

Interview with Colonel A. V. Ussher, OC 10th Scottish Rifles, in a ward of the Queen Alexandra Military Hospital Millbank SW on Saturday, October 2nd 1915. He was hit in the knee just after passing the first line of German trenches.

The Colonel showed me his own field service map with a dark pencil line showing the route marked out for the battalion.

'The whole thing went like clockwork', he said. The orders were carried out to the letter. The whole battalion gave perfect satisfaction. It was all due to Scott and Pringle, splendid fellows. Had adequate reinforcements, guards for choice, been sent up promptly there was absolutely nothing to stop the advance to Lille or anywhere else. When it was decided that two companies were to lead, I found they were all equally keen to lead, so I drew lots. The lots came out in order of seniority : Major Scott first, Captain Pringle second.

'The excellent behaviour of the men in battle was due to the men who were with me throughout the training more especially Scott and Pringle and Duncan the Adjutant, but I loved them all.'

The Colonel then showed me a letter to himself from the Brigadier, General Matheson complimenting the battalion on the splendid behaviour, and informing him that the losses of the brigade in the attack were 2270 men and 76 officers.

From J. C. Pringle

13585 CSM Baxenden, J. 10th Cameronians (Scottish Rifles) BEF, 11.12.15

I am writing to thank you ever so much for the gifts of mits, cookers, and cocoa which you sent to us. I have seen them delivered, as far as possible, to men of the old 'B' Coy, and it is in their name that I am expressing this thanks.

I wanted to write to you 'ere this and am glad of this opportunity. I wanted to express to you my admiration for your late husband. I wanted to tell you the company's opinion of him. I wanted some of his honour to reach you.

I was QMS of the company at the time before the charge and also in England. I often used to admire the splendid patriotism in his work and the way he realised what Duty was. We had lots of work to do in England, irksome, tiring and dull work. His work was the most of all for he was the OC Company. I never heard him grumble. To do his duty was a pleasure to him. He was just a splendid Briton.

His conduct in the attack was just what we expected it to be. All the chaps realised that the Captain was just the man to help them in a corner. They were all resolved that where he went he'd have someone to follow him.

On the Thursday evening he went through the details of the plan of the attack and seemed in excellent and his usual jocular spirits.

He was early over the parapet on the Saturday morning. The advancing line halted and lay down – a lot of the men had been mown by machine guns and it was necessary to wait for D Coy., to come up.

During this time the Captain fired about 150 rounds out of the rifle of a dead soldier. Most of these told for he was a good shot and the Germans were rather hastily moving out of their front trenches and running back over the top.

Just past the first German line he was wounded slightly over the eye. He did not stop to have this bandaged. Then everyone was too much engaged with the enemy to notice much but it was observed that the Captain collected the men when past the third German trench and all swept on up Hill 70.

His wonderful courage was, at this critical moment, a great incentive to the attack. Nearly all the other Company Commanders were casualties by this time and he had a long line of men to control. He sent back messages just as we did on manoeuvres at Bordon, Morrell – his servant – taking them.

Just over the crest of Hill 70 he was shot badly in the right arm. His servant bandaged him up and filled his revolver, which he made good use of with his left hand.

In the dusk of the evening the line had to retire. The cause of this does not lie with our regiment. The Captain was in a shell hole. His servant asked him to come back. He refused. This was on the farther side of Hill 70.

Beyond this I can give you no further details.

When we collected after a day or two it was hard to realise how things were. It was agonising to find one's friends gone. I, personally, seemed horribly lonely. I went round with Captain Baillie (since killed) to try and find out who were due rewards. The name of Captain Pringle was mentioned first in every case. He won the VC twice over.

I am proud to have been commanded by such a man. You must be prouder still to have had such a husband. He was a big factor in that attack. He set a glorious example which I assure you was followed by his men.

I sincerely hope that these details will not bring you pain for I should be loth to do anything that would do so for your loss is great. You are not alone in your sorrow. His country feels his loss. We share your bereavement.

In the name of the old company I offer you the deepest condolence and sympathy.

(Signed JOHN BAXENDEN)

Narrative of Lieutenant Paton of the 10th Scottish Rifles. Given to me at his father's house 36 Alleyn Road, West Dulwich SW. 9.10.1915.
Three months ago we were opposite Maroc 1 mile south of Philosophe and next to French troops. I never saw any of them wearing steel helmets. None of us had them. A man wearing a helmet in our lines would run a serious risk of being killed for a German.

For the attack on the 25th September we came up from Philosophe, thence to 'Quality Street' and thence to the trenches. Our bombardment went on through Tuesday, Wednesday, Thursday and Friday 21st, 22nd, 23rd and 24th September. There was practically no barbed wire left in front of the German trenches. B Company (Captain Pringle) C Company (Major Scott) went into the trenches on Thursday night; A (Robertson Durham) D (Tronton) went in on Friday night. The alignment for the attack was as follows :

Captain Bailey, second in command of B Company, and Captain Grant, second in command of A Company, were left behind and went up hours later.

Besides Captain Pringle there attacked, with B Company, Maul and Stenhouse, subalterns Paisley (? subaltern) and 3 NCOs.

The objective was Cité St Auguste : the brigade was to turn half right after passing Loos. It was anticipated that the British gas would be enormously successful, putting not only the enemy infantry but also their gunners out of action to a depth of three miles. In point of fact the gas was blown back by a gust. The men wore their smoke helmets but threw them off to charge. The London Division on their right, on the other hand, were said to have reached the German wire unseen under cover of the smoke.

The country is very open and level, little coal pits here and there with a village round each. On Saturday morning (25th September) all fires were to be out at 8.30 a.m. so the men had their breakfast before that, cocoa biscuit and bully beef. They all took emergency rations with them, and some bread as well which they had bought for themselves. They had these in their haversacks together with waterproof sheets and towels. Officers did not carry rifles, but revolvers, 30 rounds of ammunition, daggers mostly of the knuckle duster type, and most of them carried 4 or 5 bombs as well. The men were frightfully keen for the fight. We were all dry when we started, though it was misty. It came on to drizzle about 10 and rained heavily in the afternoon.

An intense bombardment started at 6.50, accompanied by 10 minutes' gas, then 10 minutes' smoke, then 10 minutes' gas, then 10 minutes' smoke. We crossed the parapet at 6.30 at the walk. Captain Pringle was hit about 200 yards from the start but went straight on. Lieutenant Paton was hit very soon after and before reaching the German trenches. He did not see Captain Pringle again after that but he heard his voice quite clearly shouting the order for the charge. 'I could not see him but I could hear him yelling' (Scots for shouting). He thinks as many as 5 platoons were got into line for the charge. Captain Pringle probably commanded the line : he certainly would if Major Scott had already been hit at that stage. Lieutenant Paton was not in either of the two leading companies, but he observed that they suffered a great many casualties 'seemed pretty well wiped out.'

Rifle and machine gun fire and shrapnel was poured upon them at a great rate and the din was tremendous. Lieutenant Paton saw a lot of prisoners being brought back. He believes Captain Pringle led the charge into the first trenches. He believes there was hand to hand fighting in those trenches.

An account of the part played by the 7th RSF on September 25th and 26th in attack and counter attack on Loos.

For twelve days the regiment had enjoyed complete rest at the pleasant little village of La Beubrière some 10 or 12 miles behind the firing line. It was the prettiest spot we had yet struck in La Belle France and the men took advantage of the light duty, enjoyed themselves in their own way and almost forgot that there were such things as trench mortars and aerial torpedoes. Still, when the rumour began to circulate that in a few days we were leaving this atmosphere of peace for the excitement of the great adventure all were eager for the fray. We left about 6 p.m. on Thursday bound for Vaudricourt another village some 5 miles distant.

Hitherto the elements had been most propitious but now it seemed as tho' they had declared themselves in favour of the enemy for we had scarcely left Hasdignent before the growl of thunder the intermittent flashes of lightening told us that we were in for a biggish thunder storm. It soon burst over us and long before we reached our destination we were all drenched to the skin the steam of soaked clothing surrounding us like a grey pall. Just before entering the village a Rolls Royce motor tenanted by a portly figure wrapped in furs passed our bedraggled companies. It would have made a good subject for a picture of contrasts; General Rawlinson passing thro' his drenched and weary troops.

Shortly afterwards we entered the woods where we had to bivouac for the night. It was indeed a melancholy spectacle. The tracks had been reduced to quagmires along which we stumbled in the dark. There was nothing for it but to accommodate ourselves to the conditions such as they were and it was wonderful how the men with their waterproof sheets and by means of branches they bent for the purpose managed to improvise little tabernacles. But I imagine that few if any got any sleep that night. Personally I tramped up and down for most of it with the minimum of clothing as I had discarded my breeches in the hopes of getting them dried at one of the many fires that now glowed like fitful fire flies in the wood.

However with day-light came the sun and consolation and before noon we had forgotten our troubles and were speculating as to the result of the terrific bombardment which was now in full swing and offered a spectacle of unparalleled grandeur. From the road outside the chateau gates we could see thousands of shells bursting over the skyline throwing up vast pillars of smoke and debris which towered heavenward while the roar of the guns was ceaseless.

All that day we wandered in groups through the wood discussing the possible outcome of the great adventure we had come to seek. We had one solemn Pow Wow with our OC and were given the different objectives for each company and then with the latest maps before us we very carefully rehearsed our various programmes with our company commanders.

At 9 p.m. in silence the battalion assembled itself in its companies in files and such kit as we were taking with us had been carefully inspected and at intervals of five minutes we set out for the enterprise from which alas so many were never destined to return. In silence we marched along a road specially constructed and designated as the Red Road and always as we marched the roar of the guns gathered volume and sound while the horizon was lit up by the countless flashes that made night as bright as day.

By half past twelve we had reached our objective and each company slowly defiled into the trenches and took up its allotted position. At intervals of two paces we lay down on the narrow trench floor and after some tea and a tot of rum which washed down the sandwich ration we had brought, tried to snatch a few hours repose before dawn. At about 5 a.m. the signal was passed down for our advance D and C Companies leading in K, B and A in support. By that time the noise from our guns was absolutely beyond description. There must have been over 1200 in action at once in our sector alone. The very ground rocked and swayed under our feet; we were almost dashed against the sides of the parapet as in some places the muzzles of the guns were within a few yards of us. Nothing like this bombardment had taken place before in the history of this Titanic struggle.

An hour or so later we received a message to the effect that the leading battalions had left their own trenches and were in full charge on those of the enemy. It was then that the guns of the enemy hitherto comparatively silent opened on us with indescribable fury. They seemed to have the range to a nicety and as we moved slowly up we began to get the first glimpse of the havoc they were making. At first pools of blood grim and ominous met our gaze and later on the shells began to fall fast and thick, until the trenches resembled in some places a shambles. The scream of the high explosives followed by their impact and rending crash, the different note of the great aerial torpedo, the smashing burst of the trench mortar, together created an atmosphere that could only be described as Hell.

It was piteous to see the scattered groups of maimed and wounded whom we passed groaning in their agony, and yet we could render them no assistance for the call of duty was imperative, and drove us forward to our goal. But the progress was slow and it must have been hours before we reached our objective, that part of the fire trench known as 7 B from which we had to make our charge.

By the time we reached this point we discovered that our gallant little captain had been hit by a fragment of shell and was slightly wounded. With some difficulty we managed to get him into the comparative security of a dug-out.

The command then devolved on Captain Ferguson who had been informed of the incident and who had hastened up from the rear of the company. It was an intense relief when at last we were told that we might leave the congested trenches and surmount the parapet for the advance. It was such a relief to get out into the open and have a full view of our objective, those grim Pylons Towers that we had watched for so many weary months and which had been such a continual thorn in our side affording as they did to the Germans such an advantageous post of observation. The enemy were still shelling vigorously – we could watch the burst of high explosive and shrapnel over the ground thro' which we had to pass. Here and there they found their billet and a few groups fell in huddled heaps of maimed or dying. But our losses were small and we steadily pushed on towards Loos watching the while the havoc that the German shells now playing on the church and miners' cottages which still remained standing.

We soon encountered rifle fire from the top storeys of some of the houses but a few rapid rounds, supplemented by judiciusly placed bombs, effectually disposed of the inhabitants or at all events silenced their fire. It was at this point that after searching the houses to right and left of us we commenced the task of organising our company for a further advance towards the crest of the now famous Hill 70. I had been given the honour of leading the first contingent and by short rushes at extended intervals we gradually made our way up towards a reverse slope which offered a splendid natural line of resistance. The enemy continued to shell the ground over which we had advanced relentlessly but by this time the men had learnt the knack of choosing the psychological moment just before the burst, to drop flat on the ground, and casualties from this source were not severe.

It was otherwise, however, with the advanced line that occupied the further side of the reverse slope where we had now begun to dig in and fill the sand bags we had brought with us. Groups of wounded men began to come through our line and many unwounded who had found the terrific machine gun fire too much for them and who now began to retire with a precipitation that almost suggested panic.

They could not a first be induced to rally but fortunately the infection did not spread to our own ranks and our line was slowly built up on a frontage of 500 or 600 yards, while with their entrenching tools the work of digging in slowly continued. The first reinforcements in constantly increasing numbers converged well to our left so we sent down volunteers asking for fresh support as the situation with us was becoming increasingly critical every minute.

Our line of fire embraced a frontage from the railway embankment on the right of Loos to a road well on the left and there was a strong probability that the enemy might develop his counter attack at any moment. By this time most of our battalion had put in an appearance on the crest referred to. A Company under Captain Burn was on my right and for some hours we were together seeing to the strengthening of our line trying to get up some picks and shovels, procuring additional ammunition and other details.

Captain Ferguson was on the extreme right and to my great joy in the early afternoon I was told that gallant little Moyna had arrived with the remaining platoons of A Company. B and D Companies were further to the left; some had advanced over the crest but these had subsequently to retire under heavy machine gun fire that caused havoc in their ranks. It was at this stage that several officers were wounded including Captain Mair, Prinsep and McQueen. Captain Skipwith who had lost his Company near Loos was reported missing and up to the time of writing has not been traced.

The weary day wore on; our company had now been reorganised and occupied, under their platoon and section commanders a position on the right of the entrenched line. Captain Ferguson was in charge of the right, Moyna of right centre, while my own platoon was stationed on the left. The bombardment of Loos meanwhile continued without ceasing. Hardly a second intervened between the enemy's shells most of which were directed on the Pylons Towers presumably to prevent any observation of their movements being made from so commanding a post. Over the crest the village of Cité St Auguste which had been set on fire by our shells flamed in rosy glare, a circumstance which was later on to prove disastrous to the Germans in their counter attack on our position. The rain now began to fall and the strain on our weary troops without food or sleep became hourly greater.

At about 6 p.m. we had a visit from our Colonel who informed us that we should be relieved in the course of the night by the 21st Division. Hope renewed itself in our hearts but the hours passed on and no relief came. It afterwards transpired that the men of this division had been marching for five days, knew little or nothing of the ground and that in consequence had missed their objective. A few platoons did actually arrive and relieved portions of the 44th who had taken their part in the original charge on the German positions and had earned a well deserved release from their labours. But the 45th remained without relief. From now onwards the enemy who were just over the crest began to send over Very lights, possibly to determine our position before making their attack and word was constantly passed down our line to keep a sharp lookout.

It must have been shortly after midnight when the warning 'Here they are' and by George so they were. For a long time the attack developed most strongly on their right facing the position held by my own company. Time and again the Huns reorganised their shattered lines; they were met by terrific rifle fire which had it been supported by machine guns would have created still more than it did. For hours they came on in scattered groups verging all along our line, yelling like fiends with bayonets held in their right hands and evidently trying to find a spot in our defence. But our men controlled and directed by their officers and above all by gallant Moyna staved every attack and must have strewn the ground with victims as was afterwards found to be the case.

About 4 a.m. the grey of that grey morning they stopped coming on and retreated in order to dig themselves in. I had been all the time in close touch with Burn on my left and Moyna on my right and occupied myself in bringing up fresh supplies of ammunition at first in bandoliers and later on in boxes of a thousand rounds. I also procured some bombs in anticipation of a bomb attack from the enemy.

At this stage their snipers got to work. Hitherto the enemy had not fired a shot. The officers who were standing behind their men for the most part offered easy targets and soon began to fall under the deadly fire of the enemy. Watson of A Company, who had done splendidly throughout and who helped me to bring down a machine gun which unfortunately jammed and went out of action, was the first to fall shot through the throat. I at once went to the left to acquaint Captain Burn of his loss. On my return I was hit through the hand with two bullets which smashed the bones and placed me hors de combat. Our right, too, suffered; McGairn our machine gun officer being seriously wounded and Captain Ferguson slightly. I could hear little Moyna close by acquainting HQ through the telephone of our losses and asking for fresh supplies of ammunition. Soon afterwards his voice suddenly ceased; a bullet had come through a sand bag and lodged in his brain. He lingered on for a few minutes, but never regained consciousness. So died a heroic soul, the kindest most modest soldier in our battalion.

For some time I remained in such shelter as the very low parapet afforded and tried to give occasional fire orders to my men who had sustained up to now scarcely any casualties. But the pain of the wound and the shaking of the broken bones made me so faint that I decided to return and have the smashed hand attended to. I am not likely ever to forget that weary pilgrimage through the shell torn Loos and the still more shell torn Lens Road which alas! proved a death trap to so many of our wounded officers and in some places presented a veritable shambles. Through Captain Ferguson I was subsequently able to complete the account of what had happened on the right. It appears that we were in touch with the 47th during the whole of the proceedings on Hill 70 and that later on about 9 a.m. orders were issued for an attack on the Germans.

In the course of the attack which resulted in the repulse of the Huns and a successful penetration into their first line of defence Ferguson was wounded but returned to give Sharer who was still further to the right with No 9 Platoon the necessary instructions. Sharer then led the attack with rifle and bayonet and met his death in the charge. I understand that the ground was strewn with the dead bodies of the Germans who had fallen under our fire. Our men deprived of all their officers and encountering terrific machine gun fire on their right flank were forced to retreat to their original position and suffered very heavily in doing so, several of the sergeant majors being killed and amongst them that splendid old soldier Sergeant Major Dunn.

Long before this I had suggested a bayonet charge to Moyna who was most anxious for it but not being the senior officer was unable to carry it out. Had we made it at the psychological moment it is possible we should not have lost so many of our officers, while we could have, if necessary, after disposing of the Huns immediately in front of us, retired in order to our original position. As it was, our losses in officers were terrible, many being killed and all the others with one exception being more or less badly wounded. We could anyhow console ourselves with the satisfactory thought that we had killed a great number of the Germans and successfully for hours resisted the many determined efforts they had made to break our line. I was given to understand from a note handed to Burn earlier in the proceedings that our battalion was considered to have saved the situation at a stage when it threatened to become gravely critical. Burn, poor fellow, was wounded on Hill 70 and was subsequently found lying dead on the fatal Lens Road where he was eventually buried. His loss and that of Captain Moyna will be difficult to replace. Poor young Watson also died from the result of his wound and gallant young

Hay fell shot through the heart on the hill that had proved so fatal to many of our officers.

From J. C. Pringle

T. Hansford-White – After the battle
I was interested to see your letter of the *Telegraph*. I was not in the Battle of Loos but in the closing stages of the war, I was there in the same old trenches with the 15th Scottish Division serving with the 74th Field Company, Royal Engineers.

The 15th Division was in the Battle of Loos in 1915 and my sappers many of whom were there at the time, told me of the fearful events of those days.

We were there in late September and early October and when the Germans withdrew and started their retreat back to Germany we followed up and crossed the Hulluch–Lens road and the plain, very open and bare to Pont-a-Vendin and put duckboard and petrol tin foot bridges across the Haute d'Curle canal and then a pontoon bridge near the destroyed railway bridge and the following day went on to Carvin and followed up the Germans to Tournai where we were held up for a day or two preparing to make a crossing of the river, but suddenly we found that the war was over'. (11th November 18)

It seemed to me to be a satisfactory conclusion for the 15th Division.

Officer (unknown) – reporting the 15th Division attack
I could not have imagined that troops with a bare twelve months training behind them could have accomplished it. Once in No-Man's-Land they took up their dressing and walked – yes coolly walked – across towards the enemy trenches. The effect of these seemingly unconcerned Highlanders advancing on them must have had a considerable effect on the Germans. I saw one man whose kilt had got caught in our wire as he passed through a gap; he did not attempt to tear it off but, carefully disentangled it, doubled up to his correct position in the line and went on.

CASUALTIES SUFFERED BY THE 15th DIVISION
FOR THE PERIOD 25th, 26th and 27th September, 1915

UNITS	OFFICERS					OTHER RANKS				
	KILLED	WOUNDED	MISSING	GASSED	TOTAL	KILLED	WOUNDED	MISSING	GASSED	TOTAL
Hd. Qrs. 44th Bde.	—	—	1	—	1	—	—	—	—	—
9th Black Watch	8	11	1	—	20	68	314	292	5	679
8th Seaforth Hrs.	5	10	4	—	19	44	362	294	—	700
10th Gorden Hrs.	—	5	2	—	7	23	221	130	—	374
7th Cameron Hrs.	4	6	4	—	14	64	255	215	—	534
13th Royal Scots	6	9	1	—	16	37	224	105	4	370
7th R. S. Fusrs.	6	11	1	—	18	63	240	83	—	386
11th A & S Hrs.	7	4	1	—	12	36	214	64	—	314
6th Cameron Hrs.	8	8	—	1	17	30	270	70	—	370
7th K.O.S.Bs.	9	7	3	—	19	12	221	404	—	645
8th K.O.S.Bs.	3	7	4	—	14	23	124	228	4	379
10th Sco. Rifles	12	5	4	—	21	68	318	239	—	625
12th H.L.I.	7	11	—	—	18	59	184	315	—	558
9th Gordon Hrs. (Pioneers)	5	4	—	—	9	21	179	64	4	268
70th Bde. R.F.A.	—	2	—	—	2	1	12	—	—	13
71st Bde. R.F.A.	—	—	—	—	—	1	14	2	2	19
72nd Bde. R F A.	—	1	—	—	1	—	1	—	—	1
73rd Bde. R.F.A.	—	—	—	—	—	2	8	—	—	10
11th M.M.G. Batty.	—	2	—	—	2	—	3	—	—	3
15th Divl. Cyclists	—	—	—	—	—	1	6	—	—	7
73rd Fld. Coy. R.E.	2	2	1	—	5	10	14	29	—	53
74th Fld. Coy. R.E.	—	—	—	—	—	3	3	1	10	17
91st Fld. Coy R.E.	—	—	1	—	1	9	32	11	—	52
45th Fld. Amb. R.A.M.C.	—	—	—	—	—	—	4	—	—	4
46th Fld. Amb. R.A.M.C.	—	1	—	—	1	—	1	—	4	5
47th Fld. Amb. R.A.M.C.	—	—	—	—	—	—	3	—	—	3
TOTALS	82	106	28	1	217	575	3227	2546	41	6389

ATTACHED UNITS

180 Coy. R E.	—	—	—	—	—	1	22	2	—	25
187 Coy. R.E.	—	—	—	—	—	—	1	—	4	5

15th DIVISION

	Officers	O.R.
44th Infantry Brigade		
9th Bn. Black Watch	8	205
8th Bn. Seaforth Highlanders	7	200
10th Bn. Gordon Highlanders	19	495
7th Bn. Cameron Highlanders	11	320
45th Infantry Brigade		
13th Bn. The Royal Scots	13	609
7th Bn. Royal Scots Fusiliers	10	598
6th Bn. Cameron Highlanders	13	600
11th Bn. Argyll & Sutherland Highlanders	15	611
46th Infantry Brigade		
7th Bn. King's Own Scottish Bdrs.	6	307
8th Bn. King's Own Scottish Bdrs.	15	509
10th Bn. Scottish Rifles	5	216
12th Bn. Highland Light Infantry	10	440
Pioneer Battalion		
9th Bn. Gordon Highlanders	9	737
TOTALS	152	5849

This casualty return, sent to me by M. G. B. Crosthwaite, was submitted while the battle was still continuing and was typed in a dugout advanced Divisional HQ, by Sergeant James, now dead. Subsequently it was found that these figures, high though they are, were, in fact below the correct totals at the time.

9

1st Division, IV Corps

Diary of W. Boddington 1/4 London Scottish
  4th July 1915 Sailed from Southampton to Le Havre.
  5th August 1915 In trenches at Cambrin.
  11th August 1915 Up to front line.
  Some extracts from diary :

Friday 20 August Air traverse looks northward – the line is a horseshoe here and I would see the Plough alongside on the left. Cassiopeia was directly overhead. Things very quiet. Haven't fired my rifle yet. Our men always let off at dawn but I have seen nothing to make it worth while.

  Saturday, August 21st 1915 (in front line at Vermelles)
  General stand-to 4 o/c as usual. A cup of tea about 4.15 and then turn in and slept till 8. On guard 9–10 Periscope but could see nothing. Fine in morning – I slept till one o'clock but in afternoon it rained. Rumoured we are moving into Camerons position further to left tonight – Germans said to be massing troops. May mean a schemozzle. Got ready to move about 10 but the Royal Scots Fusiliers (6th) did not come up till after 11, then they relieved us by coming up *outside* the trench. If the Huns had put a machine gun on the line it would have been fatal. We had to carry picks and shovels and rations and as the trenches were narrow in places it was absolutely hell getting through. We relieved the Camerons. Had a 'dust up' with Troop? Gilly and I won. On duty all night – it was nearly 3 before we were all settled down.

  Sunday, August 22nd, 1915 With the dawn we could see the German line half right – a ridge loopholed. Airslie was out in the 'sap' – 150 yards from Fort Hohenzollern the German fortress. My guard 10–11 and again 2–3. It was a sunny afternoon and I was in a particularly sunny corner. Blue sky and white cloud and the buzzing flies. Shutting my eyes I could dream I was in Richmond Park. On coming off had a fatigue making a new fire position in traverse and though it was hard work putting up sandbags, still it was fine when it was done. Captain Syer complimented us on it. Must make a special note. Managed to wash my hands – some water that had already been used. But it was a delight to eat food with clean hands. Trench mortars sending over heavy stuff – shook our mess tin on our fire. Evening was a sunset more glorious than any I have ever seen except one September at Huntley. It was like molten copper and while I was on guard 6–7 everyone noticed it. Then the moon almost full came up. Gillispie, Airslie and I were on a fatigue clearing up the latrines – the most disgusting fatigue out here. We had to dig a hole out at the back in full moonlight. We had just got it done and were back in the trench when a pip squeak came to the place. Must have seen us.

Monday, 23rd August Had my first shot at the Germans this morning. The moon was beautiful and thin filmy clouds were lit by it like a picture at home. After midnight a sound of working party in German lines so A and I put a shot over. It stopped them for 10 mins.

Tuesday,24th August Morning was a glorious one. Sunny. Aerial torpedo came over. First one report and the torpedo could be seen coming down. I got the periscope on it and saw it burst after a moment on the ground. A great red sheet of flame, a loud report and a dense cloud of smoke. Our artillery replied but 2 shells were short bursting 20 yards in front of us. Got rather scared, we had a large store of bombs in the gap. Were relieved at 8.

24th August To billets in Verquin.

Thursday, September 2nd, 1915 Reveille 6 and tea was served at 7. 7.15 a route march until 8 – we went as far as St Hilaire des Cottes and on way back noticed that the country was prettier than that up the line. Little hills with woods made it more interesting than the flatness of Vermelles. Hurried over breakfast – parade at 9 with water sheets to go shooting, 5 hits at deliberate and 4 hits rapid (only 4 –) in 30 secs. We came back by a much shorter way by 12.30. After stew found that we had to parade to attend a football match. A Company against Camerons. The skipper was playing so the whole Company was marched down. Most of us lay reading under the shelter of a hayrick.

Had Crieff cake for tea and then was detailed for billet guard with Airslie and Williamson. My spell 12–2 and from 4.40–6. Rained all the time – scene a row of trees as usual and the ubiquitous smell of mildew and the constant drip of rain. Very dismal indeed. Went spirit visits to pass the time!

Friday, September 3, 1915 Relieved at 6 o'clock but raining still. Breakfast at 8.15 Rifle and billet insp. 10 – cleared ammunition. (*pour passerle temps*) It was pouring in torrents but they kept us employed all morning and finished lecture 11.30–12. Afternoon No. 2 Platoon supposed to have baths but we never went out. Wrote Miss Randal and slept. Very cold and raw (still raining) until we were invited over to the *estaminet* to warm ourselves by the fire. Very grateful, then to parade for new bonnets, *comme l'armée* Kitchener. Given blue touries(?) to put in. Altogether rather an improvement on Glengarries. Evening still raining so turned in early. A rum ration served out. Fairly coarse stuff but I took it after I had turned in. Very unhappy night, a foretaste of winter and it does not make one look forward to it.

Saturday, September 4th, 1915 A battalion route march at 10 o'clock with full marching order. A Company met the other boys at the corner of the road. We all looked uniform and rather fine in our new bonnets. Major Lindsay as CO looked almost handsome! In afternoon spent a sunny afternoon in the orchard writing Lillie. It seemed very far from war and I was wishing I were back in England.

Short evenings nowadays and after tea-time there is no time for anything.

Sunday, September 5th, 1915 Reveille 6.30, breakfast 7.30, Church Parade 9 back about 10.45, 11.30 parade for inspection by CO full marching order. That was rotten – mainly for emergency ration – bully beef, tea and sugar and biscuits. Got back 1.30. Had to parade at 2.30 to clean up the road. As all the local middens seem to drain individually they find their way to the roadside and it was perfectly offensive. We were on it till 3.45 then I finished my letter to Lillie and turned in. Having a candle it was possible to read – got *Anne of the Barricades* by Godett.

Monday, September 6th, 1915 Reveille 6 and tea about 7 and parade 7.15. We were for an hour doing extended order drill. This gives the idea that an advance is probable and that we'll be in it. The Black Watch say we are going over the parapet even before the rest is over the month. Breakfast 8 and parade again 9.30. Away up the lane to the 2 windmills where we practised attacking from a trench and we came back the 3 miles across ploughed fields first in sections and then in extended order. Afternoon parade again (after having the Platoon photo taken) 2.30. We went off up the lane again and did outpost work there till 4.30. Evening parade at 7 for night work. 2 Platoon had to make a crossing of river and 6 of us had to borrow a ladder and two planks from a brickworks. The man came while we were at it and I had to explain. We went off and in the dark we were very quiet. Crossed the river at 8.25 but the ladder broke and we thought we made a dickens of a row, but we got over and up the crest to the 4 tall trees in extended order. Tins rattling for machine guns. Back by 9.30. The cow had calved!

Tuesday, September 7th, 1915 Reveille at 6.30 these mornings are so bright – walk up the orchard as usual and got an apple. I wish I were on holiday. No parade before breakfast. Porridge 9.30. At A Company HQ sorting out ammunition – all B marked served out with other to make up. Told that night work was a success and carried out very quickly. No parade in afternoon. I wrote Griff and then went down to Lespe (where battalion HQ is) to look for stray parcels. Evening. Just at dusk I went for a lovely stroll up the hill. Looking NNW to home, had such a longing for home – the long line of trees on the horizon – the hollow of the village on the right and the 4 lovely trees on the right – waited till dark fell. Got another candle and wrote Annie Peters then wrapped myself in great-coat and fell asleep.

Wednesday, September 8th, 1915 No early parade as Syer and Sparks were up at the trenches looking over positions. Looks suggestive of an early attack. They say Fort Hohenzollern at Vermelles is the objective. Mr Macgregor in charge. Did square drill for an hour CSM and Andrews and then practised digging ourselves in and protecting lines of trenches.

Afternoon off. Had date duff for tea and as a parcel came from Nellie and Rennie we finished with biscuits.

Night came down swiftly and we tried to write letters in the barn. As usual sent in to persuade Madame to give us some *chauffé l'eau* for *café au lait*, then went out and flirted with Mademoiselle while she milked the cow. Smell of cow byre pleasant. She wanted to know so much – whether my Mother worked on a farm, etc., etc., etc.

Thursday, September 9th, 1915 Mess orderly with Airslie and Williamson so had to get up at Reveille. Fried bacon for breakfast so a greasy 'dixie' at breakfast time to clean. Airslie did it and we did the greasy stew one at 2 p.m. Morning – a battalion outpost scheme. Supposed enemy to SW. We were on picket and had quite a soft time after I had got a message to Captain Syer. Running after a mounted officer is no game at all on a warm September day. Parade again 2.45 but very short. Everybody got wind up again – we are to get our bayonets sharpened. My boots to be mended. Parcel from Lillie. Photos that I gave to the photographer at Lieres proved no good. Very unhappy. Rumour that we start work tomorrow at 4.30 a.m. Hope not!

Friday, September 10th, 1915 Too true! Wakened 4.30. Breakfast 5.15 and parade 5.45. At 6 we were moving out of Lières (A Company) with 2 Platoon carrying spades and picks. Up to the mining village and from 6.30–7 our Platoon dug a trench and covered it cunningly with branches about 30 ft. long. Lay there waiting for enemy – other three companies had to hold it till 1 but attack developed at about 10, we had to leave our trench. Back to a brickyard where our section held a stack (brick) until it was almost too late. The rest of platoon under Sparks retiring and I went with them through wire and down a 8 ft. back – only I tripped and fell on my arm. Afraid it was broken at first could not feel my fingers. Lay still although enemy lined the bank and went out at right angles. I kept my white brassard low down. Cease fire sounded after half hour and I rejoined without being captured. Sent down to dressing station. Dr G. not sure about fracture. Afternoon, another cold bandage on it. Bath, home at 3. Concert in evening A. in Nily Billet – no piano but good. Queer scene, men sitting all round on the floor by the light of 6 candles on table. Sparks there and Worloch and Macgregor. Sergeant Pickford sang Mary Morison with a fine Scotch accent. Mulled wine ad lib free gratis and for nothing.

11th September Convalescent camp at Rillens.

12th September Developed trench fever. Hospitalised.

23rd September To hospital at Arques.

Saturday, 25th September Throughout the night the bombardment sounded heavier; the rumour was that the attack was to take place morning of 25th. Raining still.

Wednesday, 29th September Left Arques fit.

Thursday, 30th September Arrived Noeux and found platoon. After a long search after dark at last found our platoon. Mac safe, Archie badly hit – hand and stomach. Only 20 of platoon left.

Tuesday, 5th October Back to trenches 3 miles beyond Le Batoire Farm.

Friday, 8th October Afternoon I was asleep and in the midst of a delightful dream that I was having tea with Lillie, when Sergeant P. came round. A Company to put all equipment on and stand by. We were being bombarded like hell. (I had slept through it all). Artillery officers came in and used our dug-out as phoning station. G. making an attack on Chalk Pit. Red House taken – later heard that it was retaken by us. Then about 5 we were moved up. Everyone thought we were in for a bad night. Up an interminable Com. trench passing wounded men but instead of 1st line we were to relieve Kings L/Pool in 2nd line. No dug-outs and being shelled. Slept resting against McL. Relieved at 3 by the N. Lancs (Scottish had offered a Company to hold in for the night for them). Back over land – dead beat.

Saturday, 9th October Heard that G attack was a complete failure – attacked in mass in 3 lines with only about 500 men. Reached within 50 yards being mown down by our machine guns – Douglas saw it. In the morning G. shelled the wall again and killed 3 men one a Scottish Corporal Matthew of B. also a 1st Gloucester and an RFA man – many wounded.

Letter from Lieutenant Perry

On reading today's *Daily Telegraph* on your writing an account of the Battle of Loos, 25th September 1915, I should mention that I took part in all the operations as a Lieutenant in a Territorial Battalion of the King's Liverpool Regiment. This battalion in which I served two years four months was part of the 2nd Brigade 1st Division – in those days there were six battalions sometimes in one Infantry Brigade.

The units were 2 K.R.R. 2 Royal Sussex, 1 Northants, 1st Loyals, 5th Regiment Sussex T.F.* 9th Kings Liverpool T.F.

In this engagement – the London Scottish and 9th King's formed a body called 'Queen's Force' whose first objective was the German front line trenches in the vicinity of the Lone Tree – as this objective was left uncovered by the diverging advance of the 1st Brigade on the left and the 2nd Brigade on the right.

Although I am now in my 83rd year I remember a great many details of the battle – the latter part of which is well described in a novel by G. Frankau. This particularly refers to a Southdown Division which released us on the 25th/26th September, followed I'm afraid by disastrous results.

The battalion spent a lot of time in this sector including the repelling of Hulluch and the German counter attack on the 8th October, for which it was mentioned in Army Orders.

As I have said I am in my 83rd year but still active enough to shoot at Bisley where I hope to attend for the second week this year, 19th/26th July. [1975]

If there is anything else I can give you with regard to this great battle please do not hesitate to ask me.

I might add that the Brigade remained in this sector till after Xmas 1915 – in January '16 it left the 1st Division to form up with all the other West Lancashire T.F. Units in forming the famous 53rd West Lancashire Division.

Letter from Lieutenant Colonel K. H. Leake (retired)

My Battalion the 1st Royal North Lancashire Regiment 2nd Brigade, 1st Division was heavily engaged on September 25th and our casualties that day were 15 Officers and 489 other ranks (I quote from the regimental history which I have).

Briefly, at 19 years old I was a replacement Subaltern sent out from our reserve battalion about September 28th so, although I was not at Loos on the 25th I was in the front line along the Lens–La Bassée road

*Territorial Forces, i.e. originally enlisted (in peacetime) for home defence only.

just north of the Chalk pit from (I think) October 5th or 6th until after the abortive attack on October 13th on Hulluch just north of us. My platoon sergeant and I went out that night to look for survivors between us and Hulluch, but with no result.

At that time our front line of trenches was subject to enfilade fire from German 5.9 guns situated near Hohenzollern Redoubt – most uncomfortable.

Except for rest periods the 1st Division were between Grenay and Hulluch until July 1916 when we went to the Somme.

I was wounded and lost an arm in November 1916.

From 1940 to '45 I was on the retired re-employed list, serving most of the war with RASC Driver Training Units.

Anonymous account

September, 21st, 1915 Move to front began, London Scots from Le Marequet Wood nr. Lapugnoy (years of leaf deposit and tree cover) thunder storm made 3000 gun barrels seem puny –

September 23rd Verquin – stubble field near large slag heap *rain*.

September 24th 9.30 p.m. move up long corn trench full of water up to knees – but rested on top of c.t. until next morning. Fosse Way trench north of Le Rutoire Farm where there existed a cement pill box, still intact 1973.

September 25th 5 a.m. moved up after gas projected – when local ladies came drifting back – 7.30 a.m. Infantry advance – orders for a frontal attack had been carried out with heavy casualties (probably Black Watch and Cameron) as belt of wire intact – 20 yds. wide – later Major Lindsay of London Scots suggested a flank attack which resulted in 600 prisoners of 51st Regiment – a fresh clean unit. Here the ground was open with good visibility – no shell holes – the London Scots moved forward and went down entirely in view of the Germans before the last rush. I was probably the last man down as I was the *extreme man* on the left flank. All the while I was glancing right and saw the casualties of the first move forward. On this open ground the Germans picked off our troops. I was so close to my next comrade who was killed as he covered my body. *Note* Orders were Gas Helmet carried on head (same material as shirts) – no respirators or steel helmets yet London Scts. moved forward and dug in facing flank but later moved to Chalk pit.

September 26th/27th 2 a.m. 21 Div. began to arrive with 24 Div. after long march (not under fire previously) Transport knocked out water bottles empty – no food issue – (I believe they had landed at Boulogne) (It was said they took off their boots and no doubt had their trousers down when the Boche attacked – the area became very quiet and still before the counterattack).

When London Scots withdrew in *fours* we passed men of Berks Regiment foaming yellow and could not notice or fall out to assist. They had occupied a trench which held the gas.

Losses 5 Officers and 260 O/R.

Later on 11th October London Scots used in counter attack as 21st Division was withdrawn for further training. Battalion was held up by wire and one Company lost all their NCOs.

The 21st Division later became a fine fighting unit and gained many decorations.

Note On October 13th authority was first given for proportion of Officers and O/R to keep out of action to be used for re-organisation.

40,000 losses on the greater front.

Lone Tree situated half way between lines was a cherry tree and used to range on. It was rumoured that an officer of 15 Division in this tree was killed and remained there for a few days.

October 3rd At Noeux-les-Mines I went to the Orderly Room to receive commission papers in the field to another regiment and withdrew before crossing the road as I thought it best not to pass in front of the Prince of Wales approaching my direction.

Note The Vermelles area was very quiet for several months in 1915 previously as trenches were wide apart – it was a corn growing area and held the most red poppies I came across.

10

12th Divison

From E. E. Lane

I was in that battle, going 'over the top' at 7.30 on the morning of 25th September, 1915, in the face of sheer hell. Having got to the German trench I was immediately confronted by the enemy and hand to hand ensued for some time. I ended up with a bayonet wound in my mouth and my front teeth knocked out. Never the less I had the satisfaction of disposing of my opponent whom I believed then to be a *'Uhlan'* – disbanded cavalry. In as much I was able to get his spiked helmet and his Iron Cross from under his top pocket lapel. The helmet was covered with a green cover and numbered 233. These I cherish very much and the present generation in this village admire these with awe and wonder and all are anxious as to what then happened.

We were beaten out of their trench later that day and I lay in a shell hole in No-Man's-Land amid white chalk until the early hours of next morning when I was able to crawl back to our trench when the stretcher bearers took me back to safety and eventually sent home on seven day's leave.

I was a Sergeant (No. 10357) in the 5th Royal Berks of the 12th Division and we suffered very heavy casualties. We had a 'Guards' Division and a Scottish Division on our flanks who also suffered similar fates . . .

From R. G. Hawkins

In response to your request published in the *Telegraph* I thought perhaps that whilst I have no letters or diaries concerning the Battle of Loos, as a participant I do have vivid recollections of its latter stages, have been the sole survivor of twelve blown up by a German 'coalbox'.

I was serving at the time as a Vickers Machine Gunner with the 12th (Ace of Spades) Division (which was then under the Command of General Gough) and our gun position was in a part of the front line known as the 'Rabbit Hole' in the Hulloch Redoubt which was overlooked by the Germans from their positions of a huge slagheap.

I recall that our headquarters were situated in the Brewery cellars at Vermelles, where I was taken after the 'blow up' and dosed with a pint of service rum to save me from shell-shock.

My father, who was also involved in the Loos Battle was then serving with the Royal Engineers with 15th (Scottish) Division and only a few days prior to my going into the line had been able to meet him at the nearby village of Noeux le Miens.

If in my memories I can recall anything that may be helpful to you, I shall be only to pleased to share them with you.

I I

7th Division, I Corps

Letter from J. B. S. Notley
I went out to replace those killed or wounded. I was a second lieutenant and stationed at Wareham, Dorset. I went out on 1st October 1915 and joined the 8th Devons at Cambrin near Béthune. I was given command of No 1 Platoon A Company which consisted of a sergeant and three men! The 8th Devons lost in 30 hours 25th/26th September, 22 Officers and 753 men. I have information from the few officers left after the battle of the part played by the Devons.

We were in the 20th Brigade, 7th Division and were 'Army Troops' and went to France July 1915. I am sending the maps and accounts of the Devons etc., to the Devonshire Regimental Museum as they have asked me to do so.

The Devons gained their objective and were waiting on the Hulluch main road for eight hours for supports, with no enemy in sight, but General French had kept the Reserves far too far behind and so the 8th and 9th Devons, or what was left of them had to retire all the way back to their starting position. Hearsay said French lost his command over this blunder . . .

[After the war Mr Notley began to teach fly-fishing and shooting. Today, aged 82, he still does so.]

Extract from History of the Devonshire Regiment in the Great War (Atkinson)
Hard hit both battalions had certainly been. The 8th had 19 officers and 620 men in their casualty list, and it was even more in the quality than in the quantity of their losses that they had suffered so much. To lose so many of the officers and NCOs who had borne the brunt of the work of raising and training the new battalion, was a shattering blow. Colonel Grant, Major Carden and Captain Kekewich had all done great work for the 8th and their loss was severely felt. The Colonel, himself a great worker, had expected the 8th to work hard and to learn rapidly. With

the keen raw material with which he had to deal his exacting demands and his high standards had been a great incentive. The 8th had been keen to satisfy one who showed himself in every respect a competent soldier, and for the high level they reached and maintained their first CO deserves not a little credit.

The 9th's losses, though less by a quarter than those of their sister battalion, came to 15 officers and 461 men,* but, fortunately, they had fared better in that far fewer officers had been killed. In the 8th, besides the officers already mentioned, the wounded included Captains James, Pryor and Broadbridge, Lieuts. Hulm† and MacMichael, 2nd-Lieuts. Nixon. Balderson, Bridson† and Cracroft, and the Chaplain, the Rev. F. W. Hewitt, had been killed. No less than 148 men were killed, 129 missing, and 343 wounded or gassed. The 9th, with Lieutenant Tracey and 2nd-Lieutenants Allan and Davies,‡ and 59 men killed, 76 men missing and 326 wounded, were almost as much in need of reconstruction.

Still the 8th and 9th could look with pride on their first battle. At that period in the war but few other battalions could boast of having captured German guns. The 1st Lincolnshires had taken a battery on the Aisne, the 1st Royal Berkshires had captured two guns at Ypres, and in this battle of Loos some four or five units shared this credit with the 8th Devons, but it was a notable achievement for a new battalion and an earnest of fine things to come. It spoke well for the battalion's training and for the spirit by which it was inspired, that, when nearly all their officers had fallen with so many of the men, the survivors should have carried on the attack with such vigour and resolution.

One survivor wrote: 'The men were simply splendid, as steady as veterans; they neither flinched nor grumbled the whole time, though they were cold, hungry and tired to death, as well as wet to the skin.' For the failure to exploit to the full the success of the first attack the 8th and 9th could not be held responsible. In capturing their objectives, and in retaining all but the most advanced positions reached, they had done all that could be asked of them. That Loos was of the nature of an experiment, that lessons were learnt there about the limitation of objectives, the use of reserves, and the necessity of artillery support for the later stages of an attack, is obvious enough when the story of the whole war can be reviewed. At the time all that was clear was that the two Service battalions

---

*On September 30th the 8th's fighting strength was 6 officers and 263 men, that of the 9th being 12 officers and 325 men.

†Subsequently died of wounds.

‡To those officers already mentioned as wounded must be added Lieutenants Martin, Upcott, Glosson and Worrall, 2nd-Lieutenants Hinshelwood and Pocock, and Lieutenant O'Reilly, RAMC.

of the Devons had borne themselves worthily, in a way which befitted the Regiment from which they had sprung, and had shown themselves fully entitled to a place in the hard-fighting Division to which they had been allotted.*

*Two of the guns taken by the Devons at Loos were presented by the War Office to the County of Devon, and were formally handed over on November 12th to the Lord Lieutenant (Earl Fortescue) and by him entrusted to the Mayor and Corporation of Exeter for safe custody. At the parade there were present about half-a-dozen officers and 40 men of the two Service battalions with detachments from the 3rd Battalion, the Territorial Provisional battalion, the Yeomanry, and the Territorial batteries. It was about the first ceremony of the kind and provided an impressive and memorable scene, which did much to bring home to the City and County the fine work of the junior battalions of the old Regiment.

12

28th Division, I Corps

Letter from Major J. H. Henderson
When we were relieved and going down the communication trench carrying our two remaining Vickers Guns we passed Brigade HQ dug-out and standing outside was our Brigadier (28th Brigade) Brigadier Scrase Dickins (I hope I have spelt his name correctly) with tears rolling down his cheeks. The only time I ever saw a General in tears. The other incident was the last seen alive of Second Lieutenant Jackson commanding No 2 Platoon, 6th King's Own Scottish Borderers, he was hanging on the barbed wire shouting, 'Go on the Borderers.'

Letter from A. B. Swaine
Before outbreak of war I was a Territorial in the Kent Cyclist Battalion. I was in camp for annual training in July 1914 and mobilized. Transferred in October 1914 to Temporary Regular Army (3 years was duration) when the Army Cyclist Corps was newly formed. There were a hundred of us drawn from various Cyclist Territorial units. Gathered at the White City, refitted and despatched to France in mid-November 1914. By a strange chance my regimental number with this new Corps was No 1.

Detrained at Hazelbrook and joined by a number of regular Troops drawn from various units. Divided off into companies of cyclists and one company attached to each division. My company went to the First Division – all were regular soldiers except for about a dozen of us Transferred Territorials.

In the Trench Warforce we were usually used, owing to quick mobility, to reinforce units which had been badly cut up. We just stored our cycles just behind the line and go in on foot. I recall two such areas, namely Givenchy and Quinchy. When withdrawn we cycled back to Bethune on several occasions. This was the winter of 1914 and early part of 1915.

Just prior to Battle of Loos we were in various parts of the line between the Hulluch Road–Vermelles Road on the Loos front and Marzot.

On the breakthrough on 25th/26th with squadron of Northumberland Yeomanry extended across the fields, my Company cycled up Hulluch Road. But short of Hulluch we ran into gas (I think from gasshells) and were ordered to return.

Soon after turning back, handicapped by a steamed up gas helmet (the old flannel bag with oblong mica front) I crashed my cycle in a shell hole. The company went back without me, leaving me to follow on pushing my badly buckled bike and suffering from gas in a minor degree.

I was reported missing believed killed, but I eventually caught up with them.

I think it was on the second day when the 21st and 24th Divisions straight out from England got caught in a barrage of 'Coal Boxes' and started to turn back, a number of cavalry men mounted, with some of my company hanging on to stirrup leather were sent across the Loos plain to try and persuade them to get back up the line. We had little success.

The 'Lone Tree' sticks in my mind. Both the German and our own artillery had registered on it. It stood in No-Man's-Land and was shattered and blasted by shell fire but never a direct hit.

My first close-up acquaintance with this wretched tree was one night from our front line, we heard calls for help both in English and in German.

Before day break I was sent out with three other men to see what we could do. We took a 'duck board 'as a stretcher and found a German warrant officer (with Iron Cross) badly wounded. On the duck board we carried him back to our support line but he died before we could get any medical attention for him. I might add that my three regular soldier companions tossed up for his Iron Cross.

My next visit to the 'Lone Tree' was with several others, to *cut it down* and drag it back behind our lines. We were told HQ wanted it cut up for them for souvenirs so I cut two chunks off it for myself. I still have them, suitably inscribed, one sizeable piece on my wall and the smaller chunk I made into a cigarette lighter. Thinking this might interest you I photographed the pieces and enclose copies herewith. The circular object just below the plate is the sawn through nose of a bullet, and below that some shell splinters.

In 1917 I returned to England, was commissioned in the Buffs, and spent the rest of the war on the North West Frontier of India until December 1919. I may as well add that in 1924 I went to Singapore as a Rubber Planter, joined the Singapore Volunteer Corps, commanded the Fortress Signal Company as a Major and finished up in a Japanese prisoner of war camp in Borneo. Starvation for three years ! ! I was better off as an eighteen year old at the Battle of Loos 1915 !

Excuse my ramblings and I should very much like to read your account of the Battle of Loos September 1915. After the lapse of 60 years one's memory gets a bit vague especially as to place names, and I have never managed to obtain a map of that area with details of villages etc.

Should there by any specific points about which you might require information and could let me know, I might be able to dig into a failing memory.

I might add that for my $2\frac{1}{2}$ years in France I was a private soldier. We were given very little information. Very often we hardly knew where we were or why we were there until we found ourselves in some unpleasant situation.

I hope you can decipher my handwriting – like my memory it deteriorates with the passage of years !

Extract from my Autobiography
From A. L. Tomlinson, The Second Cheshire Regiment
(he was just 19)

Prior to launching our attack, our artillery had sent over a gas barrage as well as tremendous bombardment of artillery fire.

We had tried to cut the barbed wire entanglements during the night before they attacked and when we launched the attack, it was still very very difficult to get through the barbed wire. The battle was a shocking one, and we were being mowed down like corn. Our objective was 4,000 yards to cover a rise in the ground away from us, and then consolidate.

We hurried over the dead bodies, in and out of the trenches and pot-holes. Some of the soldiers had been lying there since the previous battle – The Battle of Neuve Chapelle.

We nearly reached our objective, but I was hit by enfilade fire, one bullet going through my arm, and one more piercing my side, smashing my ribs and chipping bits off my spine, the bullets fortunately did not lodge in the body but went straight through. I lay there helpless for nearly seven hours and during that time recovered consciousness. For all that time, there was no-one in sight. Bullets from the Germans just missed my head, artillery shells were bursting near to, making terrific holes, the soil covering and nearly burying me.

In spite of all this, I became fully conscious and managed to get my right hand into the corner of my tunic to an iodine bottle which was sewn into the left-hand corner of the jacket. I somehow was conscious enough to cover the blood patches in my arm and side with the liquid iodine. Whether that saved me from tetanus I do not know.

I lay there and prayed hard until a wounded Welsh soldier crawled past me. He seemed to have a shattered hand. He said he would report that I was there. He must have saved my life, because after what seemed a long time, stretcher bearers risked their lives through the shells etc., and found me. Because of the nasty corners in the connecting support lines between the trenches, the stretcher bearers, (two men) could do no other than to lift me high above their heads. Shots were whizzing past me the whole of the time. They were taking me back to the First Dressing Station in the front line. We eventually reached the first Casualty Dressing Station and I remember asking the Doctor : 'Do you think I did my duty?' As if he would know. He replied : 'Of course you have.' The reply seemed to satisfy me during this anxious semi-conscious state. I was getting weaker and weaker through loss of blood.

I was later taken further down the line and placed, still on the stretcher, at the side of a large building in the street, together with hundreds of other wounded. A padre came to me and asked for my name and address.

He took it from some papers I had on me and sent a brief note to my family, saying that I was wounded, but was doing alright. This was a great relief to my parents, brothers and sisters.

At the end of the day, I was put on a train, the destination being Le Treport on the Coast. The wounded were dying on my left and right. I watched some die and taken away.

At Le Treport I was put on my first bed in the Second Canadian Hospital. We were under canvas. There was a tremendous number of wounded going to the different Hospitals, which I understand, were run by the Canadians on a voluntary basis, but there were so many casualties and they were so terribly busy and short-staffed, it must have been a nightmare for them at that time. There were said to be 50,000 dead or wounded in the Loos Battle offensive within the two days. The hospital staff just could not cope.

In the next bed to me, the man had obviously been hit in the head with a bullet or shrapnel. I tried to attract the attention of the men's orderly to tell him that blood was squirting from the poor man's head at the back and onto the tent itself. I just watched him die.

I myself was in a pretty bad shape. I was in agony with the call of nature. For what seemed like hours, I asked someone who might pass for some reason or other, which was very rare, if they could kindly bring me a bottle.

After hours, I was whipped off for an examination and told I was

One of the most famous Bairnsfather cartoons

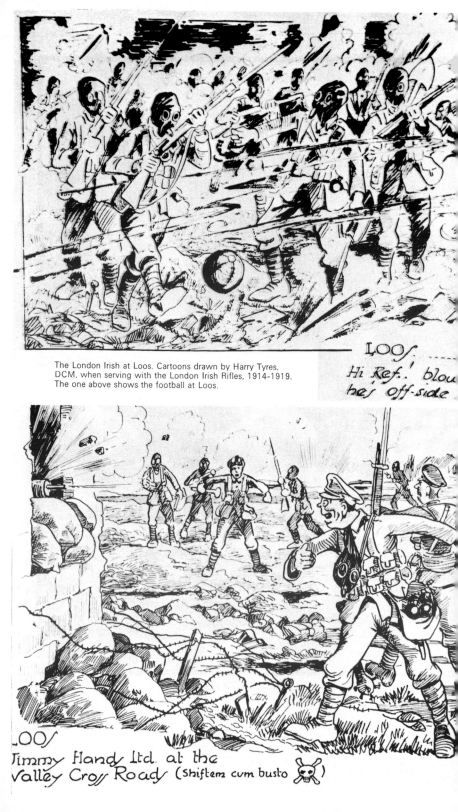

The London Irish at Loos. Cartoons drawn by Harry Tyres, DCM, when serving with the London Irish Rifles, 1914-1919. The one above shows the football at Loos.

Loos barbed wire captured during the battle

Captured German trench. Note machine-gun emplacement covering barbed wire

Loos. Vermelles road after attack. The view towards Loos shows wrecked transport and MG limbers of 21st and 24th Divisions. In the foreground a shell hole in middle of road, old German support trench on extreme right.

(*Below*) German dead at Loos

Loos, October 1915

Postcard supplied by Mr. F. E. Heninghem. These pictures were considered to be good for everyone's morale.

"Y" AT HOME IN GERMAN DUG-OUTS

A typical wet trench

(*Below*) A shell hole

e-Major Robert Mackenzie. He played the
KOSB over the parapet although shot in
h legs. He died of these wounds.
)sequently he was awarded the VC: He was
r 60 years old.

Piper Laidlaw, VC, another piper at Loos,
congratulated by Captain Grant.

e Emilienne Moreau. When only 17½ she
s caught in the battle of Loos, where she
d. She was helping in a first aid post when
ame under sniper fire. Taking a revolver the
ran out behind the houses opposite. In one
found and shot two German snipers. She
n went back to her work. She was awarded
ilitary Medal and a Croix de Guerre.

A piece of the Lone Tree, showing tip of
sawn-off bullet and shell splinters

Loos 1976

The battlefields of Loos, 1976. Note the absence of cover for advancing infantry

The cemetery at Loos

going home on a hospital ship in two or three days. I learned afterwards that the hospital ship which had sailed before the one I was on had been cruelly torpedoed by a German submarine and sank with no-one saved. On a stretcher, I was taken to a cabin of the ship. I was unconscious at that time, and how they got me on to a bunk, I do not know.

I remember two of the men's orderlies saying that they could not, or would not, get the stretcher by the side of my bunk, and that as soon as we arrived at Dover, I would have to try to stand on my feet. When we arrived at Dover, the stretcher was placed outside the door. I stood up, and with their help was placed upon it. I must have become unconscious with doing this for I remember nothing further until I was put on a British train. The nurses were like angels to me although they were overwhelmed with work, but they were helped by men orderlies. I was in a very weak state. One man orderly, or at least I think he was an orderly, but whoever he was, went from bunk to bunk on the hospital train and asked each wounded soldier whether he had any francs. If so, he could change them into sterling currency for them.

I had quite a pocketful, as before the bayonet charge, we had been paid, and I did not smoke, and had nothing to spend my money upon. The cad of a man referred to on the hospital train, with my permission, took all my francs. There was no-one to stop him, as he hurried down the corridor of the train. The nurses were so busy, they hardly knew what we were talking about. This wicked cad thief never came back, and must have collected a terrific amount from the wounded soldiers, because there were hundreds of helpless men on the train. On arrival in dear old London, I was almost out of this world.

I was taken to Endell Street Military Hospital, which was an old workhouse turned into an emergency hospital. It was organised by a most wonderful organisation, (women only) – The Women's Hospital Corps, the founders being, I think, the famous Dr Garret Anderson and Dr Flora Murray both highly skilled women.

I was taken up to the 3rd floor in a lift and put on a bed at 11 o'clock.

I had not been there long, when one of the nurses in her hurry touched my bed as she passed and I shouted with pain. This drew the immediate attention of the Sister, and I was then whipped off to the operating room for an urgent operation. My back and side were cut wide open, the loose rib extracted and bits removed from near to my chipped spine.

My parents were sent for, as I was on the danger list and my mother came overnight, and was put up at the Bedford Hotel nearby.

Extract about the Loos Battle, 25th September 1915 Taken from *The History of the Cheshire Regiment in the Great War* by Arthur Crookenden, Colonel of the Regiment

Loos

This battle was intended to result in the capture of the German positions from Loos to the La Bassée Canal.

The British attack, opening with success at many points was held up by the evening of the 25th September.

On the extreme left of the attack, immediately south of the La Bassée Canal, the 2nd Division had had the misfortune owing to a change of wind, to be overwhelmed by their own gas, and their attack failed completely. On their right however, the 9th Division had achieved a remarkable success. From a slag heap, known as the Dump, in rear of the German front line, the enemy had observation over the whole of the Rutoire plain which lay between the British front line and Vermelles. To protect the Dump, the Germans had constructed a projecting work, strongly mined, known to us as the Hohenzollern Redoubt, a map of which is in the text.

Early on the 25th, the 26th Brigade of the 9th Division had carried the Redoubt and gone forward as far as Haisnes, 1200 yards further East. Owing to their exposed flanks, and in spite of reinforcement, these advanced troops were driven in.

The 84th Brigade, in which was the 2nd Battalion, meanwhile was moving forward, by bus and march route, to a position in reserve at Bethune. Heavy fighting continued for the recovery of the Dump during the 26th and 27th. On the 28th, an attack at dawn was driven back and in the afternoon the 85th Brigade made another attempt with no better success. At nightfall, the British front line was still in the Hohenzollern, but the enemy had footings in Big and Little Willie.

The close and desperate fighting on this day and on those which were to follow can be taken as an outstanding example of trench warfare, and for which the Germans were better prepared than we were. They had more and better bombs and many more machine guns. The close hand-to-hand fighting, the congestion in the shallow trenches, the break-down in the means for removing wounded, make it impossible to follow the progress of the battle or to ascertain the local situation. Often orders were issued by Divisional HQ for a position to be captured which had been won and, at such heavy sacrifice, that it had been lost again before the orders arrived!

Fighting continued on the 29th and under constant bomb attacks, the

85th Brigade held fast. Through the incessant bombardments, the trenches had by now become recognizable.

The 84th Brigade was ordered into the line on the night 30th September/1st October in relief of the 83rd Brigade. The Northumberland Fusiliers and the 2nd Battalion were in the front line in the southern portion of the Hohenzollern Redoubt, and adjoining trenches. The 2nd Battalion was to occupy the west face. No opportunity was given to reconnoitre the trenches or even the way up to them. The communication trenches were very narrow and deep and most complicated for newcomers.

When the 84th Brigade was trying to move in, three disorganised brigades were using all available means of leaving the front line, and Central Alley, which had been allotted to the Fusiliers and ourselves, was a funnel into which poured to the rear scores of wounded and leaderless men from many units.

The loss of the Brigadier and Brigade Major of the 85th Brigade at the outset of a difficult and confusing situation handicapped the troops very seriously. Throughout the operation the great difficulty was the movement of troops along the trenches. Parties arriving at the wrong places, and having to retrace their footsteps, found the places allotted to them occupied by other troops. This hampered and delayed all preparations for offensive movements. To keep the troops supplied with water, bombs and food, required the ceaseless employment of large fatigue parties. These parties took many hours to come and go and so the troops in reserve got little rest.

On this day, the 2nd Battalion had received its first issue of Lewis guns, in the use of which Lieutenant Cole and four men had some elementary instruction. The guns were taken into the line. Trenches, so full of dead, and so knocked about that they averaged only 18 inches in depth, were taken over from the Royal Fusiliers. Part of this line was a piece of the German second line, about 300 yards long and terminated at each end by a barricade, on the other side of which were Germans. The trenches were taken over under a fairly stiff barrage of shelling from guns, minenwerfer and hand guns. Many men had been lost through the machine gun fire on the way up.

In these circumstances, it is not surprising to learn that the battalion had hardly finished taking over, about 9.30 a.m. on the 1st, when it was found that the Germans were occupying a portion of the line allotted to the Northumberland Fusiliers on our right, near the point of junction of the Hohenzollern Redoubt and Big Willie. When this report reached Divisional HQ, howitzers were turned on to the point and on all com-

munication trenches leading to (the point and on all co) it from the
German side. The Northumberland Fusiliers attacked, but in spite of
every effort, did not succeed in turning the Germans out. Bombing continued all day, and towards evening our men began to establish some
superiority.

On the night of the 1st, an attack was ordered, on the 'Chord' by us,
and on Little Willie, on our left, by the Welsh. At first, it was thought
that we had captured the Chord, but daylight showed that we had not.
The fact is that the Chord was unrecognizeable even by day and still
more so by night among the maze of trenches and ditches with which this
area was covered. Although Major Roddy had reported the state of
affairs and advised making no further attack, there is no doubt that
brigade and superior headquarters entirely failed to realize the condition in and around the Redoubt, and ordered attack after attack in a
way that can only be described as ruthless and senseless.

The troops were bombed all day, and although there were officers and
men in this maze of trenches they were completely disorganized, and
mixed, mainly owing to the heavy loss in officers and senior non-com-
missioned officers. It was beyond the power of human endeavour to
collect and sort out the men for an organized attack. However, all through
the 2nd, in the most gallant way our men, Northumberland Fusiliers
and Welsh delivered individual bayonet and bomb attacks in their efforts
to dislodge the Germans and to comply with orders.

One of the many plucky deeds performed during the fighting was the
way Lieutenant Cole, Sergeant Remington and his section served their
Lewis gun. During an enemy attack, the gun, fouled with mud, jammed,
and the section were all killed, Lieutenant Cole persisted in his efforts
to clear the gun, but was himself, too, finally killed.

After nightfall, the Suffolk Regiment made an attack on Little Willie,
but was heavily repulsed. The only thanks they received was a demand
to rally and attack again. This was beyond human endurance and was
not done.

On 3rd October, the Germans attacked all along the line of the 84th
Brigade, but were repulsed except on the left where they gained a footing. Our men put up a wonderful resistance. All our bombers were
killed. A bayonet counter-attack, led by Major Roddy, was met with a
hail of bombs and driven back to the British front line. Brigade HQ
ordered fresh attacks but this was quite out of the question, having in
view the exhaustion of the individuals and the congestion in the trenches.
It was quite clear to anyone who visited the front line that further attacks
were not feasible, even by fresh troops, until the congestion of wounded

and dead had been overcome. Nevertheless, another attack was ordered and gallantly carried out by the East Yorkshire Regiment and one company of the KOYLI early on the 4th. This attack, too, failed, at great loss of life, and confirmed the judgment of Major Roddy which he had given in a report to Brigade HQ on the evening of the 1st.

Later in the morning, the Germans swung in a surprise attack on the left of the 84th Brigade, drove through the Welsh, and swept down on our men in their trenches. Our war diary says, 'The enemy broke through part of the trench occupied by the Welsh on our left flank and advanced with great rapidity, throwing hundreds of bombs, their bombers being supported by machine guns and riflemen. The attack came as a complete surprise.'

Our line was driven back till the Germans were held up by C Company of the Northumberland Fusiliers at their block at the end of Big Willie.

On the night of the 5th/6th October, the Brigade was relieved by the 2nd (Guards) Brigade. The relief took 13 hours of daylight, although ample time was given for reconnaissance by officers, the trenches cleared of all obstacles to movement, and all arrangements most carefully organised. This shows, in some measure, the impossibility of the demands made on men of the 28th Division during the previous five days.

Our casualties were very heavy. Six officers, Major A. Rowland Hill, Captain F. L. Lloyd, Lieutenants S. Cole, D. C. B. Brien, W. E. Hartley, and M. McGregor, and 43 men killed; 7 officers and 153 men wounded and two officers and 166 men missing, of whom none were ever recovered.

The survivors had all but reached the limit of human endurance. This phrase is often used, but it is, unfortunately, justified. The unpreparedness of England in 1914 threw in a handful of her willing servants a burden which demanded the most extreme exertions of which the human frame is capable. Their bodies were sustained by their spirit superior to all trials and dangers.

In this battle, the first of our New Army Battalions made their appearance under fire, the fith Battalion in the 58th Brigade of the 19th Division and the 11th Battalion in the 75th Brigade of the 25th Division.

The 58th Brigade, whose Brigade Major was Major H. S. Adair of The Regiment, attacked on 25th September against Rue D'Ouvert, North of Givenchy and reinforced the attack of the 9th Welch Regiment, but was held up by uncut wire and machine gun fire.

Captain Symons particularly distinguished himself in bringing in wounded from the wire during the night and three men won the DCM.

Letter from Sir William Hildreth

Thankyou for your letter of the 19th June about the Battle of Loos, in which I played a small part as Lieutenant in the 1st York and Lancaster Regiment.

I now have 60 diaries for each year since 1914 and the earlier ones are very difficult to read.

I have, however, copied the diary from Thursday, September 23rd, 1915 to Thursday, October 7th, when the Y and L marched away from that mismanaged episode.

If you want further information, I should be glad to see you most afternoons or early evenings if you will give me a ring.

I am surprised that you received so many as 120 replies. I thought most of us all would be dead by now; and it is reassuring to know that so many are alive.

The following is the diary of Sir William Hildreth (then Lieutenant Hildreth) from Thursday, September 23rd, 1915 – Thursday, October 7th

Thursday, September 23rd, 1915 All ready and left billet with the band at 8.0 and marched past the General in Bailleul Square. Went to O near Bailleul. Here men got a barn. Hollis and I a clean room, Lucas and Halcomb beds in a nearby cottage. HQ a long way off.

Friday, September 24th Started to rain. A long route march. Letters. Played cards and read at night.

Saturday, September 25th News from the front that some attack was in progress and that we might be wanted. Stand to, to move at short notice. Paid out, got to bed early and read some magazines. This was at a place through Bailleul called Outersheene.

Sunday, September 26th Woke at 4.30. Without breakfast or any drink, marched 12 miles through the brisk little town of M, and then on to R. Billetted here and got a splendid billet at an *estaminet*. Made friends with the girls there but marched off at 2 and went 3 miles and stopped, waiting. Heavy bombardment; all tired. Suddenly about turned and went back to R. Same billets. Washed, had tea and a very night. Heard our valises were lost. Had a splendid night in a good clean bed. Halcomb ill and saw the MO.

Monday, September 27th Marched off and got into buses. Grateful for a good night. Through Bethune. Lines of wounded; great excitement; through B to a field behind V which was being shelled heavily. Heard we were going to trenches but cancelled. Stayed in cold field and marched off to a field near firing line at 3 a.m.

Tuesday, September 28th Got some sort of breakfast; very cold and much shelling. Marched into a communication trench and passed heaps of wounded and dead lying on top. About turned into a reserve trench where it rained and got into dug outs.

Wednesday, September 29th Was sent to take up ammunition to the Hohenzollern Redoubt. Never saw such sights as on the way up. Walked over heaps and heaps of dead and got to the trench. Our men retired and Buffs charged into the trench in front. Bombs, Bombs, Bombs. Supported the charge and worked back to support trench. Lucas ordered us to fix bayonets. Suddenly came the order to charge. Got out and commenced to run. All quiet for 10 yards and then it started. Hail of bullets and bombs. Got across 200 yards and followed Captain into a trench. Ordered to go right. Poor Hollis shot under the armpit and I was called back to see Lucas shot in the leg. Left several men on top. Saw Lucas off and worked my way along the trench and got to a corner with about 40 men. Thought I was cut off. Gathered about 50 men and met Turnberry with some other men. Drenched through and bitterly cold and tired. Halcomb was missing. Urgent messages for help wanted. Sent NCO and 20 men to reinforce Turnberry and 15 to help A Company who were apparently cut off. Finally went across the top and saw Major of the Buffs. He said help no use without bombs. Brought the 15 back and waited about, sent off report to Headquarters as to where I was and reported casualties. Stayed in trench where I was and kept in touch with flanks. Never so cold before or so wet. Managed to gather about 70 altogether. What a day!

Thursday, September 30th After the coldest night we ever spent we got moving. Halcomb and Sergeant Taylor turned up, finally formed about 100 of the Company. Cleared dead out of the trench, cleaned up and read letters, most welcome parcel had come with cake, quiet day, thank the Lord and at night were relieved. Felt cold and quite done up. Going out, never felt worse or more tired. Got out and sat on the dump with Cresswell, pouring with rain. Heard that Roberts and Foster and Howard and Cole were dead. Ellison, Buckley, Ashton and Adsetts were wounded. Sat on the dump feeling like nothing on earth. Manned a trench for the night, got some straw but never got warm once.

Friday, October 1st Sunny but cold, letters from home, Cissy and Daisy etc., Heard with deepest sorrow that Chippey (Adsetts) was dead. Spent an hour of misery. At night went out and spent an hour in a field that was being shelled. Then marched to Cambrin. No tea, no billet. Had to find them. Slept with D Company.

Saturday, October 2nd Sunny but cold. Spent early part cleaning up.

Got Wales to take on my cook as servant and p.m. Went through wounded and killed officers' kits – a sad service. Went through poor little Chippey's and wrote down the Will, remembered rugs etc., kept his Panatellas which he had said were for us both. At night for first time managed to get warm and had an excellent dinner. Wrote Daisy, Cissie, Adsetts' Father and Professor Wynne. Got down in straw. Wales takes over A Company.

Sunday, October 3rd Ordered to move at 11 a.m. postponed till 1 got some letters off. Marched through Vermelles and halted in the road. Germans shelling trenches hard with coal-boxes. Marched up to a support line and were told the Redoubt was lost. King's Own and East Yorks were going to attack and we were to support. Big dug-out here so Halcomb and I sat and waited.

Monday, October 4th It started, never heard such rapid fire. No artillery. Wounded pour back from the firing line and we learn the attack was not successful. We move up with the next trench and sit in the wet all day. At night Adjutant sends us into the firing line which has to be cleaned up and wire put out. Welcome letter from home and a parcel from good old Peter Davies. Confectionery came in a treat at midnight.

Thursday, October 5th Shelling the Redoubt all day and night. At night supposed to be relieved. Icy cold and waited all night. Relief arrived at 6 next morning and we got out at 8 o'clock.

Wednesday, October 6th Got back to Annequin and got the same billets. Cleaned up and fed and at 1.30 marched away. Halcomb rode ahead to find a place for tea and I had the Company. Marched through Bethune and halted in a field for tea. Marched away and arrived at G. Men in a theatre and we had beds in an *estaminet*.

Thursday, October 7th Cullen arrived and took over the Company from Halcomb. Very smart appearance. Above all our valises arrived.

13

9th (Scottish) Division

Letter from Mrs P. J. Williams
My father was the Sergeant Major of the 2nd Battalion of Gordon High-landers. He wrote to my mother on the 24th September, also to her brother. His letters prove so much of how the soldier of the day put his regiment first, family second, (or so it seemed). He describes his feelings as he knows he must be killed. He says his regiment was chosen to 'go over the top' leading the battle and what an honour it was and though afraid, he hopes he won't let the Regiment down, etc.

He was killed. A letter (which I read, but have not got) was written to my mother by his commanding officer, a Captain Miller. He tells her that he, Dad! survived the battle. He was taking the roll call at 6 p.m. (25th) when a sniper's bullet hit him in the knee, and as he fell, he was hit in the head and killed.

Account by Captain Wyllie, Royal Scots Fusiliers (written in 1952) sent in by *G. P. Keef*
The 15th September 1915, found the regiment at Bethune in which town we arrived after an all-night march of 27 miles. I am afraid I am not absolutely certain of the actual date as I have not my diary with me, but the date I give above will be approximately correct. In the account which follows I have to rely entirely on my memory as none of the details I am about to commit to paper have ever been recorded. For years after these events, there were many blanks in the sequence of happenings which my memory has only been able to fill in the course of time and in this I have been assisted occasionally by accounts from one or two men from the platoons who were themselves in the battle. These accounts although not always relevant to this narrative, nevertheless, served to jog my memory and piece together the events which took place as I actually saw them, and although I am well aware that many details are being left out through defects in my memory, I feel that the lapse of 37 years has helped to co-ordinate my recording of events rather than the reverse.

The regiment was commanded by Colonel H. H. Northey with Captain Purvis as Adjutant. I do not remember who commanded A coy as Major Goodeve had been killed not long before, in fact I think he had been 2nd in command. Captain Turnbull commanded B coy, Captain Brodie C coy and Captain Robertson commanded D coy.

With regard to the march, we had all had about enough of it by the time we marched into billets the next morning, and I well remember that when dawn broke I noticed one of the men in the platoon in front of mine, marching in his stocking soles through which blood oozed at the heels, particularly one foot. The man had his boots slung round his neck by the laces. I have no doubt that there were others in the regiment in the same condition. The march was conducted in the usual manner, i.e. ten minutes halt every hour, but we had one hour's halt half way through the night. It was obvious that the whole division (9th) was on the march. During the halt for one hour, we happened to halt in the middle of a village and I remember finding the scraper at a cottage door a convenient gadget on which to rest my head as I lay partly on the step and partly on the road.

Towards the end of the march and during the usual ten minutes halt, we did not sit down, but continued to stand. This kept the blood from forming in the blisters on our feet and greatly reduced the pain in our feet when we started on the march again. I do not remember anyone falling out, but the men were very tired towards the end and several subalterns were carrying rifles to help some men along and just at the end I found myself with three, and I have no doubt that others had the same.

This march, however, was not without its amusing incidents, one of which I must recount before I leave this subject. Lieutenant Boyle (The Hon Alan) commanding No 12, Platoon, developed an attack of malaria not long after the march started. Captain Brodie kindly lent Boyle his horse and he happened to be riding directly in front of me. I could see by the way that Boyle was gently swaying in his saddle, he was fast asleep. We were marching through a small market town at the time where, I suspect, the Square was situated some distance off the line of march. I rather think the square in question contained the usual drinking trough and it was this the horse probably smelt, for it started to leave the column carrying the sleeping Boyle on its back. I was greatly amused and made no attempt to interfere. An NCO, however, stepped out of the column and led the animal back. Boyle was much amused when I told him about the incident the next morning.

The regiment had been in billets in Bethune several times before, and

I was lucky enough to get my old billet again which was clean and comfortable. The woman who owned the house had a son who was a prisoner of war in Germany and I was able to give her a few cigarettes to send to her son – which pleased her greatly.

The Line was not very far north of Bethune and the roar of the guns could be plainly heard from the town. Now and again an 18 pr gun would be brought in for repair having received a direct hit, and then there was the continual passage of ammunition columns and other supplies in addition to troops of various branches of the Service. Above the continual drum fire of the 18 pr batteries, could be heard the deeper note of the heavier calibre guns – right up to the massive 15 in. hows. All these signs and many others made it quite clear that a colossal battle was shortly to begin although we had no idea of the exact date of the attack. In actual fact, it was to be the biggest battle ever recorded in history up to that date. Needless to say, there were many conferences at Battalion HQ and there was a great deal of detailed information which each officer had to memorise.

In addition to this there was a good deal of detail which had to be jotted down with regard to signals etc and there was also an issue of the latest map showing the enemy lines and strong points, taken by air reconnaissance, relative to our frontage.

Over and above all this, platoon training continued as usual, starting with running parades by individual subs every morning before breakfast. About two or three days before we went into the line, at least one Sub from each company (two in the case of C Coy) were taken from their Companies and sent to the Base to bring reinforcements up after the battle. One of these was Boyle who commanded No 12 Platoon C Company. (I had No 11 Platoon C Company) I will never forget the look of acute disappointment on Boyle's face when he saw his name in Battalion Orders. He was so upset that on leaving the tobacco factory, where the men were billeted, he started walking back to the Mess in the wrong direction and I had to run after him and bring him back. I was secretly glad that he had been detailed as he was a charming fellow and I felt at least this would be the means of him living a little longer than the rest of us. Boyle, as the Directory states, is still alive after the most amazing adventures which took him to Egypt, among other places, after France.

About two nights before we marched out of Bethune, a division of Kitchener's Army (2nd Army) (we were incidentally the first division of Kitchener's 1st Army) marched through to go straight into the line at dawn. I could see that the men were all very exhausted and at the time would be of little use in a fight. I heard long afterwards that there had been a change of generals at the last moment and about three divisions had been overlooked and when they were wanted in the scheme of things they were thirty miles further back than they should have been. I think I am correct in stating that this is referred to in the book Peter Jackson, *Cigar Merchant*. The man who wrote that book must have been in one of these three divisions.

Meanwhile the drumfire continued night and day and as far as the eye could reach the horizon was one incessant glow of flickering light like summer lightning.

Now the 9th Division, so far as Infantry was concerned, comprised three Brigades, 26th all Highland, 27th half Highland and half Lowland, and the 28th which was all Lowland. The 6th Royal Scots Fusiliers were in the 27th Brigade which consisted of the 10th Argylls, 6th Royal Scots Fusiliers and the 11th and 12th Royal Scots. There was, I think, a Pioneer Battalion also making up the Brigade the 9th Gordons, but they were probably divisional troops.

If I remember correctly, the Division moved up into the Line early in the night before the attack and regiments had each approx 25 officers and 900 men including other ranks. The 26th and 28th were the attacking brigades while we in the 27th were in reserve and went forward after the attack some hours later. The night before the attack was spent in making certain that we had all our information correct and checking rations, water, ammunition etc etc and finally issuing rum. By this time we had discarded all pretence at using trenches and just worked in the open. The attacking brigades went over at dawn at which time the gunfire reached a crescendo and the din was terrific. I could see the German wire torn from their steel posts and it lay like straw on the ground. (I must mention here that there were notable instances where this was not so and the taking of the line a costly business.)

The Battalion was moved forward in front of the 18 pr guns which at this part were lined along a slightly sunken road. The guns could not have been more than about one hundred yards behind us and I really felt that had I lifted my head, my balmoral would have been torn off. I do not remember how we were able to get into this position, I think the guns must have ceased fire to let us out in front. I remember that the guns were lined gun wheel to gun wheel, with a gap of about one gun width separating individual batteries. I think one gun in each battery was kept silent in succession to allow it to cool. I also remember a small stream near where we were and from this the gun crews were collecting buckets of water which they were throwing over the gun barrels to cool them, which, I should have thought, was extremely bad for the gun! The men were stripped to the waist and were streaming with perspiration and, no doubt, very thirsty. It was an extraordinary sight to see so many guns as far as one could see on each side, recoiling under the force of the charge as often as a shell could be rammed into the breech. At this stage, I think the guns were concentrating on the German Front line.

Much to my relief, we moved forward into what was our original front line trenches and it was from these trenches that we launched a gas attack before the brigades went over. The wind was light and variable and the gas got half way towards the German line and then came back on to us. The attacking lines were through it too quickly for it to do them any real harm except in one or two cases. One battalion was so badly gassed that only one platoon attacked the German line, the rest being incapable of climbing onto the parapet. I met the sub commanding this platoon in Salonica, some years after. Needless to say his platoon was wiped out, he getting a bullet through his right lung before he had gone a few yards.

It was here that Piper Laidlaw won his VC by marching up and down on the top of the parapet while the entire German Army on his front fired at him. (KOSB) He had every drone shot off his pipes and the bag punctured in several places. It was not very long ago that I saw his death in the papers. Incidentally, it was not long ago that I saw the death of Bugler Dunn, VC of the South African War, but I forget at the moment the actual battle in which he won it though I well remember the account of the incident.

The trench which we occupied was stocked with gas cylinders and there were a number of dead and wounded lying in the bottom. We had, by this time, put on our gas masks as a precautionary measure, but found that this was not necessary after some time had elapsed. We soon had all the wounded out of the trench and put on the top outside to be clear of any gas which might be lying in the foot of the trench. By this time the guns had ceased all except the heavier calibres, but this was because the attacking line had gone beyond the objective on which they had been firing.

From our new position we watched the 18 pdr batteries galloping up the Hulloch Road, which was situated on our right. The guns wheeled round in circles at full gallop and took up positions in the open, the guns coming into action almost as soon as the gun trails hit the ground. I do not remember how many batteries were involved, but it was a wonderful sight to see these guns coming into action and also the gun limbers galloping down the road for more ammunition.

Further to the right, I could see squadrons of cavalry massed in a depression in the ground, waiting for the order to advance and exploit any break-through – which never came. By this time a constant stream of wounded passed through our lines from whom the men in the regiment eagerly enquired 'news of battle.' The information we received was at times conflicting and, of course, confined to what each wounded man could see on his immediate front. The ground in front of us was strewn with dead and wounded as the attacking line lost considerably in the advance. It says a great deal for the troops in the German line who put up such a fierce resistance while being subjected to such a terrific barrage. I must here mention that there was little or no opposition from the German batteries and I heard later that the Huns had withdrawn nearly all their guns as soon as the attack started. They, of course, knew all about the attack before it was actually launched.

It was, I think, about 4 p.m. in the afternoon that the battalion was ordered to advance. We came out of the trench line (the original front British trenches), but received little opposition, and that from our extreme left and also from the top of Fosse 8 which was a large slag heap at the top of which there appeared to be a mine shaft with a shed round it. We took no notice of this firing and the Battalion advanced in column of half companies, D Company leading. I was ordered forward with the first half of C Company followed by Captain Brodie, Lieutenant Eales-White and Lieutenant Peck, with the second half. The other companies followed on in the same formation. It was just before we advanced that we sustained a few casualties which included Lieutenant Staples killed.

It is at this juncture that I have to record a very serious blunder for which I was solely responsible and which probably had a marked effect on the situation two days later and resulted in heavy casualties. It appears that certain men were given boxes of Mills bombs to carry in addition to their full equipment. I came across one of these men in the trench before we went over and he reported to me that the boxes were heavy (which was true) and that he could not carry them very much further. I ordered him to carry the box as far as he could, which I remember was done. What I should have done was to have the bombs taken out and distributed among the men and taken one or two myself. I had one or two already in my pack and could quite easily have taken more. Two days later, we ran short of bombs and these would have been invaluable. To this day I can't think what I was thinking about to let an opportunity of this sort go.

We advanced for about half a mile in columns of half companies, the Colonel with the second half of C Company. Just at this juncture, the

Colonel passed the word up to halt in front. I intercepted this message and ran back to the Colonel and reported that the Brigadier was leading the first half of D Company ahead. The Colonel evidently did not know this when he ordered the Battalion to halt. It was shortly after this that the Brigadier halted the regiment and, so far as I remember, we formed up battalion in line just as darkness was falling. I might here mention that all the towers, Church steeples and other landmarks behind the German lines and which we were using as guides to marching, were promptly blown up by the Huns.

As darkness fell, various fires in the villages behind the German lines began to show as a red glow in the sky and this was added to by the flicker of intermittent gun fire. At this juncture it began to rain, a fine drizzle. This made the sky overcast and increased the blackness of the night. Our position was about ¾ mile in front of our original front line and well beyond the German line of trenches, which were badly battered. However, there seemed to be few German dead about so I take it they must have withdrawn most of their troops when the advance began. It was very quiet by this time and the only sound in evidence was the thud of long range bullets which were falling in considerable numbers and which were responsible for a number of casualties.

Some thoughtful person at home had sent me out a tin of frozen methylated spirits – so arranged that it formed a stove on which water could be boiled. By arranging my overcoat very carefully, I was able, with the help of my servant, to light this stove and make some tea for a few of the wounded of whom a considerable number lay about. Long range bullets continued to fall throughout the night and it was just about this time that it was reported to me that my Platoon Sergeant had been hit. I went along to him and found that a bullet had passed through his spine – cutting the spinal cord. He was finished, poor devil, and I felt very bitter at such a thing happening as there was nothing I could do to help him. I remained with him as long as I could and I promised to write to his wife – which I was subsequently able to do and got a very plucky letter back, which I still have in my records. The man himself was first class and absolutely reliable. This was Sergeant Gibson and he was a locomotive fireman on the London & North Western Railway. The same night two more good men were killed, Corporal Trig and Private Horne, both shot through the head. There were several more, but I can not remember their names. I can remember the Brigadier passing me in the darkness going on and speaking to Captain Brodie, and then going on towards the direction from which we had advanced, so far as I could tell. I mention this because later on in the night, he was taken prisoner with the whole of his staff in a small quarry quite near our position although I was not to know this until a long time afterwards. He returned after the war much to my relief – the reason for my anxiety I will explain later.

As the night wore on, I was conscious of sounds of movement some distance on our right flank, but could not make out quite what was causing it and I dare not open fire in case it was some of our own troops.

Later in the night, while happening to be looking towards our lines, I noticed a considerable number of troops rushing towards our original lines. They were well to our right rear and I would not have been able to see them at all had they not been silhouetted against a streak of pale sky. By their attitude I was certain they were Huns, but I could do nothing about it as they were too far off. I, however, reported the incident to Captain Brodie as a matter of form.

It was just about this time that I realised my batman Jones was missing. He went off to give a wounded man a drink who he said was quite near and I never saw him again. I felt it too risky to send any men out into the darkness to look for him in case they walked into a trap, as it was some-time before I woke up to the fact he was not there. Meanwhile a steady stream of wounded continued to pass through our line, probably from the attacking line, and those who felt they could walk further, continued on in the darkness in the direction of our original lines. The rain continued, but not very heavily and the men continued to carry great coats in their packs as it was not deemed wet enough to justify wearing them, especially as the night was not very cold.

About half an hour after I had seen what I thought looked like Huns in the distance, I heard more movement in the darkness, but this time it was directly behind the right half of the Company and where I happened to be standing. I peered into the darkness, but for a while I could see nothing, then I was able to make out very faintly a dark mass of people which was moving towards us and then came to a halt. I estimate they could not have been more than seventy five yards away. It was quite obvious that whoever they were, they were just as uncertain of us as we were of them. Complete silence now reigned.

I thought of the reserves we had been told to expect and I thought of the mysterious figures I had seen in the distance and resolved to take no chances. I called out into the darkness, but not committing myself to any language; the call was answered in German. I have quite forgotten to mention that the moment I became aware that a body of men were advancing towards us, I immediately took every other man out of the line, faced him about, and this made a firing line of about thirty men, heel to heel with a space of about two yards between the lines. This allowed me room to walk about without falling over men in the darkness. This was quite easy as the men, who were all in the prone position, heard the advancing column as soon as I did and being trained, they expected something of this sort to happen. All I had to do, therefore, was to walk along the Line, touch every other man on the heel and tell him in an undertone to get up, face about and keep quiet.

The whole manoeuvre was carried out with hardly a sound. The men were already in position when the German gave the position away. I at once ordered rapid fire. There was a blinding flash from the rifles which made it quite impossible for me to see anything, and after each man had fired about four rounds, I ordered the cease fire. For some little time I was completely blind and could not form an opinion as to the effects of my fire so it was several minutes before I was satisfied that the black mass I had seen originally was no longer there.

Just then, I had to dash off to Captain Brodie who was calling me for the purpose of finding out what this sudden burst of firing was about. When I returned to my position and was satisfied that there was no longer any danger, I withdrew the men and put them back into the line as it was in this latter direction our real danger lay in spite of the fact that our attacking lines were somewhere ahead of our position. I was never able to investigate the result of the fire myself as just then, a Hun walked right into the middle of us with his rifle slung on his shoulder. I got Captain Brodie to see him and then handed him over to a Sergeant for safe keeping. The Sergeant subsequently shot him under the pretext that he tried to escape, but I was very doubtful and was furious with the Sergeant, but could say nothing as I lacked evidence to the contrary.

I think it was just then that I heard one of the men in the line near me say 'Retire', and immediately every man started to get up on his feet. I heard the movement and ordered the men down again. I am certain I know who it was who tried to cause a stampede, but here again I had no evidence. I mentioned that I never discovered what had actually happened when I opened fire, but five years afterwards, I met a man in the street in Glasgow who stopped me and asked me if I was Mr Wyllie, he asked me if I remembered the night I opened fire etc and then said he was one of the men I took out of the line and while I was away talking to Captain Brodie, he crawled forward and counted eighty-seven men dead in the grass. I well remember the look of almost savage glee in his face and he was almost dancing with joy when he recounted the incident. I know quite well why he had said nothing before because he knew he had no business to crawl forward without permission.

I was quite glad to hear the sequel of this episode and have the question as to who they were finally settled. You can imagine how thankful I was, therefore, when I heard that Brigadier Bruce was a prisoner in Germany and, therefore, had not been in the party of Huns who walked into the rear of C Company. There were from time to time, various bursts of firing at different parts of our Line, but I do not know any details. The Medical Officer was with us, Dr Dunbar, and he did what he could for the wounded.

Sometime before dawn we were ordered to withdraw and Captain Brodie ordered me to cover the withdrawal of the Company and bring back the wounded. I had by this time about forty-five men unwounded and several with slight wounds. I gave the Company about five minutes start and then attempted to carry out my orders. It was quite evident that bands of Huns were roaming about more or less all around us and I had to have flankers out as well as one or two bringing up the rear. These men had to be quite close to the main body of the platoon, otherwise I would have lost them in the dark. I also knew there was a quarry slightly to the left of our direction and I had to be careful not to fall into that. I have no doubt now that it was the quarry in which the Brigadier had been taken prisoner earlier in the night with all his staff. I soon found that it was quite impossible to carry out the part of my orders which related to the wounded and to my everlasting regret, I had to leave them behind. It was quite the worst decision I had to make ever, I had no stretchers or any other means of carrying wounded and at the time I had to decide whether I dare risk my small force by using them to carry wounded as best they could and gamble on my chances of getting through or retain the force as a fighting unit. I will never know the answer to this as we moved much faster as a fighting unit and kept more or less on the tail of the Company. I was eventually greatly relieved to see the names of one or two men who I left behind that night – in the German Casualty list, also the death of my Sergeant who I knew could not have lived, but I felt dreadful at leaving him behind and felt I had betrayed him.

Dawn on the 27th was breaking as I rejoined C Company and, incidentally, the rest of the battalion and once again we were near our original front line from which we made our advance. As the light grew stronger, we were subjected to a certain amount of fire from the top of Fosse 8 to which I have previously referred. The range was about a thousand yards, but we took no notice and I do not remember hearing that anyone had been hit. I was quite thankful to get into a position where we were not surrounded, once more. Sometime later on, we were withdrawn, to a position inside a large quarry, the walls of which had been honeycombed with dugouts by the Germans. Tnis quarry was inside the original German defence line system. When dawn broke we found that the ground on which we had halted was strewn with dead and wounded – some of the wounded I recognised, having seen them there when we went over the day before.

I was very glad to get into some form of shelter as the men were looking very much the worse for wear. We called the roll and the result was shattering to say the least of it as I had little more than half my platoon left, and so far as I could see, other platoons were no better. Rifles were cleaned and examined, but it was a ghastly parade and I am afraid I could not see well enough to know whether a rifle was clean or not. We, must have got a little sleep here and also some food and water, but it was not for long for, about four hours later, we were suddenly called up again and put into one of the old German trenches to the left of our position and about five hundred yards due south of the big slag heap which now towered up above us. These trenches had been occupied by battalions of the 2nd Army who were forced marched through Bethune a few days before, I heard afterwards that their first line transport had been parked during the night on the Hulloch road and when dawn broke it was pounded to bits by the German guns and completely destroyed. The regiment that had occupied the trenches in which we now found ourselves, had been moved forward into the German trenches which ran close along the steep sides of Fosse 8 and which were very deep and, consequently, it was impossible to ascertain what was going on in them. The trenches in which we were, had been well pounded by shell fire by our guns and consequently were now more like broad ditches than trenches.

I remember standing in a trench, a short portion of which had escaped our terrific bombardment to a greater extent than the rest and, out of a small hole in the wall of the trench, which I would never have noticed had the movement not attracted my eye, peeped a little field mouse. It had obviously been the pet of some German soldier who had been located in this trench for some little time as there was a distinct track along a narrow ledge leading from the hole. I put my finger forward and the mouse approached and let me stroke its neck and chin and as the little creature had obviously been a long time without food and water, I gave it a nibble from one of my biscuits and a drink of water from the tip of my finger which I dipped into my water bottle. It would seem that Hun and British were friends alike to field mice and I trust that this should be true.

The question now arose as to what was going on in the trenches at the foot of Fosse 8. Were the trenches re-occupied by the Huns, or were they still held by what might be left of the British battalions which had originally occupied them? I may mention that in the middle of all this scene, batches of Huns who had been hiding in various pockets, now came out with their hands up. Captain Brodie now ordered me to go forward into the front trench system and find out what had happened. I took six men with me and we advanced in extended order at a walk. We were much too tired to go forward at any faster pace.

The top of Fosse 8 was still an efficient German OP and I had no sooner started than a heavy shell fire opened up from the German guns. They were using shrapnel, but the range was just out as the shells were bursting just over our heads while the shrapnel itself went into the ground behind us, doing no harm although making a loud noise. I had about 350 yds to go and lay down twice in this distance for a rest.

As soon as I got up the guns started again, but retained the same error with true German precision. I soon slipped into a communication trench and proceeded cautiously up this. The Huns were watching me as they followed me all along the trench with shrapnel which burst just above us, but doing no harm. At this stage, I met an officer from an English battalion who overtook me and who, I believe, belonged to the regiment holding the deep trench in front. He seemed quite certain that some of his regiment was still in front and I felt much safer when he went on ahead of me while I followed closely in his rear.

When we reached the T head I found that his surmise was correct, but unfortunately, I have forgotten which regiment it was. As soon as I realized that all was well, I proceeded back down the trench, which I now began to notice was lined more or less by German dug-outs with sacks over the fronts of the doorways. The Huns were still intent in trying to bag our little force and as soon as my position in the trench permitted, restarted a heavy fire, again with shrapnel – perfectly timed, but once again they drew a blank.

The rain had ceased falling about an hour before dawn and we were gradually drying. I don't seem to remember what happened immediately after my return from the forward German trench, for the rest of the day, but in all probability we were again withdrawn to the quarry where we got some badly needed sleep and fresh supplies of ammunition. As darkness came on that night, however, we were on the move again and were in the line further to the right of Fosse 8 with the 10th Argylls in trenches in front of us. For some mysterious reason, a stampede started in the Argylls, and they came tearing along the trench – past a junction at which I was standing. I made no attempt to stop them and it was not long before they all came back looking very shame-faced, which I could not fail to notice even in the dark.

Before darkness fell, I remember a half-hearted attempt to drive the Huns off the top of Fosse 8, by a small party of Highlanders. The Huns came out of their lair on the top and there were casualties on both sides and the dead and wounded lay on the steep slopes of the Fosse, but little resulted from this as it lacked drive on our part. A nest of machine guns hidden in this mine head was going to cost us dearly the next day. Having foiled the attempt to drive them out, the Huns disappeared into the wheel house while our people returned to the trenches at the bottom of the Fosse.

Shortly after dark, we advanced in much the same direction as we had done the night before, but in this case Captain Brodie led the leading half of the Company while I brought up the 2nd half behind. If I remember correctly, Lieutenant Eales White and Lieutenant Peck, were with their own platoons and went with Captain Brodie. I can remember earlier on in the night, being approached by an NCO if I would allow two of my men to carry a wounded man – who was a mutual friend of the two men – to a dressing station which was quite near in some trenches roughly about 500 yards away. I knew who the man was as I had seen him lying there about thirty hours earlier. I told the NCO to parade the men to have a look at them and when they arrived I saw that they were reliable men and I thought they could be trusted.

Such a request was an unheard of thing in the middle of a battle – allowing two fit men to leave the line to carry a wounded man to a dressing station – was quite outside the rules which are supposed to govern warfare. I pondered over this for some time and finally consented, but I spoke to each man separately and made him give me a promise that they would be away as short a time as possible and would each in turn come to me personally and report their return. This they did, and I told the NCO they could proceed. I soon forgot all about this incident and the fact that as an officer I had no right to allow such a thing to happen. It was some $\frac{3}{4}$ hour later that a dark figure loomed up through the darkness and reported that he was one of the men who had helped to carry the wounded man away, and then a few minutes later, another figure appeared to report its return also very much to my relief. I also remember, during the hours of daylight which preceded this incident, stopping a private from some Scottish Regiment (Lowland) who seemed to walk out of the blue and was proceeding through our lines.

This man told me that he was going to look for some help to get his officer back to a dressing station as he had got him in a dugout in the village of Hulluch, which had been over-run by our attacking waves. The man informed me that there had been a wounded German officer in the other bunk in the dugout, but he had killed the German officer before he went off for help in case he did any harm to his officer, while he, the private was away.

I pointed out to this man that such an act greatly reduced his officer's chances of survival should the Germans enter the dugout during his absence. I could see that this point of view had not occurred to this man before as his face fell when I said it. I told him that, much as I should like to have done so, I was quite unable to send any men to help him to get his officer away – which, of course, he quite understood. He then proceeded on his way and I never saw him again. I have often wondered who the officer was and how he fared – just as I have wondered about so many things which happened during these days, as the years go by.

As I was relating, we were on the move again in much the same direction as on the night before, but we did not hold this direction long, and after going for about half a mile, we changed direction left and proceeded in a westerly direction thus we had Fosse 8 on our left and the German Hohenzollern Redoubt on our left also, as it lay roughly, so far as I can remember, East of Fosse 8 and quite near to it. I must explain that this redoubt consisted of a maze of trenches packed with strong points in the shape of machine guns, trench mortars, bombing posts and arrangements for hurriedly blocking up the trenches at various points and defending them against an enemy who had penetrated the trench system. It was all at ground level and a very level and a very formidable nut to crack. It had been cracked however, as it was more or less clear of German troops when we skirted it in the dark on the night of the 26th/27th. I make this statement with reserve as it has been prompted by the fact that we were not fired on as we passed.

We moved forward until we arrived at a German trench called Little Willie on our maps. This trench was actually a long German drain trench, at least $\frac{3}{4}$ mile in length. It was dead straight and about 2 ft 6 in deep and ran from the trench system around Fosse 8 almost due North, but it curved sharply East at its North end where it seemed to have joined another trench system. At this point, there was another branch of this trench running due west and this probably connected up with some more trenches. When we arrived at this drain trench, which was slightly muddy, but no water in it, the Regiment halted and occupied this trench. This placed the Fosse 8 about 1,000 yards on our left rear, estimating from where I was stationed which was about the centre of the Regiment.

The right flank of the Battalion was completely in the air*, i.e. D Coy. Next to D came C Coy, and then the other two Coys. On the left of us were the 10th Argylls and next to them were probably the 11th and 12th Royal Scots, all regiments now reduced to what was probably half their strength. The drain trench continued past and very close to the slope of Fosse 8. With regard to the strength of the Royal Scots, they must have been reduced to much less than half as one of these battalions was entirely gassed except for one platoon, as I have already indicated. Although we were not affected by the gas visibly, most of us suffered from the after effects and I remember it took from 1915 to 1928 before I could definitely say I was clear of gas. The nearest trenches to the rear of our position were those fringing the Hollenzollern Redoubt and my map gave those as 500 yards. These were occupied by British troops.

The men were very tired and, on arriving at this trench, they soon fell asleep. This was quite easy as all they had to do was to stand in the trench and lie forward over the ground. There were only a few hours before dawn and as I had posted no sentry, I decided to do the watching myself. At the faintest sign of dawn, I woke the platoon up and had the men cleaning rifles – which they badly needed. As the daylight strengthened, I searched the ground in front, but there was nothing to be seen. The ground was dead flat for at least five hundred yards and then this was broken by a line of what looked like hedge in which were a line of poplars so typical of the roads in France. Behind that again, a Church tower stood and this might have been on this road side or at least not very far back from it.

The men had hardly been working on their rifles for more than a few minutes than the Huns opened up with a gun of about 11 in. calibre, and shell after shell continued to hurtle into the slopes of Fosse 8, raising large clouds of coal dust. I knew that the Fosse was occupied by the Huns at the top, and I was certain that the German gunner would know it also and I was completely at a loss to discover what this manoeuvre could mean, but I knew it meant something and, therefore, I was uneasy. In spite of the noise from the shelling, the Companies on my right and left continued to sleep and as there was no sign of movement in any direction, I saw no occasion to wake them. I thought of gas, but this did not answer as the dust was drifting in a great cloud towards the east from where the Huns might come, although they were just as likely to advance from the north – which would be in the nature of a flank attack. I remember standing up on the trench while in the process of puzzling out the reason for this shelling, and there were some Huns up in the church

*Meaning separated from any other unit and thus exposed to flank attack.

tower, to which I have referred, who were shooting at me. I was the only person that they could see and although I did not know it at the time, it was very important to them that I should not stand on that trench.

They fired about twenty rounds, some bullets coming in very close, but none actually hit me, finally they ceased firing as I gave no indication that I heard their bullets going into the ground at my feet. Their shooting was good at that extreme range. The ground was damp from recent rain, and, therefore, there was no evidence from the bullets going into the ground.

I forgot to mention that the night before Lieutenant Eales White was shot through the hand, but had it bound up and continued to serve with the Regiment. The sleepiest man in my platoon was just finishing the cleaning of his rifle and I was still standing on the trench, when a peculiar sound caught my ears. I can't describe this sound and it was not like anything I had heard before. I looked up and, through the haze of coal dust, I saw a solid moving mass of field grey slowly approaching from the distant line of hedge in front. The whole landscape seemed to be on the move.

I gazed at this incredible sight for at least a second before I realized that it was a colossal German counter-attack and then I knew the reason for the shelling. I glanced to the right and left, but all but No 11 Platoon were still fast asleep. This was not important as the direction of the attack was aimed towards the trench junction at the foot of Fosse 8, and therefore, we would not get the full force of the attack. I jumped down into the trench to make sure if the platoon had a target and found I had one, but the sound of the advance was much fainter inside the trench than out.

My opening range was 500 yards and I opened up with a slow fire. At the sound of my firing, it was amazing how quickly the fire travelled along the line. As the attack approached, the men in the front poured out of the line and those behind stepped over them. I was sitting up on the trench at this stage in order to command a good view of what was going on and as I watched, I remember thinking of the wheat fields at home, the stalks of wheat trembling for a moment and then going down before the invisible knives of the reaper; and so it was here.

The Huns came forward at a walking pace, shoulder to shoulder, with their rifles at the trail. I soon brought my range down to the standard 200 yards as men are inclined to fire high in an attack anyway. The attacking force wore the spiked helmet and this indicated that they were reserves which had been rushed in as soon as they arrived. There must have been, at a conservative estimate, at least two thousand men in a line and there could not have been less than seven lines deep. I might mention that all junior officers were ordered to carry rifles and, of course, I had one, but I never used it at this stage as I was much too busy. As a drill movement this attack was superb, but it was just sheer slaughter.

It was not long before I could begin to see daylight between the legs of the lines that were still left and as soon as this became evident, I stopped firing and allowed the machine guns to finish the job. The supply of ammunition to a mobile force continually in action is one that is always a difficult problem and it was the ever present fear of running short of ammunition that prompted me to stop firing at the earliest possible moment. It was not long before the firing died out all along the line, but it continued longest away on my left in the direction of the Argylls as this was the point where the attack was the most concentrated. Finally – firing ceased altogether and then there was a deathly silence.

The ground in front was grazing land and the grass stood about six inches high. All the way across that wide open space as far as the line of hedges and trees which formed our horizon, was grey with the field grey of the dead. In some places they lay thicker than in others and in these the bodies lay higher than the grass. This may have been due to a change in the rate of traverse of the machine guns. In those days, we only had four Vickers Machine guns per battalion, but they were water cooled guns and could be kept firing, if need be, until the barrels wore out. They were heavy guns and it is a mystery to me how it was possible to cart these guns about at the rate we did and their ammunition supply in addition. I watched the ground for quite a while, but not a single body moved that I saw. Not long after firing had died away, I looked up and saw two Huns approaching my part of the trench – all that was left of that colossal attack. They were carrying their rifles at the trail as all the others had done.

As I look back on that scene now, I think they must have been drugged as indeed all the others probably were. My first impulse was to take them prisoner, but they still retained their rifles. I was in a straight trench where a round from one of these men could kill, possibly, six of my men. The men were only about thirty yards from the trench and I had to come to some decision quickly. What if they were shamming until they were close to the trench!! I decided to take no risks as I felt I owed it to the men. I turned to an NCO and ordered him to have these two men shot. The NCO turned to two privates and ordered them to shoot the men. Two rifles were slowly raised from the ground, there were two reports, and two men fell dead about twenty yards or so from the trench. A few jokes on this episode were made and that was the end. On the face of it, it was a cowardly thing to do and I hated having to do it and ever since I have thought of all the many other ways I could have done instead of shooting them, but every other way had an element of risk in theory though in actual fact when I look back on it now, there probably was little risk. I hated making that decision whether it was right or wrong, and would gladly have taken them prisoner. Captain Purvis, who spoke German fluently, could probably have extracted some valuable information from these two men had I taken them prisoner.

Just about this time, intermittent firing started from the Vickers gun in D Company away on the right flank – directed, evidently, at small bodies of Huns who were moving about in the far distance. I was a little uneasy at this as it served to locate our position in the far end of the drain trench and further more, it was not a good target for a machine gun at any time and even less so when ammunition must have been running short. The HQ were evidently uneasy themselves because messages were passed along the trench from time to time – 'Watch the right flank' and others having the same urgency.

By this time the roar of firing had begun to fade in our ears and, luckily for us the wind although light, was blowing towards the German lines and therefore blowing the cordite fumes away clear instead of all round us. When this happens it leaves a horrid taste in our mouths and makes the men terribly thirsty. It was quite evident that the HQ were fully expecting the Huns to launch a flank attack from the trench system at the far end of the drain trench, and this is exactly what happened. It must have been about 10 a.m. when the German bombing attack was launched from the trenches at the North end and a good deal of bombing took place at that end. I heard long after that Lieutenant Lord Stuart and Lieutenant Allan were both killed by one German bomb and in the process of the attack Captain Robertson commanding the company was knocked unconscious and later taken prisoner. This meant that there were no officers in D Company left to organise a counter attack against the Huns. One Sub – I don't remember who he was – came racing down along the top of the trench to see if he could obtain bombs from the Argylls as the various urgent messages passed down the trench had failed to produce any bombs except a few – which were not nearly enough.

It was at this point that I realized to the full my crass folly in failing to load up with bombs two nights earlier in that trench. The incident of the Sub applying to the Argylls for bombs is referred to by Ian Hay in his book, *The First Hundred Thousand*, in, I think, the last chapter. He also makes a reference to the Regiment and pays it tribute. Ian Hay was, at the time of that attack, Captain Beith in the 10th Argylls. He had been a master at Loretto. He was Lieutenant Beith when I knew him first when we were in the same mess together at Talavera barracks Aldershot in September 1914. A tall dark serious man who did not look as if he had a spark of humour in his make up, but this was far from the truth.

Things got from bad to worse on the right flank and even the supply of bombs from the Argylls failed to save the situation. The men started to crowd down the straight trench as they were completely exposed to the German attack in a straight trench and here another and unexpected development occurred which was inadvertently caused by me. I jumped up on the back of the trench with a view to doing something to stop the attack on the flank, when the men immediately jumped up on the top also, this movement was so rapid that it could not be checked as it formed an avenue of escape for the moment from the German fire at the far end for the time being.

This quickly resulted in what was left of D Company and half of C Company forming a crescent facing the German trench system which ran at right angles to the drain trench, thus – half the Regiment was now in the open, the other half which was further down the trench on my left, remained where they were. It immediately became apparent that the trench system at the far end of the drain trench was packed with Huns as large numbers of these came out of the trench under the impression that we were on the run. There was nothing we could do to retrieve the situation except get the men who were out in the open, down in the prone position and open fire on the advancing Huns. This I did and many Huns were shot down. I did manage to get a certain number of men back into the trench, but by this time the Huns had mounted a machine gun at the far end and several of these men were killed. I think it must have been this gun that killed Captain Brodie and wounded Captain Purvis, the Adjutant.

I could see the bullets from this gun kicking up the soil along the edge of the trench, but I could not see the gun itself. We were no sooner in the open than we were subjected to a very heavy fire as I could see the ground jumping all round me wherever I walked. The Huns in front had stopped advancing and were still being shot down, but there were many left and I felt that it was essential to take that trench. I ordered the fix bayonets and as the men were expecting such an order, the bayonets were out and on to the rifles in no time. The noise of firing was so great that I could not make either my voice or my whistle heard.

The moment I got up, however, every man was up on his feet in a moment as they knew what was coming. I stepped out of the line a few paces so that they could all see me and we advanced at a walk. Every man was in correct dressing and as I looked down the line I saw one long line of gleaming blades and a roar went up from every man in that line. The Huns gave ground as fast as we advanced and that was a heart breaking situation. We were under a murderous fire from some distant machine guns and although I did not know it at the time, under fire from the guns on the top of Fosse 8 as well. I remember searching the trees behind the German trenches, but could detect no sign of hidden guns. As we advanced, the men were pouring out of the line and I saw at once that there would be hardly anyone left if I continued the advance.

I brought the line to a halt and continued firing and was able to shoot down most of the Huns that were left in the open before they could get back to their trench. We were still under heavy fire, but the target was much less and consequently the losses were much less in the prone position. Before the advance with fixed bayonets, I happened to look up and saw a Hun standing aiming at me, I don't know how long he had been in this position, but I expected to feel the kick of his bullet at any moment as he was only about 250 yards away. I raised my rifle at a venture and pulled the trigger just as the butt touched my shoulders. Nothing happened for a moment, and then the Hun slowly lowered his rifle, it then dropped out of his hands onto the ground, and he pitched forward on his face and never made any attempt to break his fall with his hands. I will never forget the intense feeling of satisfaction at killing my one and only Hun, in distinction to my feelings when I ordered the other two Huns to be shot. Later, I left my rifle lying on the ground a few yards in front while I dashed out and brought in a wounded man who was masking the fire of the line. It was only a short distance, but the man was killed by another bullet while I carried him, this was the second time this had happened to me and in both cases the men were dead when I brought them in. 1 left my rifle out in front as I felt there was more lead flying out in front than where I was in the line, but I still had my revolver which I now drew out of the holster. We had shot down a large number of Huns and I began to wonder how many were still left in the trench. I don't seem to remember what was happening in our old trench a short distance on my left, but I remember seeing Lieutenant Eales-White, who had come out of the trench and who was behind me, get a bullet through his chest very close to the heart and Lieutenant Peck, whose platoon went forward in the bayonet charge with me and who had already been wounded, was also out in the open and was being propped up by his servant to see his platoon go forward, when he got another bullet right through his head. I believe he was somewhere behind me, but I only heard this long afterwards, from one of the rank and file.

I am afraid there are many gaps in the sequence of what happened during those fateful days, but they are gaps in my memory which I don't seem to be able to fill. I have heard some strange things from some of the survivors at different times – some I am afraid, relating to myself, many of which are quite impossible and therefore, quite untrue, but we all know what the rank and file are like in these matters. I now remember an incident that happened just before the time that the northern half of the drain trench was evacuated. The Vickers gun at the far end in D Company was knocked out by the Huns as they put a bullet through the side plates. I remember Lieutenant Galloway, racing up to this gun, along the top of the trench with spare side plates to see if he could do anything about it. I remember watching him pass me as I stood in the trench and expecting him to go down at any moment as the bullets were falling all round him like rain. Galloway, strange to relate is alive to this day. During the attack (earlier) he was stationed further down the trench with one of the other guns, where the counter attack was much more concentrated. All the men on the gun had been shot down by the machine gun next at the top of Fosse 8 – very much nearer to him than we were. I met one of the gun teams years after, and he related to me the following story, which I believe to be true :

This man stated that every man in the team had been knocked out except Mr Galloway and himself – (No 1) As the Huns approached the trench in a solid mass, Mr Galloway was acting No 1, and he was acting as No 2. Just as the Huns were within five yards of the trench, Mr Galloway got a No 2 stoppage and then the man said, 'I thought we were finished', but he went on to say that Mr Galloway cleared the stoppage at lightning speed, but by this time the nearest Hun had already passed the end of the muzzle. The officer drew his revolver and shot the Hun dead. He fell forward, striking the gun a glancing blow as he fell. The No 2 grabbed the Hun and pulled him head first down into the trench. Galloway then was able to give the gun a short traverse which cleared a gap round the gun, and then a longer and wider traverse, and the situation was saved.

On hearing such a story, many people would say that such a tale was all nonsense because they would ask why the Hun did not kick the gun over when he was so near, but those who know anything about war, know that in action the subconscious mind plays a big part and a man ceases to think normally and only carries out what he has been trained to do on the barrack square and field at home. I would here mention that I have seen men in action, carry out to the letter orders I have given them when I could see perfectly well from the vacant expression on their faces, they were not really conscious of what they were doing and, therefore, we get back to the saying – which I know to be a very true one – 'The soldier is made on the barrack square'. Therefore – this story, however fantastic it may seem – is, in the circumstances, quite feasible and, furthermore, the way the man told it carried conviction. If the officer has been taught to think in action successfully, then the combination is a good one.

The situation in regard to the right half of the Company, as it now stood was somewhat better, but was still causing me the greatest anxiety. We were lying in a long extended line right out in the open within about 350 yards from a trench manned by the enemy. This trench appeared to be a normal trench, probably at least 6 ft 6in deep with a firing step, until it made a junction with the shallow drain trench. I do not remember how far this trench extended Eastward, but I expect it connected up with another trench system further north and east. The Huns who had, by this time retreated into this trench, had no pack or heavy equipment and only about four bandoliers of ammunition slung across their chests and their rifles.

We, on the other hand, were loaded down with heavy equipment which, of course, was essential to our sustained advance into enemy territory. I noticed that the Huns, as soon as they jumped into their trench, disappeared from view altogether, but as soon as a man stood up to fire at our line he got a bullet through his head unless he was very quick about it. The situation would not have been too bad had we not been under fire from distant machine guns in addition. I was afraid to put any more men back into the drain trench on my left as I could see that the Huns still had a machine gun at the top end of this trench as the bullets from this gun tore up the ground along the top of this trench from time to time and must have caused heavy casualties in the left half of C Company – which still remained in the trench, although looking back on things now, I can't see they would have been any better off had they come out in the open where I had landed myself much against my will at that time.

I knew that if we remained where we were much longer, we would be completely wiped out, so I resolved to make another advance with the object of taking the German trench and just as I was about to order another advance, I got a bullet through my right hand which also hit the butt of my revolver and smashed it to pieces. The impact turned my wrist, forced the revolver out of my grasp, snapped the leather strap as if it had been thread and sent the revolver flying into the air – where it went to, I don't know as I never saw it again. A number of small pieces of ebonite from the butt went into my hand, but gave no trouble. Luckily, the bullet passed through my hand between the bones and, consequently, I hardly felt it at all. The blood oozed out of the wound for sometime after, and then ceased. The loss of my revolver was disconcerting, as I was now completely disarmed and the training I had undergone on the barrack square in Aldershot and elsewhere, had not embraced such a contingency.

I now returned to the question of another bayonet advance (I can't call it a charge) and was in the act of getting onto my feet and was actually rising off the ground when I got a bullet through my balmoral which flicked my scalp, but did not penetrate or draw blood. This made me sit down on the ground again in rather a hurry. In doing this, I automatically lay forward to present as small a target as possible – ie, in the prone position, and I had no sooner taken up this position than I got hit in the throat by a spent bullet which was a ricochet off the ground. The blow was very severe and at the impact I sprang at least a foot in the air. The wound was not a deep one as it only tore the throat open, but here again it did not bleed for very long, but it twisted the muscles of my neck rather badly and made the throat swell up to such an extent that I could hardly make a sound. I noticed that the first bullet came from my right front, almost entirely from the right, while the second came from my direct front. I hastily put a field dressing round my throat as it was bleeding quite freely when it started.

Very shortly after this, I was hit on the right side by another ricochet off the ground, but in this case, it did not penetrate and caused no damage, that totalled three bullets from the right flank and one from the front – all long range. I found afterwards that another bullet had ripped up the flap of the right hand breast pocket of my jacket, but I don't know when this occurred. As soon as I had patched up my throat, which really did not hurt, but felt rather queer and as if it was made of wood, I got up on my feet and tried to order another charge, but absolutely nothing happened, I could not understand what was wrong and became furious at the line for ignoring the order until I saw one of the men who was lying at my feet, turn round and look up at me with an expression of surprise on his face.

I then began to realize that I was unable to make a sound. I must have been trying to do some work with my whistle when I realized that my voice had gone as, afterwards, I found the pocket of my jacket where I kept my whistle, matted with blood, evidently from the bullet hole in my hand. This effort therefore, was a complete failure, and I was in the act of lying down again when I got another bullet right through the leg at the top of the thigh. This bullet came in from the back and I now realized that it came from the machine gun nest at the top of Fosse 8. Here again I was lucky as the bullet missed the bone, but the leg gave a violent kick and the blood poured down the leg in a great flood quickly followed by a numb feeling as if the limb did not really quite belong to me. The blood poured down the leg at this rate and felt much hotter than the leg itself and as the bullet passed right through the leg, there were two holes from which the blood flowed. This did not last for long however and the stream slowed down to a steady flow which I noted had a welling action corresponding to the beat of the heart, I managed to rip my bedford cord breeches up from the knee to the top of the leg and put my last field dressing on this wound and with the unbounded optimism of youth I thought that the wound was not anything to bother about especially as I discovered that I could still walk about on it so long as I kept the knee rigid. Actually – the bullet passed through the main vein near the top of the thigh, but in doing so, it also passed through the outer and middle coat of the femoral artery – leaving the thin elastic coat intact.* This elastic coat bulged into the opening in the main vein and to a great extent, stopped the bleeding, otherwise I am told I would have bled to death from the main vein in a few minutes.

Sergeant Telford, the Red Cross Sergeant, who was in the trench not far from where I was, came out and bandaged my leg for me, and he also did the same for Captain Purvis the Adjutant who was also shot in the thigh, but who died afterwards as a prisoner of war in Germany some months later. Sergeant Telford received a decoration for his work during this battle – which he well deserved as he took colossal risks to help the wounded. I am glad to say he survived the battle. I seem to have done a certain amount of walking about on my wounded leg which worked quite well so long as I kept the knee rigid, but I can't remember what I did about the line, if anything. I know that before very long my sight began to go from loss of blood and everything began to look milky white. I finally collapsed and crawled into a shell hole to die like a wounded animal.

I remember I had a horror of being shot through the head and as my vitality slowly ebbed, the primitive instinct of self preservation began to assert itself in spite of the fact that I was fully convinced that I was going out.

*In 1943, in Italy, T. G. K. Bishop, Lancashire Fusiliers, was shot through the femoral artery. It clotted rapidly and he survived. Today he has no ill effects. Pre-war he played Rugby football for the Harlequins.

By this time my leg began to swell a good deal and fill up with blood inside. The inflammation inevitable from such a deep wound acted on all the nerves in the top of the leg and resulted in a great deal of pain and, therefore, the prospect of death seemed by no means unwelcome. When eventually I faded out, the line was where I had left it when I became no longer capable of doing anything to help it.

I heard years afterwards that Captain Dunbar, our Medical Officer, took off his Red Cross armlet, rallied the men who were left, and took the German trench which I had failed to do. Knowing Dunbar as I do (as he bore a charmed life and is still alive) I think this story circulated by the rank and file very probable. Such an act, as we all know must be kept very hush hush as it is strictly against the Hague Convention.

And so ended my active share in the Battle of Loos, but before closing this record of these events I wish to pay tribute to the rank and file who did so splendidly and were so standfast and loyal. Their training was undoubtedly sound and this enabled them to anticipate any orders that had to be passed along the line regardless of the stress of circumstances. I have dim recollections of seeing many acts of courage performed by those men and I only wish I could remember them clearly enough to recount them. The second episode concerns myself personally, but the detailed account of what happened can only be justified by the many acts of courage and comradeship, I was myself able to witness in the process of being forcibly dragged from the German Line.

In the preceding account I had come to the stage where I had crawled into a shallow shell hole to die – as I fondly believed. By this time, everything I looked at appeared to be enveloped in a milky white mist. There were by this time, many dead and wounded near by and, what was left of the right half of the Battalion, lying out in extended order with, so far as I know, no one to look after them. Bullets seemed to be raining down into the ground as thick as ever and I remember lowering my head as much as possible below the lip of the shell hole as I had a strong objection to being hit in the head. The time must have been about 11 a.m. as near as I can remember.

I must have been completely out for some hours; when I came round sufficiently I found that my vision had cleared considerably and all firing had ceased. Quite close to the place where I was lying, two German officers were standing – both looking over my head towards our next line of trenches which I knew from my map were 500 yards away. One of these was pointing out to the other something in our lines which appeared to be engaging their attention. Immediately I saw them and grasped the situation – the old training on the barrack square at home began to assert itself and the thought went through my mind – 'I must kill those two officers'.

Without making a move I glanced round for my rifle to find it was not there. This discovery was disconcerting and then I remembered that it lay out in front beyond my reach. My thoughts then travelled to my revolver and very slowly my hand crept down to the holster at my belt only to find that this was also empty. This discovery came as a severe shock, as for many months past I had never been a single day without this loaded revolver at my side. It had been used several times in action and had crept into my subconscious mind as being part of myself. Many hours had been spent in the Old Country in learning to shoot from the hip, and almost as many in the billets behind the Lines.

This discovery, in addition to a sense of shock, brought in its wake a feeling of complete helplessness and dismay followed by a sense of guilt that I had gone so far as to allow myself to be unarmed in the middle of a battle. I had enough sense not to move or make any sign that life still existed in that bundle of blood stained and mud encrusted rags that lay so close to them. It took me sometime to piece together the events which had taken place and resulted in this alarming discovery and the whole sequence was only finally verified when I slowly withdrew my hand to a position where I could see the blood stained bandage.

It is quite evident from this that I had ceased to experience any discomfort from my hand, the bullet having passed through the hand between the bones, and this made all the difference. I quite realize now that I had not the strength to handle my revolver – much less the rifle. I had hardly become aware of my complete inability to do anything, when I blanked out again completely and, so far as I can remember, knew nothing until I came round on the morning of the following day to find the field strewn with dead only – the Regiment and all wounded having disappeared.

I have never been able to find out what really happened during these twenty four hours except that I know that a ding-dong fight went on in which the drain trench was occupied alternatively by the Regiment and the Huns. I think there is no doubt that Captain Dunbar, the Medical Officer, took off his badge of office and rallied what was left of the right half of the battalion, and re-took the top end of the drain trench, or the extension of the drain trench which ran at right angles to it. It was years after when I met Dr Dunbar, and when he had recovered from his surprise at seeing me alive, he told me that shortly after dawn on the second day they re-took the ground and he was able to mop up all the wounded he could find. He said that he saw me and thought I was dead, but admitted that he did not go very close to me. I tackled him on the persistent rumours that I had heard concerning himself, but of course he ridiculed these and would tell me nothing. Nevertheless, the Huns took some of our men prisoner, among whom was Captain Purvis, the Adjutant who, some months later, died in Germany from heart trouble I believe. His people received a letter from the German doctor giving details.

As I say, when I again became conscious (about 10 or 11 in the morning) only the dead were there and I believe the Regiment had been withdrawn from the line. So far as I can ascertain there were at least 108 men left and one subaltern unwounded, but there may have been more. I don't know that I was at all overjoyed at finding myself still alive. It was a clear sunny day with some white fleecy cloud and had not been raining since we were in action. I recognized Fosse 8 and this gave me my bearings. My wounds seemed to have ceased to give me any trouble and all the sounds of battle had died down. Again the training began to assert itself and I felt I must do something about proceeding to a dressing station if possible. I found I could stand up if I kept my leg stiff at the knee, and I managed to walk out of the shallow shell hole I was in. I had hardly done this when the battlefield began to spin round and I collapsed. I don't think I was out very long and when I came round again I realized I still had my heavy equipment on including my pack. I managed to undo my belt and shoulder straps and slip out of my harness and having done this, I realized that I had buttoned up my shoulder straps from force of habit. I tried standing again and felt the relief at the absence of my heavy harness.

I started to walk towards our line when suddenly I blanked out and again knew nothing. When I became conscious again I was in no hurry to try walking and just lay on my face on the ground. I had not been there long when I heard the thud of running feet and the sound of hard breathing and on looking up, I beheld two stretcher bearers racing towards me. They had raced out from the trenches about 450 yards away having, I suppose, seen my efforts to get to their trench. It was a very good show on their part and it was just one of the many links in the sequence of events which directly resulted in my surviving. I do not remember that I was experiencing any trouble from my wounds nor did I experience the pangs of hunger or thirst although it must have been at least two days if not more since I had had any food or water.

The two stretcher bearers helped me to my feet and I proceeded to walk in with an arm along their shoulders. I remember arriving at the edge of the trench and seeing a long line of men and rifles looking up at me – and then I went out again. While I was being helped in, the Huns opened fire and I could hear the bullets thudding into the ground all round us, but the two men never quickened their pace. I do not know what regiment held the trench except that it was an English battalion. I don't think either of the stretcher bearers were hit and I know that I was not.

When I became conscious I was lying at the heels of the men in the trench who were all at the ready. I had not been conscious for long when a clump of shells landed at the back of the trench not far away. I felt the reaction of the men at once and realized from this that they were raw troops. Unofficial news came down the trench to the effect that it was gas (this no doubt, was prompted by the acrid smell of the fumes from the explosion – there were no gas shells in those days.)

This rumour started what I was afraid was going to result in a panic. I knew that something had to be done quickly, but how to speak loud enough with my throat in the condition it was and at the same time with sufficient conviction, was quite another matter. Lying on my back in the foot of the trench gave me an excellent view of the sky and, from this position I noticed that the clouds were passing over towards the lines being held by the Huns. This gave me my cue and the following dialogue took place between myself and the nearest private soldier whose heels were touching my shoulder. 'Which way are the clouds going?' The man looked down at me with a look of surprise on his face, probably thinking that I was dead or nearly so, and, after recovering from his surprise, he slowly turned and looked up into the sky and, after contemplating the clouds for what seemed to me to be an age – said, 'In that direction', pointing towards the German Lines.

I replied 'They are going towards the German Lines aren't they?.'
The man replied, 'Yes.'
Then I said – 'The wind must be blowing the same way, isn't it?' to which the man again replied, 'Yes.'
I then replied, 'Then, how the hell can it be gas, pass the word down the line – NO GAS.'

I had the satisfaction of hearing the word 'Officer says no gas,' being passed along the line until it gradually faded away in the distance, and then I must have blanked out for a considerable time because the next thing I knew I was no longer in that trench, but was being half carried – half dragged through by three men from the Regiment, none of whom I knew by name as they were not in my platoon, but they were obviously very alarmed at my general condition and I must confess I was often unconscious and, therefore, unable to help them in their efforts. By this time the incessant twisting and handling I received began to have its effect on the wound in my leg and I was soon getting a great deal of pain.

After a while, there were only two men instead of three, the other going off to try to find a stretcher, which would have been quite useless in such a narrow twisty trench.

At one stage in the proceedings they found someone who had some rum in his water bottle and they poured some of this down my throat. This well-meaning act should have finished me and it certainly had the effect of making my wounds, which were still oozing blood, bleed a little faster. The immediate effect of the rum however was to make me get up on my feet and stand on the firing step looking for Huns – like the intoxicated mouse who said, 'Where's that blinking cat?'

The next thing I knew – the wall of the trench suddenly went flying up in the air past my nose, and I knew no more for another long spell. We were in the Hohenzollern Redoubt and, when I came round, it was obvious that the Huns had managed to get a footing on the fringe of this and were attempting to re-take the redoubt, in which they eventually succeeded.

Shells began to fall in all directions, mostly shrapnel, and I could hear the men saying to each other that they must hurry up and also that I was sinking fast and they would never get me to a dressing station in time. Some parts of the redoubt seemed to be quite empty of troops while other parts were fairly full. Men were being hit by shrapnel which was accurately aimed and perfectly timed.

At one stage I was being carried by one of the men at my heels and the other holding me by the shoulders. A shell came into the trench and burst about one foot above my waist. I did not hear a sound when it exploded, but most of the shrapnel went into the wall of the trench. I remember seeing a flash and the man who was holding my heels suddenly turned a perfect back somersault and ricochet round the bend in the trench and completely disappeared from view. I was conscious that I had landed on my back on the floor of the trench and, on looking round, I saw the man who had been holding me by the shoulders, returning from the other bend in the trench. Both these men arrived back to where I was lying at the same time and greatly to my relief they were both un-hurt. The amazing thing about it was that several men who were behind the men who were carrying me, were wounded.

The sudden contact with the ground seemed to have somewhat revived me as I well remember that a piper who was hit in the leg and blown down by the blast was heard to say, 'Mind my pipes – mind my pipes.' I told him that he must go off to a dressing station (where I imagined he could find a dressing station in that redoubt – I can't think) but that is what I said.

He replied that he would not go to a dressing station, but would get up on the top of the trench and 'Gie them a blaw'. I replied most emphatically that he would do nothing of the kind, to which he replied 'I beg your pardon Sir, I didnie ken you was an officer.'

I got everyone I could into a dugout until the intensity of shelling became less, and then we proceeded on our slow, and I can truthfully say for the three of us – weary way. I will never know how it was that the three of us were not blown to pieces by that shell. As we proceeded the sounds of fighting grew louder and I became seriously alarmed for the safety of these two men, at the same time it did not look as if we would ever get out of the redoubt. By this time the wound in my leg was giving me hell – so much so that I had no wish to go on.

I finally told the two men to leave me where I was and to save themselves as I was not going another step further. Private Orr, the leader, whose name I subsequently found out, replied that they would not leave me and that if I decided to go down, they would go down with me. At that they both picked up their rifles and stood on the firing step.

This was too much for me and I had to consent to be dragged on toward some imaginary goal which we never seemed to reach. I must have faded out for a long time for when I came round, it was just getting dark and I was being lifted onto a stretcher in a dressing station and, in the semi darkness, two men crawled along the floor on their hands and knees and lay down against the wall like a couple of exhausted dogs.

I managed to ask the surgeon if he would look after these two men and I remember him promising that he would. I was so weak by this time that I could only just manage to frame the words. I have dim recollections of being taken along the Hulloch road on a stretcher on wheels and hearing the long range bullets pattering down like drops of rain, and when we were held up through congestion of traffic I could hear the orderlies making free use of the password, 'Officer', 'Officer.' Which seemed to have its effect. The orderlies had no wish to remain any longer than it was absolutely necessary in such a locality, for which I did not blame them.

My journey to the base occupied two or three days of which I have little recollection. When I was brought into the first dressing station, I was inoculated against tetanus and new dressings put on my wounds. I have dim recollections of various casualty clearing stations in which bits of one's clothing were cut away to gain better access to wounds as the occasion demanded, but it was not until I arrived quite near the base that my boots were cut off and when I finally arrived in No 1 Red Cross which was the Duchess of Westminster's Field Hospital at Le Touquet, I was fully dressed except for my boots and I was left on the floor on a stretcher for the night as the head surgeon did not consider I would live out the night.

On being found alive in the morning, I was put in a bed and my service jacket taken off me and put in a locker and the rest of my clothes cut away by knives and scissors. I remember persuading a nursing sister in some dressing station during my journey down the line, to give me a post card and I was then able to write a card to the Old Folks at Home to say I had been slightly wounded and would be home shortly, blissfully unaware of the magnitude of my wounds.

When I had written the card, I found that there was a smear of blood on it from my hand so I had to explain that I had been hit in the hand. The Sister brought me a card with such bad grace that I was afraid to ask her for another one. I quite sympathized with the Sister when I reflected that dozens of others must have asked her for the same thing and the cost must have mounted. I think I am not far out when I say that we put over the top eighty seven thousand men in three days and suffered just under fifty thousand casualties. The surgeons and sisters were sleeping on their feet from sheer exhaustion.

The bullet that went through the top of the thigh, cut a 'halfmoon' out of the main vein, which accounted for the terrific flush of blood. Luckily, the bullet also went through the outer and middle coat of the femoral artery. This left the inner coat undamaged, which is an elastic coat, and this coat bulged into the recess cut into the main vein and saved me bleeding to death from this very large blood vessel.

The first thing they did in hospital was to X Ray my throat, which they swore had a bullet in it. My opinion on the subject was politely ignored. After photographing my throat from every possible angle, they finally admitted that there was no bullet there. Meanwhile my heart began to get stronger and my leg began to swell up to almost twice its normal size. They kept telling me that they would probably have to take my leg off the next day, and as each day dawned they decided to wait a little longer. This did not worry me in the least and became quite a joke, but I noticed that the surgeon was not very happy about things. Finally, about ten days after I got the bullet, the femoral burst and my bed was soon swimming in blood. Three doctors and three nurses made what I think I can describe as an ugly rush at me as soon as I told them my leg was bleeding. The artery was held where it crossed the pelvis ridge, and everyone took turns at holding it down, to rest their thumbs.

I was immediately chloroformed in my bed and carted off to the operating theatre where the leg was cut open and about ¾ of an inch cut out of both the femoral and the main vein and the four ends ligatured. The two pieces were put in a bottle of spirits and shown to me after. This was the first time such an operation had been performed and proved successful; all others had resulted in amputations.

I was six weeks in this hospital before I was sent over to London on a stretcher, and from my experience during that time I can't speak too highly of the efficiency of that hospital and the way in which the Duchess worked.

During the time I was there, most of the visiting surgeons in France came and inspected my leg and I was very definitely exhibit A. I arrived at a hospital in London on Guy Fawkes Day and after being at a convalescent home near Farnham, I was home for Christmas, armed with my service jacket that was thoroughly bloodstained all round the collar and the right pocket where I kept my whistle in addition to evidence that it had been in close contact with bullets – furthermore, the brass buttons were green with gas. I left the family to lick their chops over this garment. I was, of course, very lame for a long time, but managed to wangle the job of taking a draft to France when serving with the Reserve Battalion (9th RSF) on the Forth Bridge. This was in February 1916. With this I found I had taken on a little more than I bargained for because it landed me with having to march the draft four miles in the snow, but I managed it all right because I used my stick. Three old ladies, who were connections, very kindly and thoughtfully knitted khaki stockings with a spiral effect which I wore in the place of puttees as the legs just refused to function if I wore a putty.

Needless to say, I called in at Le Touquet and saw them at the hospital. I must say they looked amazed when they saw me turn up only 3½ months after I had been in the hospital. I remember while travelling in the train from the base camp to Le Touquet, there were three young subalterns in the carriage. They all looked at me for some little while and then one asked me what it was like in London. I replied that things were much the same. Silence for a little and then the same individual ventured the question as to when I thought I was going on service. Having been asked this question and remembering that I had been told I would never see service again, I rather felt, for the first time, that I was out of it and that I had said goodbye forever to the comradeship that I prized and valued so much.

For a moment I was rather shaken and, quite unintentionally, there was a catch in my voice when I replied that I had been told I would never see active service again. Each subaltern turned and looked me straight in the eye and said in turn, 'I beg your pardon.' They were fresh out from Sandhurst and full of buck and were on their way to join their regiments.

I remained with the 9th Battalion until July, during that time I, as second in command to a Company, kept as many men with the regiment who had been to France as I could and sent all the other ones to France ! !

Just about this time, volunteers were called for to serve with a Battalion to be designated The 1st Garrison Bn, Seaforth Highlanders, to serve in Egypt. The stipulation was that only officers who had been wounded and unfit for Active Service were eligible. I reasoned out that if I remained long enough with the 9th, I would eventually be sent back to France. The prospect of being sent back to France to serve in a battalion in which all the old associations would by then be missing, terrified me, so I at once volunteered and hoped I would get away with it. I rather think I did some wangling, but eventually I joined the 1st Garrison Battalion Seaforths with a medical category of C and by the end of July I reported at Tillicoultry where the Regiment was forming.

All this time I was quite ignorant of who the men were who risked their lives so often and worked so nobly to get me out and, to whom, together with those two stretcher bearers, I owe my continued existence on this earth. It was just before I was transferred from the 9th that two private soldiers turned up at a house in Glasgow with a very soiled and crumpled card and asked to see me. This was the house in which the old ladies I have already mentioned, lived.

I must explain that when the tattered remnants of the Regiment returned to billets in Bethune, all parcels out from home, addressed to Officers who were either killed, wounded or missing, were distributed among what was left of their platoons and it was a card from one of these parcels which these two men had. Letters were returned to senders and mine were marked 'Killed in action' in red pencil and this had been crossed out and in blue pencil was written 'Wounded and missing', meanwhile, of course, my people at home knew what had happened to me.

To return to the men and the crumpled card – the old ladies told me that when the men were told that I was not there, their faces fell, but they, having heard about my rescue, promptly plied the men with questions and then there obtained the names of the two men whom I had been wanting to get for so long. Having obtained these, I wrote to Private Orr at once for information, but on hearing from him I was distressed to hear that Private Lane, the other man, had already been killed. It was with great sorrow that I eventually learned that Orr was killed himself just before the end of hostilities, but not before I was instrumental in getting him an MM, which I know he well deserved and I am glad to say I was, much later, able to execute a wish he expressed to me in his letter (which I have in my possession) in a manner I think would have pleased him had he lived.

And now I think I have come to the end of an episode which is full of human emotions, almost incredible experiences, but which is dominated throughout by courage, comradeship and loyalty of the highest order displayed by the private soldier.

14

Indian Corps

Account by George Wilfred Grossmith, 2nd Leicestershire Regiment
Attached is the copy of a letter which, over fifty-five years ago, I wrote to Maud, then my fiancée, as I lay in hospital at Le Touquet. I have just re-copied it from the original, which we have kept all these years but which is too faded for photo-copying.

In writing it out again I have altered nothing, and omitted nothing except a few personal words at the beginning and end; the rest is word for word.

Reading it over again after all this time I find it difficult to understand how I thought that such a detailed account would interest her. And perhaps it will not interest the few members of 'family' for whom I have now re-done it, as it was put together in rather a flat, factual style. But it may be borne in mind that it was written only two days after the action, and that I was only twenty-one years of age at the time.

I have a lot to tell you, and do not know where to begin. First of all, I must tell you that I am only slightly wounded – a bullet through the right thigh. I have been fortunate beyond words, considering the experience that my regiment and many others have been through. My battalion, as such, no longer exists; it was decimated, along with nearly all the other regiments of the Meerut Division of our Indian Corps. Of my battalion, there are only two officers and a few men who were not killed or wounded. Our Colonel was shot through the arm, and the adjutant, Captain Romilly, one of the finest men I have ever met and a hero of Neuve Chapelle, killed. Captain Wilson, my company Commander, wounded, and the two other officers in my company, Brown and Wilkinson, both killed. Tanner, of B Company, with whom I came out in July, is here in the next bed to mine, with a similar wound.

The Great Offensive! I cannot get to hear any reliable news about the other attacks, north and south of us, but gather that they were more or less successful. Some weeks ago I know, as we all did, that it was coming (and so did the Germans) but I could not of course, write to you about it. But I know now, only two days later, that the attack north of Loos by our Indian Corps was a feint only, and doomed to failure. Our success or otherwise was not important, it was merely a holding attack, while the real mass attack was to the south, by combined British and French forces. It is of this attack that I am anxiously awaiting news.

For the last fortnight we have been listening to the roar of heavy artillery to our south, smashing the German lines in preparation for the infantry attack. That is where our artillery was massed. We had very little on our particular front, though it appeared to us that the lines opposite were being well pounded.

However, this letter is to tell you about the part played in it all by my regiment, and of my own experiences. The programme was well thought out and prepared. In the reserve area an exact replica of our front line and the enemy's was pegged out and clearly marked, to full size, and we carried out dummy attacks over it. Our attack was to be preceded by a release of gas from cylinders. And so, for the first time in this war, we were to use chlorine gas to asphyxiate and kill the enemy; and with how much success you will see as my account carries on. The gas programme was to be followed only if the wind was favourable; an alternative programme (B) was only to be used if the wind proved to be unfavourable.

We fell in at our billets at six o'clock on the evening of Friday the 24th September and marched to the battalion rendezvous or 'nest' as we called it. I have never seen the men more cheerful. They had all been told, days before, exactly what they were to do and what was expected of them, but as they marched they sang and cheered as I would not have thought possible for troops who knew that in a few hours time they would be first over the parapet towards probable death. And it was not forced cheerfulness. I felt it myself. There was an atmosphere of confidence and victory in the air. We all sang!

After marching for half an hour or so we entered south Telleloy Street, one of those terribly long communication trenches about a mile and a half long. It was 11 p.m. before we were in position in the front line and support trenches. A Company was supporting B Company and together we formed the left half battalion. The whole battalion was divided into four lines of attack, and I was in charge of the left half of the third line. The men did not have a very comfortable night, they had to get what rest they could in the bottom of a wet trench. I had a dugout with Captains Wilson and Rolph, and got an hour of sleep.

There were a good many things to attend to, such as bombs, picks and shovels, respirators, and ammunition. We knew we were going over at six o'clock, one hour after daybreak, so we stood-to at 5.30, wearing our smoke helmets rolled up on our heads like a cap comforter, ready to roll down again when the time came to advance through our own gas. Nerves were tense. Everyone was tuned up and excited, and there were tears (though not of fear) in the eyes of many. Perhaps they had very dear ones at home (as I had) and were thinking (as I was) that they stood little chance of seeing them again.

At 5.48 the big mine under the German front line, 200 yds to our left was exploded, and up into the air went over one hundred yards of their trenches. Two minutes later the zero signal was sent up from the Headquarters of the Bareilly Brigade, 200 yards to our rear, by the firing of about twenty rockets of various colours. This was the signal for the release of the gas (the wind was favourable then) and the opening of intense bombardment by our guns.

At 5.59 our first line got over the parapet and formed up, going forward immediately, the other lines crowding up the "cuts" and following them. At 6 o'clock the gas discharge ceased, and the artillery lifted its range one hundred yards. During this period, about ten minutes, our shell fire had been fast and furious, but the Germans had not sent much back in reply, only steady shrapnel. I got over the parapet, with as much of my line as I could see.

From this point the tragedy began. I am afraid that from now on my account may be rather disconnected. But before I can continue I must explain that at the time the gas cloud was being released the wind was blowing southwards at the rate of only two miles an hour. As our line at this part of the front faced southeast this meant that the gas drifted slowly along in a direction half-right from our front. The gas had rolled out of the cylinders in dense sickly looking yellow clouds and after a time seemed to pile up instead of going forward, as the feeble wind was now dying. Flanking the gas front for a hundred yards on either side we had smoke candles which generated a harmless dark brown smoke to go over with the gas, the idea being to screen everything from the eyes of the enemy and especially from their artillery. Of how much use this was I do not know, as I was not near a flank and anyhow the whole attack was quickly a failure.

To continue my personal story; we got over the parapet and moved forward. We soon realised that none of us knew where we were going. The gas hung in a thick pall over everything, and it was impossible to see more than ten yards. In vain I looked for my landmarks in the German line, to guide me to the right spot, but I could not see through the gas and smoke. Inevitably we scattered. I went forward, thinking I knew the way. Others, clearly disorganised, were running or walking in the direction of the German trenches, looking like ghouls in their gas helmets. I felt stifled in mine. Out through the little rectangular window of mica I looked for a way over the ditches and shell holes. I passed men gassed, and then saw Brown, obviously dying but motioning with his hand the way forward – a sight I shall never forget.

I crept blindly forward, a percussion bomb in one hand and holding my gas helmet tightly round my neck with the other. Then I came across some of my men lying in a row waiting for the gas to clear before going forward.

I stopped here awhile and then hoping for the best took off my stifling helmet and threw it away, as the gas appeared to be thinning. Not now sure of even the general direction of the German lines I got out my compass, although I knew it would not tell us our lateral position. We went forward, and reached the German wire, only to find it intact. Now, the artillery always blow to pieces, with high explosive shells, the front line wire before an attack, and so I felt sure we were in the wrong place, but whether to the right or left I did not know.

It would have been foolish to attack an unbroken front line with ten men, so we crawled away to the right, but in doing so I lost several men hit by rifle or machine gun fire which was sweeping between the lines the whole time, and the shelling also continued. We still could not see above ten yards. Then a parapet loomed ahead, and so uncertain was I of our position that I did not know whether it was ours or theirs. Heads appeared above the parapet and as we were not fired on it was clear that we were back at our own line.

So, with my few men, now only six, I climbed over, as I wanted to find out our position. They turned out to be the 3rd Londons, and a corporal in the traverse, to make sure I was not a German in disguise took me to his officer, which was a matter of form. This officer only knew vaguely where the Leicestershires were. He was under the impression that some of our men were 'in' on the other side.

When I looked round for my men, they had disappeared, so I went out again alone, to see if any of our men *had* achieved any advance, and if so to join them. The gas and smoke was still thick. I came to a ditch about three feet deep and in this were about a dozen wounded men, including Gurkhas. They asked me for water, which I was able to give them from my bottle. They also wanted to know the way to our lines, which I was able to give them after a look at my compass. I crawled on.

I could hear rifle and machine gun fire coming from every part of the German front, so concluded that all our men had been repulsed. I came across a party of thirty men under an Officer. They were the Brigade Grenadier Company and were armed with bombs and grenades of all descriptions. Half of them were Gurkhas. The officer, an elderly man, was shot through both cheeks and was half-dazed. He did not know where he was, or whether to go forward or backward. I could give him no advice. While I was talking to him a lump of shrapnel cut my left breast pocket to pieces, missing my flesh by a hair's breadth but it blew my wallet to pieces, and with, dear, those two photographs of you which I have had with me all along I was grieved about that. I had hoped never to lose them. There was also one of your letters which I had specially put with the photographs and 150 francs in notes (£6).

Then, looking back, I saw a party of about forty men run from our parapet and advance half left towards the German line. I thought that these men might possibly be some of my own, reorganised and making a fresh start, or perhaps the regiment in support following up, so I started to make for them. Suddenly I felt a sting in my right thigh and fell. For a few seconds it was very painful and then the pain eased. I looked at it, saw two holes in my breeches, and took my pocket knife and ripped my breeches up. I had a field dressing on me, so I unwrapped it and bound up the wound. The bullet had gone right through the fleshy part of my thigh.

I now thought it was time I gave up trying to find my regiment, so I started to crawl back towards our lines. Then suddenly I realised that the smoke had practically cleared and that I was out in the open, a target for both sides. A few obviously aimed bullets cutting the ground close to me told me that I must keep still if I would live. It was now about 7 o'clock. I had the choice between two alternatives; to crawl back the remaining hundred odd yards to our line and be almost certainly killed on my way, or lie out there, between the two parapets, motionless until 7 at night-dusk. I chose the latter. It was a fearful prospect twelve hours in the open under all kinds of fire, on wet ground, and wounded. However, it had to be done.

I would not care to again go through twelve such hours. The minutes seemed hours – the hours days. All the time the Germans were shelling our positions with heavies and all kinds of guns. The noise was infernal and nerve racking. Occasionally I was picked out by a German sniper, who did not hit me, although I was fired at intermittently all day. I got cramped, but dare not move. My stomach began to ache through being in the wet for so long. I was most uncomfortable. I was lying on my revolver and four pouches full of revolver ammunition, and after an hour or two they felt very hard indeed. My head was towards our own lines and half-left I thought sometimes that I could hear mutterings and sub-dued talking, but was not sure.

I began to get cold, even though the sun was shining weakly, and then I remembered that your brandy flask was in my haversack which was strapped on my back. How to get it was the problem. By moving my arms very slowly I was able to get at the buckles and undo the haversack without getting noticed, but it took me an hour. These efforts, although very slowly made, seemed to make me less cold; but I was soon to want the brandy. At 3.30 clouds gathered and it started to drizzle. At 4 o'clock it came on heavily, to my utter discomfiture. The eternal minutes went by, and it seemed an age till half past four.

Up till that time I had resolved to stay out until dark in spite of the rain, but I was now wet to the skin and very cold and felt inclined to risk crawling back, especially as the firing had now died down and the sentries not quite so alert in the rain. Very slowly, I undid my equipment and crept out of it. I had to leave it all, or I should have been too obvious. I also left behind my revolver, waterproof, canteen and other sundries.

Lifting my head out of the mud for the first time since being hit, I noticed a line of shell torn, stunted trees running towards and at right angles to our parapet, about twenty yards to the left. I reasoned that there ought to be a ditch running along by the trees – there usually is in this part of France. I started to crawl half left to strike the ditch half way along, working with my hands and feet and so pushing my way slowly through the mud and patches of wet grass. My bandage came off, and so the open wound had also to skid across the mud.

At last I reached the line of trees, and sure enough there was a ditch. I rolled into it. I was now, at last, covered from fire. I glanced along the ditch towards the German lines, and in it I saw what at first I took to be a party of Germans, and thought that I was to be captured after all my efforts. But a second glance, and the unconcerned way in which they looked at me, showed me that they were Gurkhas. One of them beckoned to me, and I crawled towards them. We could not understand one another. They were not wounded, but seemed to be patiently awaiting their fate. I do not believe that they knew the British from the German lines, which was not surprising – many of our men must have crawled into the wrong lines that day.

I now realised that the subdued voices which I had heard whilst I was lying out in front must have come from these Gurkhas. I tried to make them come along and follow me, but they would not. By regulation for infantry officers in the forward lines of attack, I was wearing a private soldier's tunic, my only badge of rank being a star on the shoulder strap. But my star was now all covered with mud, so probably they were not satisfied that I was an officer. Anyway, they would not move. So I turned about and left them, and crawled along the muddy ditch, which was choked with barbed wire, brambles, and other obstructions, and was by now inches deep in water. And here and there was the half-decomposed body of a British or German soldier.

I now faced a very difficult problem, how to get over the parapet and into our lines without being shot by our own sentries, probably Gurkhas at that point in the line, or by German snipers of whom I should be in full view, even though visibility was no longer very good. Fifteen yards from our parapet I had to stop as I came to a mound which completely blocked the ditch, and I would be fully exposed when climbing over it. So finally I decided to make my presence known, and, crouching behind the mound called out as loudly as I could, 'I want to speak to an officer'. I called this out several times, then glanced over the mound at the parapet. They saw me. I saw the heads of several sentries. I waved my arm, but there was no response. I thought they were levelling their rifles, and so I got my head down again. For some time I kept my head down, as I thought they might have their rifles ready set taking me for a German.

Knowing now that they were Gurkhas, and that they address an officer as 'officer-sahib'. I called out 'officer sahib' several times and showed my hand and arm above the mound. I knew they saw and heard for there was sudden talking, but no reply. I waited a few more leaden minutes, and took a sip of brandy, for it was still raining heavily and I was sodden and clogged with mud. I came to the point where I could stand it no longer. I crawled over the mound – and no one fired. Another mound now blocked my way, and I crawled over that to find myself in a ditch running up to the foot of the parapet. It was half full of water, but what difference did that make by now?

By the time I got to the end of this ditch and close to the foot of the parapet it was six o'clock, and still fairly light, so my troubles were not yet over. Another wait, and the last of the brandy, and I felt ready to take the last risk. I was so close to the parapet that our own sentries could not see me as I climbed up it, and the Germans did not notice me, so I scrambled over as fast as I could and fell onto the fire step on the other side with such a feeling of relief and reaction as I have never felt before. During twelve hours of misery and danger my dream of Heaven had been a British front line trench. And here I was; in one.

Two Gurkhas were standing in the bay. They took my sudden appearance quite calmly. I was able to walk, after a fashion, so went through into the supervision trench, asking for 'Leicesters' and met a Major of the Black Watch (or was it the 4th Seaforths?) Major Cuthbert. He was kindness itself, lending me a stick, and giving me an orderly to take me to the dressing station. I left a message about the Gurkhas in the ditch, so that after dusk they might be led in.

Our communication trenches were a foot deep in water in many places, with duckboards floating about. At the dressing station in the Rue Tilleloy my wound was bandaged and I was treated to a glass of whisky.

From now on my adventures became more commonplace. I was put on a trolley and pushed down the wooden railway as far as the 2nd Aid Post. On the way I was joined by Hemphill of B Company. He had a shrapnel wound in the shoulder and an accidental bayonet wound in the leg. We related our experiences to each other. Up to that time I had no idea how the regiment had fared in the matter of casualties, but from Hemphill I learned the worst. He also had been out all day, in a shell hole quite near their wire, with about twenty men, several of whom got shot during the day. They had waited until dark and crawled in.

At the 2nd Aid Post we were put on stretchers and taken by ambulance car to La Gorgue. Here we were given hot tea and food. We were also given dry shirts and pyjamas, leaving our clothing to be destroyed, as it was in rags and useless.

From La Gorgue we were motored to Merville, and taken into a hospital there. It was nice to get into a bed. The Colonel was there, wounded. The next day, about one o'clock, we were taken out on stretchers and placed in a hospital railway car. This car was simply splendidly fitted out and equipped. It was a palatial car, with everything provided for our comfort. We were in the train about twelve hours, and arrived at Le Touquet, about twenty miles south of Boulogne. From there we were taken by ambulance car to the Duchess of Westminster Hospital, which is where I now am. Hemphill was put in a different ward, but when I woke up in the morning I found Tanner in the bed next to mine. We were both glad about this, but I am sorry that his wound is a very bad one, although it is in the same place as mine.

The hospital is palatial. It was a casino before war. The sisters, nurses, and all the staff are extremely kind and attentive, and on the whole I am very very comfortable.

15

24th Division

Letter from Lieutenant Colonel S. Vincent

Recently I read in my newspaper that you were writing an account of the Battle of Loos (September 1915), and were asking for diaries, letters, etc, relevant to this battle and it occurred to me that you might find of interest extracts from a letter which I sent to my parents after this battle and I enclose a copy thereof herewith. I was then a Corporal in the 24th Divisional Cyclist Company; this unit was formed from personnel in the infantry battalions of the 24th (Kitchener's Army) Division in February, 1915. I had previously served in the 8th (Service) Battalion of The Bedfordshire Regiment (16th Foot). Later, some time after Loos, we were amalgamated with the 50th (Territorial) Divisional Cyclist Company to form the 5th Corps Cyclist Battalion.

For obvious reasons I was not able to tell my parents how bitter members of 21st and 24th Divisions felt after the battle of Loos; some criticism has been made about their performance during this battle but any blame there was should be placed on those in high authority who planned and carried out this battle. We were told that our two divisions and the Guards Division would be reserve corps for the battle, that the Guards would go into action first and we would follow; actually the reverse happened and the Guards came up after us, and did a good job but there could not possibly be any justification for putting two inexperienced divisions into such a battle without any experience of being under fire or of working in or from trenches, nor for keeping them for three weeks so far from the battle area and then bringing them up by forced marches and sending them in a tired condition into a battle which was already becoming confused and which obviously was not going according to plan; possibly the intention was to keep the enemy from knowing these divisions existed but I doubt very much if this was the case.

As you will see from my letter, we had the task of guiding the divisions up to the battle area so I had ample opportunity to see what sort of mess they were in, even before they reached the battle area and they then had to march several miles along roads already very congested with traffic, transport, ammunition, ambulances and walking wounded. To us all this seemed evidence of the crass stupidity and incompetence of higher authority and, unfortunately, I was, during more than two years' service in France, to see more such examples. The premature use of tanks was one such example, as you probably know, these were first used, in small numbers toward the end of the Somme battle. I was then in charge of a detachment of my regiment attached to a Divisional Headquarters and we picked up a message dropped from an aeroplane, which read, 'Landships advancing through Flers, accompanied by infantry marching in column of fours'; we asked ourselves what the hell were landships this operation whilst shewing up lessons which needed to be learnt, also gave away to the Germans what was supposed to be a secret.

Later, in the Battle of Cambrai, in November 1917, some 400 tanks were used but here again I saw evidence of incompetence of those in higher authority; the idea, we were told, was that the tanks, together with infantry, were to break through the enemy lines and then the cavalry were to exploit the position and finally, we, the cyclist, together with the other Corps mounted troops, were to pass through the cavalry and establish an outpost line beyond the river Escaut; I still have the maps, details of roads, bridges, etc, which we were to cross, which were issued to use at the time. Unfortunately once again in the reserves – the cavalry – were kept too far back and were not able to exploit the breakthrough as had been expected. We remained on instant call, ready to move, for several days but did not move until, after it became clear that the hoped for complete breakthrough would not be achieved and the line once again became more or less stable, I had to take our Lewis guns up to support the infantry and narrowly escaped capture during the unexpected and, at first, successful counter attack mounted by the Germans.

Examples of how much higher authority seemed to us to be out of touch occurred during the 3rd battle of Ypres. I was engaged on traffic control behind the battle area and though fortunately for me I did not have to experience the horrors and miseries endured by the troops fully engaged in the battle, I saw enough to make me feel that it was wrong and stupid to continue the battle for so long. There may have been some justification for starting the battle and it was unfortunate that it started to rain almost at once and continued to do so for some time but to me, as a farmer, and with previous experience of the Ypres salient, where the soil was of a fen type with a high water table level, it was quite clear that if the wet conditions continued, coupled with the effects on this type of soil of intensive artillery bombardment, it would not be possible for troops to dig deep enough to obtain cover from enemy fire and that conditions would render the task of supplying food, drink and ammunition to the troops engaged in the fighting extremely difficult and so it proved to be.

It has, I know, been argued that this prolonged battle of attrition so badly affected the manpower position and the morale of the enemy that it made a significant contribution to our ultimate victory. This may be true but we also suffered in the same way and, I think, paid dearly for the damage we inflicted on the enemy. I do not think we could have endured this damage but for the knowledge that the arrival of American men and material in France would restore and maintain the superiority in manpower and resources needed to achieve final victory. The Germans obviously appreciated this point and so mounted the massive attacks they made during the spring of 1918. These attacks were very successful at first but eventually failed and the consequences of this failure led to the eventual defeat of the enemy; I am quite sure, however, that during the fighting of the spring and summer of 1918 many of those engaged in this rearguard action must have had grave doubts about the outcome of it and when it ended the words of the Duke of Wellington after the battle of Waterloo must have been in many minds.

You will think, quite rightly, that I have been critical of higher authority and I appreciate how difficult it was for men engaged in battle to fully understand the problems facing those who planned the battle in which they were engaged so I have read many of the histories of this war but must confess that I still retain as strong an impression of the failure of those who planned our battles to realise fully the condition under which the battles they planned would be carried out. I hope my comments may be of interest to you.

Extracts from a letter written by Corporal F. Vincent, of 24th Divisional Cyclist Company, to his parents on 5th November 1915 (after the end of the battle of Loos, September 1915)

We left Brookwood at 10 a.m. on 30th August, 1915 and arrived at Southampton at 11.20. We were messing about all day, got on the ship at 5.30 p.m. and sailed at 7 p.m. We arrived at Le Havre at 2.30 next morning and got off the boat at 7 a.m. We hung about the docks all day on fatigues, etc, until 5 p.m. when we marched to the station, entrained at 9.30 p.m. and started on our journey at 10.30 p.m.

Well, about 12 mid-day we got off the train; there we had to unload some wagons for the ASC* and the RE's; then we started off to a place

*Army Service Corps.

called Bimont; as we passed through Montreuil-sur-Mer I saw some of
the 8th Bedfords who told us we had to go 9 miles, but our officers got
lost and we went nearly 30 miles and if one of our fellows had not been
able to speak French we should not have found it yet. Well, eventually we
arrived there dead beat – in fact they had to pull up once or twice to let
the chaps have a rest as half the company was falling out and to make
matters better as soon as I got there I was put on guard ... On Monday,
13th September we left Bimont, where we could only just hear the big
guns occasionally and went to a place where we could hear them quite
plainly. We were there sometime, until the end of the week, when rumours
went round that we were on the move. Our Captain told us that there
was a big attack coming off, and that the 11th Corps, that was the 21st,
24th and Guards Division were to be reserves and when the attacking
party had broken through we were to pass through them and put the
finishing touches to it. We slept with our kit packed and our boots on for
three nights and on the Wednesday, (22nd September) at 6 p.m. (now
comes the part which few people know about) the division marched
through a place called Fruges to a place called Laires, arriving there in
the early hours of the morning – in fact, about 4 a.m. We stayed at
Laires, that is the 73rd Brigade and Divisional troops – the 71st and 72nd
were away on the left. About 7.30 p.m. on that night they started off
again and arrived next morning all round a place called Busnes. I believe
the 71st Brigade marched 28 miles that night. They had to rest all day
and part of the next.

On the Friday afternoon they started off again and arrived at Bethune
dead beat at 2.30 a.m. on the fateful 25th. They were in a pretty fine
mess I can tell you as I lay on the side of the road outside Bethune all the
Friday afternoon and all night waiting for the Division. They marched,
I believe, over 20 miles each night and not on roads like you get in England; a good part of the way being on cobbled roads and about 2 miles
of them would make any man's feet sore with a full pack. Well, they left
Bethune about 9.30 a.m. on the 25th and we followed. The roads were
full of transport and wounded and ammunition and it was about 5 or 6
o'clock before we got anywhere near Vermelles a distance of about 7 or
8 miles. We stopped about a mile behind Vermelles for an hour and then
the Division went up to the firing line. The poor beggars had had no
food or water for two days and it was wet and miserable so you can tell
what a mess they were in.

We got to a place called 'Suicide Corner', where there was a notice
up as follows : 'Do not loiter on this corner as it is being constantly
shelled'.

Well, just behind the village were an 8 inch howitzer and a 6 inch ditto which the Germans were trying to shell. I suppose they thought anywhere would do for us so they billeted us right at Suicide Corner. Well, we were tired, having been up guiding the Division all the way up, so we got down to it. We slept as well as the noise of the guns behind us would allow (and they shook the place every time they were fired) until about half past three the Germans found a spot and dropped a shell in our billet and that was where poor Pearson was knocked out. We were lucky that it did not burst in the middle of the room instead of sliding down the end wall, or I should probably be pushing the daisies up, as the saying is, or enjoying myself in England. There were 17 of us in there so you can guess how lucky we were. Well, we stopped there until about 11 o'clock the next morning (Sunday). I don't think I shall forget that Sunday in a hurry. Well, we got on our cycles and pedalled away to the trenches until we came to a communication trench, and there we left our machines and got into that. I don't know whether anyone told the Germans we were there, but as soon as we got there they sent a few 'coal boxes' over and shrapnel, just as a word of welcome. One of the high explosives burst on a transport wagon close by and killed 4 men, wounded another 4 and killed the mules and nearly smothered us with dirt.

After a bit one of our platoons had to carry some rations along for the Bedfords. When they came back the rest of us had to take some ammunition up to a place where stood a single tree – we called it the 'Lone Tree'. 'We started off carrying two boxes between two of us; when we got about half way up we came to a battery of RFA. Just as we got there the Germans started to shell it; we had to drop down every time a shell was coming anywhere near to us. One of them burst up in the air about 50 yards in front of me and my two chaps and a piece as big as an egg buried itself in the ground about two inches in front of my nose. I thought I would dig it out and keep it as a souvenir but it was buried too deep and I had no time. My two mates hooked off with one box and left me with the other. They preferred going along the trenches to going along in the open, in fact, they seemed very nervous.

I had a laugh at them and was still laughing when I heard a shell coming with a rather vicious scream to it so down I went behind a trench and the shell burst the other side not two yards away. The next went just behind me and the next to the right so I thought it was a bit too warm and picked the box up by myself and walked away until I found my chaps a bit further up the communication trench so I chucked the box into the trench and we joined up again and toddled along.

Well, we got up further and had to get on top as the stretcher bearers were in the way. We kept on along the open until we came to another battery and just as we got there they shelled that and every shell went between the guns as nice as they could wish, but they only put one gun out of action. We took our ammunition and toddled back, had a rest and went up again with some rations just as it was getting dusk. It was pretty quiet then except for a few stray bullets. Then we went back to Vermelles, except two platoons who went up with some water. About 8 o'clock I went down a cellar and went to sleep feeling as tired as ever I have done in my life.

About 3.30 next morning we were awakened by the sergeant (no guns kept us awake that night, although they were at it all night) and we moved back to a place called Sailly Labourse. We spent that day in a field – slept in a ditch with my feet up one side and my head the other; in the pouring rain, woke up to find the water had drained down the banks and it was rather damp. Two platoons spent the night picketing the division out of the trenches, that is, guiding them. The next day we were paid and that night all the Company were guiding the ASC, REs, RAMC, etc. The next day we left Bethune and cycled to St Hilaire – stopped there until the Sunday – it was Wednesday when we got there – left there on Sunday – had had no food since Friday'.

Note

The rest of the letter describes our journey up to the Ypres area and events up to the date of the letter; the last part of the letter amuses me now when I read it.

'You will probably think when you read this that I have been through a bit of a rough time but that is merely a flea bite compared with what it is in the trenches up to your knees in mud all the time; I am glad I don't have to go into the trenches.

'This is a decent job – I do 24 hours on guard and the same off and we can always get a warm bath and get our clothes washed and one night out of two get our boots and clothes off too and have a good sleep. The people here (Poperinghe) do not seem to worry much and food is not scarce. We get bread, butter, bacon, jam, meat, cheese, condensed milk and sugar for our rations so we don't hurt. We get that every day bacon for breakfast always, and we pinch potatoes out of the fields so we are all right.'

I was obviously trying to quieten down any fears and troubles in my mother's mind.

Letter from E. Blasdale, 12th Sherwood Foresters Pioneer battalion (digging trenches etc, most units took a turn at this very important work)
I was interested in your letter of May 28 in the *Daily Telegraph* as I was at the battle of Loos, but I did not write forthwith as I thought I could not be of much help. However, on second thoughts I decided I would get in touch giving you what information I could. Unfortunately all our letters were censored and we were warned against keeping records which might fall into enemy hands.

I was a sergeant (aged 20) in the 12th Sherwood Foresters (Pioneers) which was part of the 24th Division. We landed at Le Havre on August 30th and it was intended that we should complete our training in France. This we did till September 21st at a small French village named St Deneoux. We then did two long night marches (some 40 miles carrying full equipment) arriving at Bethune on September 24th.

I have not delved into the official history of the war, but for what it is worth, I believe our Division was rushed up to the front to hold the line after the Australians or New Zealanders had made the breakthrough. Our information was that the Guards were detailed to carry on the offensive but had not arrived in time owing to some poor staff work.

We spent the night of September 26th in the reserve trenches and went over the top at 11 a.m. on the 27th. We met a hail of bullets and gun fire suffering very heavy casualties becoming disorganised and getting mixed up with other battalions. We were relieved about 8.30 the next morning and stayed in the area doing salvage work until October 1st.

Letter from Group Captain J. H. S. Richards
I was then a 1st Lieutenant (two whole pips) in the East Surrey Regiment. 72 Infantry Brigade 24th Division and was in the first and leading wave that went over at 11.00 hours Sunday morning September 26th. I survived across the Lens–La Bassée Road and survived well up the far Western slope until I was hit just short of the German wire – but I managed to get back late in the afternoon.

East Surrey Letter
Though in the battle line at the time of Loos, my Regiment did not take part but my father's Regiment, the 9th East Surreys did. I can only pass to (you may already know this) a point or two.

The Surreys kicked two footballs when going over the top in a bayonet charge† on the Loos mine towers (cage lifts) footballs can be seen in the

Note Rumour about Anzacs – it was in fact the Scots.

†No. That was on the Somme in 1916.

Surrey's County HQs Kingston on Thames or in the Museum at Lambeth.

There was a shell shortage for our artillery. Tin hats were not in issue then. A gas mask known as a PH helmet (hood type) was carried.

A very famous first aid post was known to men of that battle, was known as 'Lone Tree Dressing Station'. There is a photo of this tree in the Imperial War Museum, Lambeth.

A cry was made by men of the 21st or 24th Division (I am not sure which Division) that the Guards Division came into action about two to four hours late. I think you will find some material for your book in the said Museum. Piper Laidlaw won his VC playing the pipes on the parapet as the men went over.

Account by V. M. Lunnon

I enclose as promised my narrative of Loos and events leading up to the battle which seem relevant. I hope the writing is legible. Had I large scale map of the area and I might have been able to place my scene of the battle more precisely.

I realise that what I have written may not be what you want, if you feel that there might be anything more I can add do please let me know. I have much enjoyed doing this little piece and wish you every success with your book.

Personal Notes, 11 Essex Regiment

V. M. Lunnon. Born 25th November 1894. Educated Alleyn's School, Dulwich. Joined Kitchener's first 100,000 September 3rd 1914 enlisting in the 7th East Surrey Regiment, encamped at Purfleet Essex. No previous military experience.

After an NCO's Course with the Guards at Chelsea was promoted to Sergeant late October 1914.

In early December I was interviewed by Colonel Radclyffe, CO of the 11th Essex Regiment, who indicated that he would accept me as one of his officers, after which I applied for and attained a commission. I was given no intelligence test, nor was I asked for a school certificate. I had a war office interview and a Medical Exam and shortly afterwards my Commission, on parchment arrived. I was apparently recommended to Colonel Radclyffe, by a relative who knew somebody who knew him. I did not even know this was being done. So many officers were needed at the time and so urgently that any more elaborate means of selection would have taken too long to organise. At that time there were enough senior officers available from the Reserve as to ensure that each new Battalion had a good CO whose experience and judgement could be

relied upon. Colonel Radclyffe had retired from the Rifle Brigade some
5 years before and I judged him to be about 55 and thoroughly fit and
alert.

The Battalion

The 11th Essex was not the first new unit of this regiment to be re-
cruited. The 9th Essex had been started at the same time as the 7th East
Surreys and was perhaps a month earlier to commence training.

Therefore the battalion had hardly got going when I joined them at
Brighton. They had spent their first month at Shoreham hutment camp
which had to be evacuated because of heavy rain and inadequate drain-
age. Now the men were billetted in small back street houses, scattered
all over the town. Most parades were on a platoon or section basis, but
occasionally they were able to come together as companies – mainly for
route marches. There were few halls available and we took turns to use
them for lectures when the weather was bad. Morale had suffered under
these conditions and there was a good deal of minor sickness.

Unlike the 7th East Surreys in which the men were mostly Londoners,
the 11th Essex were largely countrymen many of whom had probably
waited to get the harvest in before enlisting. East Anglians are good
natured, deliberate and durable and suffered those mean billets with
fortitude.

The officers were quartered in the Royal Hotel, at that time a tem-
perance establishment. The proprietor, who still lived there, did not
approve of drink, but like Shylock 'bore it with a patient shrug'. No
doubt the army had given him adequate compensation for occupying
his hotel which would have otherwise been half empty.

The hotel was big enough to give each officer a bedroom and quite
good sized lounges and a mess. It also accommodated Battalion HQ staff.

Under such conditions the CO had ample opportunity to assess the
character and personality of his officers, a necessary process since we
were a mixed lot. There were quite a few who were well over 40, some
of whom turned out to have little or no experience to compensate for
their age. There were one or two alcoholics and a few spongers. They
had not, it was quite evident, been selected by the CO. These disappeared
quite quickly. However, there were two senior majors who were indis-
pensable in their way, a first class Welsh Schoolmaster of about 35 and
as Adjutant we had a young regular of the first Battalion who had not
yet been to the front with his unit because of sickness. The young officers
were mostly undergraduates from Oxford and Cambridge and very
bright they were.

The CO kept us pretty hard at work both with the men in normal training and collectively at evening study i.e. lectures on discipline, King's Regulations and various aspects of military training. Every officer was required to lecture in turn and was advised to study his subject before doing so, since he would be expected to answer questions. Having had some Art training I chose Field sketching and luckily no one else seemed to know much about it.

We had a first class regular Reservist as Regimental Sergeant Major but under the conditions in Brighton his job of selecting and training NCO's was much more difficult. He virtually had to wait until we could return to Shoreham before he could really see the junior NCO's on the job. It all came right in the end.

Most of the men had been issued with a nondescript blue uniform and forage cap; these served their purpose for a time, but there was a shortage of overcoats and boots and quite a few men were in civvies. There were no more than enough long Lee Enfields for musketry demonstration and dummy wooden rifles for drill.

The weather was extremely bad for most of January and improved a little in February and then late that month we were back in the Shoreham Camp, now better drained and waterproof.

This gave us the opportunity to open up the training for which we were blessed with the run of the South Downs. Also more kit began to arrive, Khaki uniforms and greatcoats, more rifles and equipment (most of which was leather and not so efficient or as light as webbing, particularly when wet).

So although our first 5 months of soldiering was a pretty thin training experience for war, we had, thanks to our good CO, got the best we could get out of it.

Coming back to Shoreham we could compare our progress with other Units in the Brigade – namely Suffolks, Norfolks and Bedfords; we exchanged visits to each others guest nights. There were Brigade lectures for both officers and NCO's and twice we had Brigade operations; i.e. lectured exercise and a route march. We also had sporting events; athletics, boxing and football. The 71st Brigade was commanded by Brigadier General Barter.

The famous Musketry Training School at Hythe was going strong with a first class staff of Regular Officers and NCO's. You were not only taught everything about the rifle and how to fire it – you were taught to teach the subject. It ended after a fortnight with a pretty stiff test which required full marks to get a D (distinguished) and a minimum of 957 to get a first. The CO sent both officers and NCO's to this course and it was remarkable to witness the change in their confidence and command of the men when they returned.

We certainly got some firing experience at the Hythe range but 303 ammunition was not available until much later for our Battalion rifle position. Indeed few of us had fired more than 15 to 20 rounds of 303 when finally we went into battle. That there were some very good shots among us was due to the CO's drive in getting a miniature .22 range going and plenty of ammunition.

Much the same could be said of grenade training. There was a Divisional School for selected officers and NCO's but the men had to be mainly content with dummy bombs which had little appeal for them. We also had a good deal of PT and bayonet fighting.

My earlier experience on the Guards course at Chelsea Barracks gave me a lasting faith in the value of drill, particularly with rifles, which had to be handled frequently to develop the stamina necessary for their use. Weighing 14 lbs they were difficult to master and only by constant handling could they become part of you. The other vital aspect of drill in that it ties each Unit firmly together, the more thoroughly and precisely it is taught, the better the rhythm and spirit of the troops. I discovered that the thorough attention to detail practised by the Guards in all movements set the standards of instruction and insistent discipline in every other aspect of their training. Drill standards were initially pretty low with the 11th Essex but gradually we improved and once we were properly equipped we became very good. If I had something to do with this it was because of the support I got from the CO, Adjutant and RSM, and of course the men of my platoon who had a good reputation to uphold.

I liked to think that the men were responsive to strict discipline in every other aspect of the training, but good instructors are not easy to find and train – so that we had a few soft areas. We were not professional soldiers yet but we were no longer amateurs. Senior officers and NCO's were alert and quick to correct weakness and everybody was getting very keen.

With three other officers I was sent to a Company Commanders' Course at Camberley Staff College in June 1915. It was a month of graceful living in peace-time conditions – or nearly so, at any rate. The silver plate and elegant tableware, the string band on guest nights, the port and the pictures and fine proportions of the mess was in contrast to our hutted camp, and the food was admirably cooked and served.

There were about 60 officers on the course which at 4 per battalion meant the potential or actual company commanders of the Infantry of the 24th Division and some others.

The Commander was a Major McCalf who had served at Mons and the Marne and there were three other regular officer instructors and some who attended for special lectures etc.

A Scots Guards Staff Sergeant dealt firmly with us at 5.30 a.m. PT and there were a number of NCO's and men for various jobs. It was all run very efficiently and every day except Saturday afternoon and Sunday was fully occupied. There were plenty of TEWTS*, mostly on Chobham Common, Lectures in the evening, occasionally by Military experts on Battles of the past and informal talks on current war experiences by the Instructors. Whilst strenuous and interesting the course lacked some of the realities of the time. It would have been a boon to have seen some films from the Front – but in those days the Army had little equipment for such purposes. We learnt about the German gas attack in the Second Battle of Ypres which was useful. We saw some of the latest weapons and missiles, the Lewis Gun, Rifle grenades, the Stokes Mortar and The Blacker bombard just introduced as a wire buster. An Engineer Officer demonstrated explosives used to demolish bridges etc., and we built and revetted a trench. This last subject could well have been more used as a regular item in infantry training at the time but I believe that the top brass was not in favour of digging in too deeply. This to my mind was a major mistake. The Germans protected themselves with deep trenches and underground quarters and defended their positions from strong machine gun points and barbed wire in considerable depth. We knew nothing about this yet. In fact the Engineers did later make some time defences which gave safety to the Higher Commanders but rarely to the troops.

The CO beamed at us on our return from Camberley and so we supposed that we had 'passed'.

By now the men were very fit and our operations were the more strenuous and testing. We used our TEWT notes from Camberley for a number of tactical schemes *with* troops and I think that on the whole they were good for us even though some of them could have been based on old wars.

In July a number of officers and senior NCO's were detailed for what we called a Cook's tour, which in fact meant going to France, Belgium and being detached singly for different parts of the front. Whilst the quieter areas were selected for this purpose we had a minor casualty or two. I was posted to the 4th Middlesex at Hooge and told to get to know

*Tactical Exercises Without Troops.

what was happening on that Battalion's front. I was given a runner to take me round for which I was glad. He knew the danger spots in the view of German snipers and the front line gunners who had a small high velocity weapons firing whizz bangs which were very very quick.

The area in the salient at Ypres was very tattered and our troops were at a disadvantage in the many places where the Germans held the high ground and arranged things so that water drained into ours. We were protected by parapets rather than trenches. The town was a distinct eye opener and when we discussed our observations with the CO on our return we were asked to make a joint report which I gather was discussed higher up. After that we did quite a lot of strenuous digging and revetting and wiring.

Our barbed wire was of lighter gauge than that of the Germans and we had begun to use concertina wire supported by corkscrew stakes which could be quickly screwed into anything but very hard rocky ground. The concertina wire coils could be quickly stretched between the stakes. The Germans took longer with their wiring, using wooden stakes, sometimes wooden X shaped supports. When our wire was shelled it was the stakes that went first and quite often the concertinas collapsed and gaps were created. It was impossible to create such gaps in the German wire by shelling and even where the stakes were blown the heavy wire remained. Had our commanders realised the importance of finding another way of breaching wire? I very much doubt whether the matter had been discussed at top level. In all battle orders I saw in the First World War it was assumed that Boche wire could be cut by artillery fire. It couldn't and hundreds of thousands of casualties were caused by the General Staff's ignorance and inattention to this very small detail. I know that the Blacker bombard came into use later in the war but we never saw it used, nor was it sufficiently developed then as to be reliable.

At least Colonel Radclyffe was responsive to the buzz of the bees in our bonnets but of course he didn't move in the rarefied atmosphere of the Red and the Gold who still had their minds upon the expected Cavalry breakthrough.

Since becoming captain, although as yet a second in command of a company, I had learned to ride but after my Cook's tour doubted whether my rather nice horse would be needed. He would, however, go with us to France and perhaps could be a means of comfortable travel in rest periods.

However, the end of July rumours were strong that we should be off to France quite soon and gaps in our ranks appeared as home leave was taken. The Quarter blokes were busy with their orders to assemble and pack stores – the camp got a lot of paint and hard scrubbing. Indeed there were more fatigues than training parades.

About the end of August we were on our way. Some of us in advance to assist disembarkation at Boulogne and others in a rear party to collect forgotten trifles, in our case one field cooker and a limber, plus a few cheerful men who had overstayed their leave.

All disembarkation was done by a very efficient landing officer and staff and so the advance party had rather a pleasant time in Boulogne. We entrained and then marched to a charming village called Estree in the Montreuil area. No doubt it was the first time that the villagers had had British troops billetted on them and we were volubly and warmly welcomed. The officers were comfortably billetted, mostly in farmhouses and the men occupied barns which had been cleared and cleaned for them. Since there were few men in the villages most of the hard work was done by the women. We could at least repay them a little by ensuring that our billets were kept clean whilst the farm lads among us lent a hand wherever possible. Our menu was improved by French cooking and whilst we had plenty of good beef and mutton to give in exchange for delicious chicken and pork dishes and pears and peaches, the French were glad also to welcome other exchanges.

With other captains we took a few rides into Montreuil where our top brass were, but after dining once at the top hotel – we reverted quickly to smaller restaurants to enjoy ourselves in a less toffee-nosed atmosphere.

The main part of our training now was to get used to moving over French roads most of which had a centre track of granite pavé with dirt or mud either side. Moving as we did in fours just about kept us together on the pavé but when we met other traffic some of us had to step down a few inches into the dirt. We might have done a little better marching in threes as in the 1939 war or just walked without formation or rhythm as did the French, who straggled but got there just the same.

We marched both by day and night and the routes were changed to exercise our map reading. We quickly realised that we should go into battle on foot and judged that we should need to cover up to 60 miles in this way. Presumably other units of the 24th Division were also billetted somewhere in the area, but we did not see them and we concluded that we were well scattered so as to give no warning to the Germans of our intentions.

On Saturday afternoon we gave a party to the whole village, many tables and forms end to end in a shady orchard, a French conjurer and punchinello for the children (including the grown-up ones) and the tables groaning with culinary masterpieces from our cookhouse. There were speeches of course from the Maire, the Docteur and the Notarie and from our CO beaming and fatherly. The wine flowed and our tongues loosened on the language we had learnt at school but never really practised.

About September 26th the CO and adjutant were absent all on a secret mission and we knew that they were receiving our marching orders.

The next day we knew all but which part of the front we were going to. Guides would be provided by the Staff to conduct us at night to three rest points en route where we would be more or less under cover during daylight. We were to enter a town behind the line in the night 24th/25th September. This town was in fact Bethune. From there we would move up by day behind the territorials and new army units in the first line of the attack and to go into action on the morning of the 26th September.

As we moved out of Estree to the cheers and tears of our French hosts, we were in good heart – our little battalion bugle band, aided by one or two other odd instruments filling the air with the songs of the time.

But as night wore on we began to feel the pinch of boots and chafing of pack straps. I soon abandoned my horse (I now was commanding C coy) for he didn't care for the pace or me. He would be better off and more useful with the transport which was beginning to collect the packs and rifles of the weaker brethren – the cooks and the clerks. Next day we exposed battered feet to cold water and sunlight and the MO was busy. Our cookers also gave of their best after which most of us managed to get some sleep. At nightfall we moved off again, the CO wisely changing the number of halts to from one every hour to one every 45 minutes – Marching with full pack at night was revealing strain although the men didn't complain. Also the roads got busier as troops from other areas converged on our route. It began to rain and on arrival at our next rest point, we found conditions very cramped. Indeed the cookers with our longed for morning tea had to be put some distance from us. During the day it rained intermittently and became colder. Our feet were getting pretty bad, but at least on the next night we should have shed our heavy packs and march more easily in battle order.

We had orders to be ready to go to cover on a whistled signal from our plane spotter. The Hun planes were very high and did no more than observe, but the alarms were frequent. We had a good hot meal at mid-day and some rest afterwards. It was to be the last decent meal that we should get for two or three days. On the march that night the converging of our division caused unscheduled halts to become frequent. There were obviously a lot of troops about including artillery on the move and the guns and limbers held us up time after time. Somewhere ahead of us was Bethune and ahead of that dismal town the slag-heaps of Loos and the front line of troops waiting to attack at dawn. We could hear the guns and see their flashes but it wasn't possible to assess the strength of our own bombardment.

By dawn we had come through the town and were moving up, still in marching order through minor roads and muddy tracks left by preceding troops. We halted between Bethune and Noeux les Mines and rested as best we could. The cooks managed tea and biscuits and the CO sent parties to forage food from the French without a lot of success. The rations had gone astray but we were rightly restrained from consuming our own rations.

Our wounded came streaming back as the morning wore on and we gathered that the German line had been broken. A few prisoners appeared, led by cheerful Scots and we saw some of our 24th Divisional artillery moving up. The forage parties came back with eggs, bread and a few chickens and most of us got one good sandwich with a cup of tea, before moving further up the line. As we moved forward the number of our dead told the tale of a hard won battle and when we finally reached the limit of the advance, a well made German trench, we reckoned that the British had gained over a mile on this section. It seemed strange that we should see no one of the unit which we relieved and we assumed that they had departed in another direction to the rear or had taken over some of the line elsewhere.

There was some shelling going on but none of it very heavy. Now and again German shrapnel burst above us with little warning sound. The German Crumps (4 in) and Coalboxes (6 in) approx calibres fired from Howitzers took longer to arrive and one could learn how to take evasive action in time no doubt.

Once settled in our trench we got busy with our preparations for the dawn fully expecting that this would be the time of our attack. We made contact with our flanks and it seemed that my Company was on the right of the 24th Division joining up with the 21st. Sentries were posted, bombs or ammunition checked and listening posts put out on the ridge in front of us. The many dead British and the fewer dead Germans had shocked us. We were new to the sight of still stiff bodies, staring eyes and mutilation. But they all looked as if they had died doing something – died with their boots on and the cries of battle on their lips. Some of us were going to be like that quite soon we thought, but never said.

The CO came up to give us cheer and encouragement as we waited, but there were no orders from 'on high' as yet and of course no rations. And yet I heard my Essex boys quietly singing as they waited.

Came the dawn and no instructions other than one from the CO for each front Company to do what it could to reconnoitre and report. My task was simple since we could keep out of sight moving up to the ridge some 200 yards in front of us and from there observe the German positions through glasses. We had no maps of the German trench system although I gather that some were in existence. Indeed our Air Survey Maps during that war were very accurate and good.

From the observation point open farmland of grass and plough stretched before us sloping down to a treelined road in the hollow. On that road to the left of us was a group of houses which I took to be the village of Hulluch and this appeared to be defended. Beyond the ground rose to the German line obviously prepared long before with thickly massed rusty wire in front of it. A Gunner observer told me he was there to register our guns on this wire and on the village and we left him there waiting for our shells to come over.

Company Commanders reported their observations to the CO and we made rough maps of our own. The HQ group would be in the centre heading for the village and the CO told us that we could take our direction from him (he would be wearing his usual white wash leather gloves) The RSM looked at me glumly – I think we all looked a bit like that; what other Commander would do this unnecessary act of sheer bravery – HQ should be behind. Well it happened that it would have been all the same wherever he was, and of course he knew that to lead himself would do more good for us than for him to come up in the rear, equally vulnerable. Finally he gave us the time of the attack. 11 a.m. After that the rain stopped and out came the sun from a brilliant sky to shine down on as we moved across 1500 yards deep of open fields.

An occasional shell from our gunners whistled towards the German line and I wondered if the RFA ammunition and our rations and rum were still somewhere back near Montreuil.

We moved forward in good extended order with instructions to leap frog forward section by section when signalled. Breasting the ridge brought the German rifle fire and we could tell by the number of spent bullets that they were wasting their ammunition. But of course going further forward we came into view of machine gun posts and thereafter moved up section by section in short rushes, taking what cover was available – very little. I noticed a half completed trench on our right about 300 yards short of the road and thought it might prove a haven if the attack failed, and by now the men were really falling. I looked for the CO but could not see him.

The company commander on my left appeared and told me that the

CO had been killed and that he was taking over battalion command. He resumed the central position but I never saw him again. My men were thinning out as their ranks became shorter. Moreover we had the road to cross and I was dead sure that it would be heavily enfiladed from the village. By whistles and signals I got the attention of a dozen of my men and hoped that those following would move as we did. In fact we crawled singly over the last 100 or so yards to the road relying on the cover which the trees lining it would give. Once near the road we would cross in line and at speed. I had spotted cover in the form of dungheaps on the other side of the road and moved forward in the direction. The fire was devastating and although I was lucky only a half of the leading dozen got over – others arrived but the final count was not much over 20 and not an officer was with them, all having been killed or wounded on the way.

Now closer to the wire I could see that there was a bit of a gully in the ground directly in front. On my right men of the 21st Division were moving forward but they faltered at and on the wire; it was impenetrable.

I decided that we could use the gully and the dungheaps as cover for a while and put some shots into the Germans in Hulluch about 300 yards away. We saw the Boche moving about and from this temporary haven did a bit of destruction. We used a lot of rounds and I called cease fire to save the rest. Had the ploy worked? It looked very much as if it had when men of the 21st Division, coming back passed over the road in safety. But we had attracted the attention of German Trench Mortar Sections and I decided to go back to the new trench I had seen to our right and there to join the 21st Division. We got there safely and took stock. We brewed some tea and ate pieces of bully beef – there. There was now food to be had if one could bring oneself to raid comrades' haversacks. We could not.

A major came running down the line beyond the parapet with rallying calls and orders to attack again. I had the beginnings of a plan in my mind but he was too excited to listen to me. No doubt he was of the stuff that heroes are made of but everybody who had seen that German line on the ridge and its impenetrable wire knew that the attack would fail. He disappeared from view but later I saw a few of his men go forward with him and fall.

My idea was to await nightfall and attack the village by surprise, from our dungheaps position on the other side of the road. But now I had less than a dozen of my men and a few others who had attached themselver. Besides it was a job for fresher troops, equipped with wire cutters' machine guns and mortars.

During the night the Guards came and took over from us and directed us back to their reserve line. They sent stretcher bearers to help ours with the wounded and as usual they were active and alert. Sentries out, trenches being repaired and deepened. They still stood upright when speaking to seniors in the line so they needed deeper trenches. My men were fed with a really good breakfast and I took my meal in an officers' mess of corrugated iron and sandbags. After that I slept for three or four hours. I had spoken to their company commander at breakfast about my little plan and he said he would have a look at the position. Whether or not he tried it out I don't know. I gather there was a good deal of in fighting afterwards and that in the end there was little to show for our losses at the Battle of Loos.

I moved to our Battalion Assembly point with my few men. Our casualties had left us with less than 200 of our original strength.

But if anybody says to me unguardedly that it was Kitchener's Army that let the British down they get a broadside from me.

To order an attack without the preparation of maps to enable us to study the ground was incompetent and that was not the fault of the men so ordered. The only possible chance of getting through at Loos on the second day was by surprise at night with troops fully rehearsed for the purpose. Indeed those concerned with the strategy of the British Army were influenced by the political pressure to boost civilian morale. Those concerned with tactics and training techniques were pretty small fry. It needed a Montgomery to break that absurd barrier, 20 odd years later.

16

Guards and Cavalry

Letter from Mrs M. Spiller

My brother who was aged 19 volunteered for the Army in August 1914 and was called up on September 3rd or 4th 1914. He joined the Grenadier Guards and when the Welsh Guards was formed in February 27th 1915, he transferred to them. He went to France the following June or July and we were not to see him again. The Guards were again in a big battle during September 1916, the Battle of Ypres, where my brother was to die of his wounds a few days later. As I was a schoolgirl at the time, my memory is rather hazy as to the month he left for France, but once there, he never had leave to come home, only the 48 hours' rest. On re-reading my brother's letters from France I find that the censorship was not as keen as it was in the last war.

I have a Press photograph of the new regiment of Welsh Guards marching through London just before leaving for the front. Captain Osmond Williams is leading them and they received their baptism of fire at Hill 70 and Captain Williams was the first officer to lose his life.

Copy of part of a letter to me from Mrs M. Spiller

Sunday September 1915

I suppose you've read in the papers by now that we've broken through the German lines and advanced nine miles along the whole British Front. We are within a few miles of them now and the big guns are kicking up a fearful din. We have had some horrid long marches night and day, but I've stuck it so far. Our CO told us that we intend driving the Germans back now and our efforts would either end the war or go a long way to do so. We were on the march yesterday when the news came through that the 1st and 2nd German trenches had been taken, of course that cheered us up a lot. We are engaged in the biggest battle of the world now and a day or two will see us in, but cheer up it will soon be over.

Guards Division 1916

This is to certify that No 266 Private F. Parry First Battalion Welsh Guards performed the following act of gallantry on 27th September 1915 at Loos.

In company with three other privates remained on Hill 70 from September 27th until midnight September 30th/October 1st in a hole between the British and German trenches with two German prisoners and a dead German officer. They lived on food taken from the Germans and returned on October 1st with the two prisoners and the papers found on the dead German officer.

This certificate is issued in appreciation of the act, but does not entitle or qualify the recipient to any reward, extra emolument or pension.

A. Feilding, Major General,
Comdg Guards Division

Letter from Captain Fox

Re your letter in yesterday's *Daily Telegraph*, regarding the battle of Loos. My diaries were handed in and my recollections are from memory.

I was Veterinary Officer to the Brigade of Guards (20th Infantry Brigade, 7th Division) from August 1914 until after the battle of the Somme 1916, when the Guards Division was formed.

The 7th Division was heavily engaged at Loos. The Guards Brigade, the night before was billeted at Bethune and we moved into battle early next morning. It was commanded by Brigadier Heyworth of the Grenadier Guards.

The High Command prepared all for battle, by stating that it was the beginning of the end and that we would go forward successfully through Germany.

The initial stages of the battle were successful. The Germans retreated, after heavy fighting and high casualties on both sides. We were not reinforced and the Germans whilst taken initially by surprise, were quickly reinforced.

When the Germans retreated I galloped into action with the Scots Greys, with very little resistance, but this success was short-lived. When the Germans counterattacked, we were forced to retreat as fast as possible to avoid capture and for the first time the Germans used gas and although prepared by having gas masks it was a most unpleasant experience. The gas did not affect men or horses as we quickly got away.

In the Battle of Loos the Guards had very heavy losses, and their officers were killed or wounded.

Letter from P. Osment; 3rd Field Ambulance, Guards Division, XI Corps
I read your letter in the *Daily Telegraph* re: Battle of Loos. I regret
that I am unable to give you any letters or diaries, in the first place we
had very little time to write letters and anything written about the battle
would have been censored. As for keeping diaries by other ranks would
have been death or any such less punishment as may be inflicted upon
you by a General Court Martial as read out to all troops regularly before
the outbreak of war.

I enlisted in the regular army RAMC. In 1912 went overseas as
Medical Orderly to B Squadron. The 15th Kings Royal Hussars was in
the retreat from Mons and on the advance from the Marne to the Aisne.
I became separated from my Unit, was ordered to join No 3 Field
Ambulance 3rd Infantry Brigade. On the formation of the Guards Division we joined the 3rd Guards Brigade, this was in the summer of 1915.
We went into the back area to form up with the Brigade. We marched
for a couple of days until we came to the battle area for Loos. Confusion
and chaos was everywhere. The staff work had all gone haywire, Brigades
and Divisions meeting at crossroads, we lost touch with our brigade for
several hours, the bearer division of the Field Ambulance always followed close behind the Battalion that was going into action. We had
done so from the Aisne to Loos. As far as I can remember we followed
the Welsh Guards; it was their first time in as a Regiment. It must have
shaken the troops what they saw going into action for the first time.

It shook us although we had been through Ypres, Neuve Chappelle,
Festubert, etc. The new troops of the 15th Scottish Division met it badly,
for weeks, all one saw was bodies hanging on the wire. Must have been
hundreds of them.

Right throughout the war it seemed as if the staff and generals did
their best to kill off as many of our own troops as possible.

I served right through the war to Cologne, Germany, from stretcher
bearer to Corporal to Sergeant.

Letter from J. H. Hardwick, 3rd Cavalry
The situation on the afternoon of the 26th September was extremely
critical, the 24th Division who had made what was at first a successful
attack was obliged to give ground and the 21st Division finding itself
opposed by strong German reinforcements, was also driven back. It was
under these circumstances that at 3 p.m. General Campbell was ordered
to occupy Loos with two regiments, as the infantry appeared to be retiring,
and it was uncertain whether the place was in our hands or not.

The 6th Cavalry Brigade fixed bayonets and advanced by three long 'bounds' down the slope into the village, the 3rd Dragoon Guards on the right, the Royal Dragoons on the left.

The line was shelled as it advanced over; one shell started up a hare which was caught on a bayonet by a sergeant. On the way the Colonel of the Royals collected about 300 Highlanders and other parties of infantry who returned to Loos and helped in its defence.

POSTSCRIPT

There are many regiments which took part in the battle of Loos which are not represented in these accounts. Probably most of the members of those regiments were killed or have since died. Their part in the battle was no less than those whose story is given in the first-hand accounts, and some perhaps endured more, if that were possible. Their experience and their sacrifice may be known from the accounts of others for if there was any battle in British history when every unit was fully committed it was undoubtedly Loos. We need say no more.

Appendix: Order of Battle

FIRST ARMY

LOOS 1915

I. Corps

Commander	Lieut.-Gen. H. de la P. Gough, c.b.
Br.-General, General Staff . .	Br.-Gen. A. S. Cobbe, v.c., c.b., d.s.o., a.d.c.
D.A. and Q.M.G. . . .	Br.-Gen. H. N. Sargent, c.b., d.s.o.
Br.-General, Royal Artillery .	Br.-Gen. J. F. N. Birch, a.d.c.
Chief Engineer . . .	Br.-Gen. R. P. Lee, c.b.

2ND DIVISION : Major-Gen. H. S. Horne

5th Brigade : Br.-Gen. C. E. Corkran
1/Queen's	2/Oxf. & Bucks L.I.	1/7th King's (T.F.)
2/Worcestershire	2/Highland L.I.	1/9th Highland L.I. (T.F.)

6th Brigade : Br.-Gen. A. C. Daly
1/King's	1/R. Berkshire	1/5th King's (T.F.)
2/S. Staffordshire	1/K.R.R.C.	1/1st Herts (T.F.)

19th Brigade : Br.-Gen. P. R. Robertson
2/R. Welch Fus.	1/Middlesex	1/5th Scottish Rifles
1/Scottish Rifles	2/Argyll & Sutherlands	(T.F.)

R.F.A. Bdes
XXXIV (50th, 70 Btys.)	XLI (9, 16, 17 Btys.)
XXXVI (15, 48, 71 Btys.)	XLIV (How.) 47 & 56 Btys.

Field Coys. R.E. : 5, 11 & 1/1st E. Anglian (T.F.)

Mtd. Troops : B. Sqdn. S. Irish Horse. Cyclist Coy.

7TH DIVISION : Major-Gen. Sir T. Capper, K.C.M.G.

20th Brigade : Br.-Gen. Hon. J. F. Hepburn-Stuart-Forbes-Trefusis

2/Border	8/Devonshire	1/6th Gordons
2/Gordons	9/Devonshire	(T.F.)

21st Brigade : Br.-Gen. H. E. Watts

2/Bedfordshire	2/R. Scots Fus.	1/4th Camerons
2/Green Howards	2/Wiltshire	(T.F.)

22nd Brigade : Br.-Gen. J. McC. Steele

2/Queen's	1/R. Welch Fus.
2/R. Warwickshire	1/S. Staffordshire

R.H.A. Bde. : XIV (F & T Btys.)[1]

R.F.A. Bdes.

XXII (104, 105, 106 Btys.)	XXXVII (How.) 31 & 35 Btys.
XXV (12, 25, 58 Btys.)	

Field Coys. R.E. : 54, 55 & 1/2nd Highland (T.F.)

Mtd. Troops : H.Q. & A Sqdn. Northumberland Hrs. (Yeo.) Cyclist Coy.

9TH (SCOTTISH) DIVISION : Major-Gen. G. H. Thesiger

26th Brigade : Br.-Gen. A. B. Ritchie

8/Black Watch	8/Gordons
7/Seaforths	5/Camerons

27th Brigade : Br.-Gen. C. D. Bruce

11/Royal Scots	6/R. Scots Fus.
12/Royal Scots	10/Argyll & Sutherlands

28th Brigade : Br.-Gen. S. W. Scrase-Dickens

6/K.O.S.B.	10/Highland L.I.
9/Scottish Rifles	11/Highland L.I.

R.F.A. Bdes.

L. (A, B, C, D Btys.)[2]	LII. (A, B, C, D Btys.)[2]
LI. (A, B, C, D Btys.)[2]	LIII. (How.) B, C, D Btys.[2]

Field Coys. R.E. : 63, 64, 90

Pioneers : 9/Seaforths

---

[1] Each of six 18-pdrs. which replaced the 13-pdrs. in June.
[2] 4-gun batteries.

Mtd. Troops : B Sqdn. Glasgow Yeo.   Cyclist Coy.

10th Motor M.G. Bty.

28TH DIVISION : [1] Major-Gen. E. S. Bulfin

83rd Brigade : Br.-Gen. H. S. L. Ravenshaw

2/King's Own	1/K.O.Y.L.I.	1/5th King's Own
2/E. Yorkshire	1/York & Lancaster	(T.F.)

84th Brigade : Br.-Gen. T. H. F. Pearse

2/Northumb. Fus.	2/Cheshire	1/6th Welch (T.F.)
1/Suffolk	1/Welch	

85th Brigade : Br. Gen. C. E. Pereira

2/Buffs	2/E. Surrey
3/Royal Fus.	3/Middlesex

R.F.A. Bdes

III (18, 22, 62, 365 Btys.)[2]	CXXX (How.) A, B, C Btys.[2]
XXXI (69, 100, 103, 118 Btys.)[2]	CXLVI (75, 149, 366, 367 Btys.)[2]

Field Coys. R.E. : 38 & 2/1st Northumbrian (T.F.)

Mtd. Troops : B Sqdn. Surrey Yeo.   Cyclist Coy.

III CORPS

Commander	Lieut.-Gen. Sir W. P. Pulteney, K.C.B., D.S.O.
Br.-General, General Staff .	Br.-Gen. C. F. Romer, C.B.
D.A. and Q.M.G. . . .	Br.-Gen. A. A. Chichester, C.B., D.S.O.
Br.-General, Royal Artillery	Br.-Gen. A. Stokes, C.B., D.S.O.
Chief Engineer . . .	Br.-Gen. A. L. Schreiber, D.S.O., A.D.C.

8TH DIVISION : Major-General H. Hudson

23rd Brigade : Br.-Gen. H. D. Tuson

2/Devonshire	2/Scottish Rifles	1/7th Middx. (T.F.)
2/W. Yorkshire	2/Middlesex	

---

[1] Replaced 9th Division in I Corps, 28th Sept.
[2] 4-gun batteries.

24th Brigade : Br.-Gen. R. S. Oxley

1/Worcestershire	1/Sherwood Foresters	1/5th Black Watch
2/E. Lancashire	2/Northamptonshire	(T.F.)

25th Brigade : Br.-Gen. R. B. Stephens

2/Lincolnshire	1/R. Irish Rifles	1/8th Middx (T.F.)
2/R. Berkshire	2/Rifle Brigade	1/1st London (T.F.)

R.H.A. Bde. : V. (O & Z Btys.)[1]

R.F.A. Bdes.

XXXIII (32, 33, 36 Btys.)	CXXVIII (How.) 55 & 57 Btys.
XLV (1, 3, 5 Btys.)	

Field Coys. R.E. : 2, 15 & 1/1st Home Counties (T.F.)

Mtd. Troops : C. Sqdn. Northumberland Hrs. (Yeo.)
Cyclist Coy.

20TH (LIGHT) DIVISION : Major-Gen. R. H. Davies

59th Brigade : Br.-Gen. C. D. Shute

1/K.R.R.C.	10/Rifle Brigade
11/K.R.R.C.	11/Rifle Brigade

60th Brigade : Br.-Gen. J. W. G. Ray

6/Oxf. & Bucks. L.I.	12/K.R.R.C.
6/Shropshire L.I.	12/Rifle Brigade

61st Brigade : Br.-Gen. C. Ross

12/King's	7/D. of Cornwall's L.I.
7/Somerset L.I.	7/K.O.Y.L.I.

R.F.A. Bdes.

XC (A, B, C, D Btys).[2]	XCII (How.) B, C, D Btys.[2]
XCI (A, B, C, D Btys.)[2]	XCIII (A, B, C, D Btys.)[2]

Field Coys. R.E. : 83, 84, 96

Pioneers : 11/Durham L.I.

Mtd. Troops : H.Q., M.G. Section & D Sqdn. West. & Cumb. Yeo.
Cyclist Coy.

14th Motor M.G. Bty.

---

[1] Each of six 18-pdrs. which replaced the 13-pdrs. in June.
[2] 4-gun batteries.

23RD DIVISION : Major-Gen. J. M. Babington

68th Brigade : Br.-Gen. E. Pearce Serocold
  10/Northumberland Fus.   12/Durham L.I.
  11/Northumberland Fus.   13/Durham L.I.

69th Brigade : Br.-Gen. F. S. Derham
  11/W. Yorkshire   9/Green Howards
  8/Green Howards   10/Duke of Wellington's

70th Brigade : Br.-Gen. L. F. Phillips
  11/Sherwood Foresters   8/York & Lancaster
  8/K.O.Y.L.I.   9/York & Lancaster

R.F.A. Bdes.
  CII (A, B, C, D Btys.)[1]   CIV (A, B, C, D Btys.)[1]
  CIII (A, B, C, D Btys.)[1]   CV (How.) A, B, C, D Btys.[1]

Field Coys. R.E. : 101, 102, 128

Pioneers : 9/S. Staffordshire

Mtd. Troops : C. Sqdn. Duke of Lancaster's Own Yeo.   Cyclist Coy.

IV CORPS

Commander . . . . Lieut.-Gen. Sir H. S. Rawlinson, Bt., K.C.B., C.V.O.
Br.-Gen, General Staff . . Br.-Gen. A. A. Montgomery
D.A. and Q.M.G. . . . Br.-Gen. W. L. White, C.B.
Br.-Gen, Royal Artillery . . Br.-Gen. C. E. D. Burworth, M.V.O.
Chief Engineer . . . Br.-Gen. R. U. H. Buckland, C.B., A.D.C.

1ST DIVISION : Major-Gen. A. E. A. Holland

1st Brigade : Br.-Gen. A. J. Reddie

  1/Black Watch   10/Gloucestershire   1/14th London (London
  1/Camerons   8/R. Berkshire   Scottish) (T.F.)

2nd Brigade : Br.-Gen. J. H. W. Pollard
  2/R. Sussex   1/L. N. Lancs   1/9th King's (T.F.)
  1/Northants   2/K.R.R.C.

[1] 4-gun batteries.

3rd Brigade : Br.-Gen. H. R. Davies
  1/S.W.B.   2/Welch
  1/Gloucestershire   2/R. Mun. Fus.

R.F.A. Bdes.
  XXV (113, 114, 115 Btys.)   XXXIX (46, 51, 54 Btys.)
  XXVI (116, 117 Btys.)   XLIII (How.) 30 & 40 Btys.

Field Coys. R.E. : 23, 26 & 1/1st Lowland (T.F.)

Mtd. Troops : B. Sqdn. Northumberland Hrs. (Yeo.)
           Cyclist Coy.

15TH (SCOTTISH) DIVISION : Major-Gen. F. W. N. McCracken

44th Brigade : Br.-Gen. M. G. Wilkinson
  9/Black Watch   10/Gordons
  8/Seaforths   7/Camerons

45th Brigade : Br.-Gen. F. E. Wallerston
  13/Royal Scots   6/Camerons
  7/R. Scots Fus.   11/Argyll & Sutherlands

46th Brigade : Br.-Gen. T. G. Matheson
  7/K.O.S.B.   10/Scottish Rifles
  8/K.O.S.B.   12/Highland L.I.

R.F.A. Bdes
  LXX (A, B, C, D Btys.)[1]   LXXII (A, B, C, D Btys.)[1]
  LXXI (A, B, C, D Btys.)[1]   LXXIII (How.) B, C, D Btys.[1]

Field Coys. R.E. : 73, 74, 91

Pioneers : 9/Gordons

Mtd. Troops : B Sqdn. Westmoreland & Cumberland Yeo.
           Cyclist Coy.

11th Motor M.G. Bty.

47TH (LONDON) DIVISION (T.F.) : Major-Gen. C. St. L. Barter

140th Brigade : Br.-Gen. G. J. Cuthbert
  1/6th London (City of   1/8th London (Post Office Rifles)
  1/7th London London)   1/15th London (Civil Service
                                        Rifles)

[1] 4-gun batteries.

141st Brigade : Br.-Gen. W. Thwaites
1/17th London (Poplar & Stepney Rifles)

1/19th London (St Pancras)

1/18th London (London Irish)

1/20th London (Blackheath & Woolwich)

142nd Brigade : Br.-Gen. F. G. Lewis
1/21st London (1st Surrey Rifles)

1/23rd London

1/22nd London (The Queen's)

1/24th London (The Queen's)

R.F.A. Bdes.
V London (12, 13, 14 Btys.)[1]
VI London (15, 16, 17 Btys.)[1]
VII London (18, 19, 20 Btys.)[1]
VIII London (How.) 21 & 22 Btys[2]

Field Coys. R.E. : 1/3rd, 1/4th & 2/3rd London

Pioneers : 1/4th R. Welch Fus.

Mtd. Troops : C Sqdn. King Edward's Horse   Cyclist Coy.

XI CORPS

Commander	Lieut.-Gen. R. C. B. Haking, C.B.
Br.-General, General Staff	Br.-Gen. H. M. de F. Montgomery
D.A. and Q.M.G. . .	Br.-Gen. R. Ford, C.M.G., D.S.O.
Br.-General, Royal Artillery	Br.-Gen. G. G. S. Carey
Chief Engineer . .	Br.-Gen. L. Jones

GUARDS DIVISION : Major-Gen. F. R. Earl of Cavan

1st Guards Brigade : Br.-Gen. G. P. T. Feilding
2/Grenadier Gds.

3/Coldstream Gds.

2/Coldstream Gds.

1/Irish Gds.

2nd Guards Brigade : Br.-Gen. J. Ponsonby
3/Grenadier Gds.

1/Scots Gds.

1/Coldstream Gds.

2/Irish Gds.

3rd Guards Brigade : Br.-Gen. F. J. Heyworth
1/Grenadier Gds.

2/Scots Gds.

4/Grenadier Gds.

1/Welsh Gds.

[1] Battery = four 15 pdrs.
[2] Battery = four 5in. hows.

R.F.A. Bdes.
   LXXIV (A, B, C, D Btys.)[1]   LXXVI (A, B, C, D, Btys.)[1]
   LXXV (A, B, C, D Btys.)[1]   LXI (How. A, B, C, D Btys.[1]

Field Coys. R.E. : 55, 75, 76

Pioneers : 4/Coldstream Gds.

Mtd. Troops : Sqdn. Household Cavalry.   Cyclist Coy.

12TH (EASTERN) DIVISION[2] : Major-Gen. F. D. V. Wing

35th Brigade : Br.-Gen. C. H. C. van Straubenzee
   7/Norfolk   9/Essex
   7/Suffolk   5/R. Berkshire

36th Brigade : Br.-Gen. H. B. Borradaile
   8/Royal Fus.   7/R. Sussex
   9/Royal Fus.   11/Middlesex

37th Brigade : Br.-Gen. C. A. Fowler
   6/Queen's   7/E. Surrey
   6/Buffs   6/R. West Kent

R.F.A. Bdes.
   LXII (A, B, C, D Btys.)[1]   LXIV (A, B, C, D Btys.)[1]
   LXIII (A, B, C, D Btys.)[1]   LXV (How.) A, B, D Btys.[1]

Field Coys. R.E. : 69, 70, 87

Pioneers : 5/Northamptonshire

Mtd. Troops : H.Q., M.G. Section & A Sqdn. King Edward's Horse.
     Cyclist Coy.

9th Motor M.G. Bty.

21ST DIVISION : Major-Gen. G. T. Forestier-Walker

62nd Brigade : Br.-Gen. E. B. Wilkinson
   12/Northumberland Fus.   8/E. Yorkshire
   13/Northumberland Fus.   10/Green Howards

63rd Brigade : Br.-Gen. N. T. Nickalls
   8/Lincolnshire   12/W. Yorkshire
   8/Somerset L.I.   10/York & Lancaster

---

[1] 4-gun batteries.
[2] 12th and 46th Divisions (concentrated behind Loos battle front on 29th September and 3rd October respectively) replaced 21st and 24th Divisions in XI Corps.

64th Brigade : Br.-Gen. G. M. Gloster

9/K.O.Y.L.I.	14/Durham L.I.
10/K.O.Y.L.I.	15/Durham L.I.

R.F.A. Bdes.

XCIV (A, B, C, D Btys.)[1]	XCVI (A, B, C, D Btys.)[1]
XCV (A, B, C, D Btys.)[1]	XCVII (How.) A, B, C, D Btys.[1]

Field Coys. R.E. : 97, 98, 126

Pioneers : 14/Northumberland Fus.

Mtd. Troops : A Sqdn. S. Irish Horse   Cyclist Coy.

24TH DIVISION : Major-Gen. Sir J. G. Ramsay, K.C.B.

71st Brigade : Br.-Gen. M. T. Shewen

9/Norfolk	8/Bedfordshire
9/Suffolk	11/Essex

72nd Brigade : Br.-Gen. B. R. Mitford

8/Queen's	9/E. Surrey
8/Buffs	8/R. West Kent

73rd Brigade : Br.-Gen. W. A. Oswald

12/Royal Fus.	7/Northamptonshire
9/R. Sussex	13/Middlesex

R.F.A. Bdes.

CVI (A, B, C, D Btys.)[1]	CVIII (A, B, C, D Btys.)[1]
CVII (A, B, C, D Btys.)[1]	CIX (How.) A, B, C, D Btys.[1]

Field Coys. R.E. : 103, 104, 129

Pioneers : 12/Sherwood Foresters

Mtd. Troops : A Sqdn. Glasgow Yeo.   Cyclist Coy.

46TH (NORTH MIDLAND) DIVISION (T.F.) :[2]
Major-Gen. Hon. E. J. Montague-Stuart-Wortley

137th Brigade : Br.-Gen. E. Feetham.

1/5th S. Staffordshire	1/5th N. Staffordshire
1/6th S. Staffordshire	1/6th N. Staffordshire

---

[1] 4-gun batteries.
[2] 12th and 46th Divisions (concentrated behind Loos battle front on 29th September and 3rd October respectively) replaced 21st and 24th Divisions in XI Corps.

138th Brigade : Br.-Gen. G. C. Kemp
    1/4th Lincolnshire   1/4th Leicestershire
    1/5th Lincolnshire   1/5th Leicestershire

139th Brigade : Br.-Gen. C. T. Shipley
    1/5th Sherwood Foresters   1/7th Sherwood Foresters
    1/6th Sherwood Foresters   1/8th Sherwood Foresters

R.F.A. Bdes.
    I N. Midland (1, 2, 3 Lincs.   III N. Midland (4, 5, 6 Staffs.
        Btys.)[1]   Btys.)[1]
    II N. Midland (1, 2, 3 Staffs.   IV N. Midland (How.) 1 & 2
        Btys.)[1]   Derbyshire Btys.[2]

Field Coys. R.E. : 1/1st, 1/2nd & 2/1st N. Midland

Pioneers : 1/1st Monmouthshire

Mtd. Troops : B Sqdn. Yorkshire Hrs. (Yeo.)   Cyclist Coy.

INDIAN CORPS.

Commander . . .	Lieut-Gen. Sir C. A. Anderson, K.C.B.
Br.-General, General Staff .	Br.-Gen. J. R. E. Charles, D.S.O.
D.A. and Q.M.G. . .	Br. Gen. A. W. Peck
Br.-General, Royal Artillery .	Br.-Gen. R. St. C. Lecky, C.B., D.S.O.
Chief Engineer . .	Br.-Gen. H. C. Nanton, C.B.

19TH (WESTERN) DIVISION : Major-Gen. C. G. M. Fasken

56th Brigade : Br.-Gen. B. G. Lewis
    7/King's Own   7/S. Lancashire
    7/E. Lancashire   7/L. N. Lancs.

57th Brigade[3] : Br.-Gen. L. T. C. Twyford
    10/R. Warwickshire   10/Worcestershire
    8/Gloucestershire   8/N. Staffordshire

58th Brigade : Br.-Gen. D. M. Stuart
    9/Cheshire   9/Welch
    9/R. Welch Fus.   6/Wiltshire

[1] Battery = four 15-pdrs.
[2] Battery = four 5in.-hows.
[3] In Army reserve at beginning of battle.

R.F.A. Bdes.

    LXXXVI (A, B, C, D Btys.)[1]   LXXXVIII (A, B, C, D Btys.)[1]

    LXXXVII (A, B, C, D Btys)[1]   LXXXIX (How.) A, C, D Btys.[1]

Field Coys. R.E. : 81, 82, 94

Pioneers : 5/S.W.B.

Mtd. Troops : C Sqdn. Yorks. Dragoons (Yeo.)   Cyclist Coy.

13th Motor M.G. Bty.

Lahore Division : Major-Gen. H. D'U. Keary

Ferozepore Brigade : Br.-Gen. R. G. Egerton

Connaught Rangers	89/th Punjabis	
57th Wilde's Rifles	129th/ Baluchis	1/4th London (T.F.)

Jullundur Brigade : Br.-Gen. E. P. Strickland

1/Manchester	47th Sikh	1/4th Suffolk (T.F.)
40th Pathans	59th Scinde Rifles	

Sirhind Brigade : Br.-Gen. W. G. Walker, v.c.

1/Highland L.I.	1/1st Gurkhas
27th Punjabis	4/King's (S.R.)

R.F.A. Bdes.

    V (64, 78, 81 Btys.)   XVIII (59, 93, 94 Btys.)

    XI (83, 84, 85 Btys.)   60th Bty. of XLIV (How.) Bde.

Engineers : 20 & 21 Coys. 3rd Sappers & Miners

Pioneers : 34th Sikh Pioneers

Mtd. Troops : 15th Lancers

Meerut Division : Major-Gen. C. W. Jacob

Dehra Dun Brigade : Br.-Gen. W. J. St J. Harvey

1/Seaforths	2/2nd Gurkhas	1/4th Seaforth (T.F.)
93rd Burma Infty.	1/9th Gurkhas	

Garhwal Brigade : Br.-Gen. C. G. Blackader

2/Leicestershire	2/3rd Gurkhas	1/3rd London
39th Garhwalis	2/8th Gurkhas	(T.F.)

[1] 4-gun batteries.

Bareilly Brigade : Br.-Gen. C. E. de M. Norie

   2/Black Watch   58th Vaughan's Rifles   1/4th Black Watch

   33rd Punjabis   69th Punjabis   (T.F.)

R.F.A. Bdes.

   IV (7, 14, 66 Btys.)   XIII (2, 8, 44 Btys.)

   IX (19, 20, 28 (Btys.)   61st Bty. of VIII (How.) Bde.

Engineers : 3 & 4 Coys. 1st Sappers & Miners

Pioneers : 107th Pioneers

Mtd. Troops : 4th Cavalry

3RD CAVALRY DIVISION : Major-Gen. C. J. Briggs

6th Cavalry Brigade : Br.-Gen. D. G. M. Campbell

   3/Dragoon Guards   1/Royal Dragoons   N. Somerset Yeo.

7th Cavalry Brigade : Br.-Gen. A. A. Kennedy

   1/Life Guards   2/Life Guards   Leicester Yeo.

8th Cavalry Brigade : Br.-Gen. C. B. Bulkeley-Johnson

   Royal Horse Guards   10/Hussars   Essex Yeo.

R.H.A. Bed. : IV (C, G, K Btys.)

Field Sqdn. R.E. : No. 3

ROYAL FLYING CORPS

Headquarters : No 12 Squadron

1st Wing : Lieut.-Colonel E. B. Ashmore

   Nos 2, 3, 10, 16 Squadrons

   Nos 6, 8 Kite Balloon Sections (R.N.A.S.)

2nd Wing : Lieut.-Colonel J. M. Salmond

   Nos 1, 5, 6, 7 Squadrons

   Nos 2, 4 Kite Balloon Sections (R.N.A.S.)

3rd Wing : Lieut-Colonel W. S. Brancker

   Nos 4, 8, 11 Squadrons

   Total : 161 aeroplanes; 4 kite balloons.

Index